We the Deplorables

Rise of the No-Longer-Silent Majority – 2015-2017

Shawn L. Belisle

DEDICATION

To my father Laurenzo and brother Wayne, who encouraged my love of history and spent countless hours over the decades discussing with me the types of topics discussed in this book.

CONTENTS

ACKNOWLEDGMENTS

Special thanks to my wife Jill for convincing me my thoughts were worth writing down and that others might find them of interest. Without her love and support this book would not exist.

My heartfelt thanks also go to Al Lavender, my brother-in-arms and fellow observer of America's long decline – and now of her miraculous resurgence. We've had each other's backs since the 1980s, have 'war-gamed' America's possible futures for many years, and have been ever ready to uphold our oaths to defend our nation 'against all enemies, foreign and domestic'.

Special thanks also to my Father-in-Law Marv Havlik – a patriot and champion of what was best from the America of his youth – for his kind but honest critiques of my work and encouragement to write this book.

Finally, my deepest and most profound gratitude goes to all my fellow Traditional Americans who, in the face of the longest odds, have stood tall against the entrenched Powers-That-Be, made their voices heard, and took the first steps towards making America great again. Though the war against those who would destroy America has just begun, we have, at long last, taken up our places on the battlefield.

Together, We are the Deplorables – the No-Longer-Silent Majority.

Shawn L. Belisle – February 23, 2017

Introduction – The Silent Majority Stirs

The time was January 2015. Obama's second term was half-over, and the politically correct Left were at the height of their power. Those humorless, puritanical, totalitarian thought police held sway throughout the West, eager to swiftly punish the slightest deviation from their secular religion of Cultural Marxism.

For decades, those who spoke out against the cultural rot were demonized and ostracized as racist, sexist, homophobic, xenophobic, and hateful. That countless reputations and careers were ruined was bad enough, but now the immense power of the state itself was also turned against those heretics – the type of traditional, salt-of-the-earth people derided by Obama as 'bitterly clinging' to their guns, Bibles, and alleged antipathy towards "people who aren't like them".

At home and abroad, America's enemies were strengthened while her people were weakened. Home-grown leftist armies of thugs and hedonists, suckled on the philosophical poisons of nihilism and collectivism, were raised to tear down the nation from within while even more dangerous hordes of aliens hostile to our Traditional American culture were imported en masse across newly-erased borders. Meanwhile, the Cultural Marxists in government, academia, and media did everything in their power to disarm Americans and render them helpless in the face of those existential threats.

There was no end in sight. All seemed hopeless. Traditional Americans had nowhere to turn – the Republican Party, who should have been the defenders of conservativism, had long-since sold out or surrendered to the globalist Left. In two years everyone expected Hillary Rodham Clinton to succeed Barack Hussein Obama as President and deliver the final *coup de grace* to the remnants of Traditional America.

It was in this environment that I finally decided I couldn't keep silent any longer for fear of reprisal. I resolved to go on record, consequences be damned, and speak out against the destruction of my country. As it turned out, tens of millions were feeling the exact same way…

You go into these small towns in Pennsylvania and, like a lot of small towns in the Midwest, the jobs have been gone now for 25 years and nothing's replaced them. And they fell through the Clinton administration, and the Bush administration, and each successive administration has said that somehow these communities are gonna regenerate and they have not. And it's not surprising then they get bitter, they cling to guns or religion or antipathy toward people who aren't like them or anti-immigrant sentiment or anti-trade sentiment as a way to explain their frustrations.

Barack Hussein Obama – April 6, 2008

You know, to just be grossly generalistic, you could put half of Trump's supporters into what I call the basket of deplorables. Right? The racist, sexist, homophobic, xenophobic, Islamophobic – you name it. And unfortunately there are people like that. And he has lifted them up. He has given voice to their websites that used to only have 11,000 people -- now 11 million. He tweets and retweets their offensive hateful mean-spirited rhetoric. Now, some of those folks – they are irredeemable, but thankfully they are not America.

Hillary Rodham Clinton – September 9, 2016

Fuck You.

Traditional America to Clinton and Obama – November 8, 2016

iii

1 – WHY A BLOG?

First Published on May 30, 2015

Although published in the blog "Counterrevolutionary Corner" in late May/early June of 2015, the first eight essays in this collection were written from January to mid-May of that year. This book is an anthology of essays adapted from the ones in that blog and span the two-and-a-half years from January 2015 to June 2017. Little did I know it at the time, but those 30 months would prove to be some of the most transformative in American political history, and my humble essays would provide a window into one man's observations of that pivotal time.

This first essay lays out the essential themes that I would expand upon in the later ones – and are essentially identical to those that would eventually sweep Donald J. Trump to the Presidency. Even though I didn't dare to hope then, what I was thinking was shared by many tens of millions of fellow Traditional Americans.

***

In a world saturated with opinion – good and bad, logical and irrational, insightful and banal – why add to the cultural static with yet another blog? The internet is filled with them, on every conceivable topic – a vast, virtual marketplace-of-ideas on steroids. Unfortunately, while many are very good, quantity doesn't always equate to quality, especially when it comes to political blogs. To paraphrase Churchill, never before have so many written so much about so little. That said, I feel compelled to do something I've never done before – to add to this thought pollution with some of my own.

Why? Simply put, because the civilization we inherited is being destroyed. Because the endowment of Western Civilization, bequeathed to us by our ancestors, has been subversively eroded since before most of us were even born and is now under overt, all-out, and possibly fatal assault. Because I can no longer watch silently while this takes place.

But what can be accomplished by mere writings in a blog? Can one man's voice have any effect whatsoever on the immense historical forces that have been unleashed by the enemies of our Traditional Western culture? I don't know. Perhaps nothing. Perhaps this effort will end up being nothing more than unread thoughts in an obscure corner of the internet. But in the current age – when our politically-correct enemies do their utmost to confuse us and convince us that good is evil and evil good, lies are truth and truth lies, that virtue is vice and every manner of perversity is celebrated as virtuous – if this blog does nothing more than to help me clarify my own thoughts and recall core principles it will have served a purpose. For it is the collective loss of clarity about those core principles that got us all into this mess in the first place.

Who am I and why should anyone bother to read what I have to say? Since our world has become such a demographically-conscious one, I will share the following facts about myself for those readers who feel the need for such context before evaluating the merits (or lack thereof) of my writings.

I was born in the United States of America. I have been on this earth for nearly half a century – old enough to remember an America that, though already past its peak, still believed in itself and its greatness. Old enough to have been raised by members of 'The Greatest Generation', whose tales of grit and courage earned during The Great Depression and World War Two were and remain an inspiration to me. Old enough to remember a world without personal computers and the World Wide Web, and to know that the new and more complex isn't always better.

I am a man of European descent who does not subscribe to the idea of 'white guilt'. Although I am not blind to the imperfections of many members of my race throughout history, I know that all other cultures have equally dark chapters in their histories as well. Many other cultures continue to vigorously write those dark chapters in blood right now. I unapologetically know that Western Civilization in general, and America in particular, is exceptional in many ways.

Although not currently a member of any particular religious denomination, I am not an atheist. I was raised Christian, and believe that the Judeo-Christian tradition, along with the classical ideas of ancient Greece and Rome, are the mortar that holds Western Civilization together.

I was a member of America's armed forces in the 1980s – one of the last of America's Cold Warriors. Although I wasn't wise enough to appreciate him as much as I should have at the time, I am proud to say that President Reagan was my Commander-in-Chief. (If I only knew then what was to come later.)

Since then I have been employed in many different jobs in various parts of the country in both the public and private sectors. Jack-of-all-trades, master of none. I greatly prefer the private sector.

Finally, I do not consider myself particularly eloquent or intellectual. I try to speak plainly and 'keep it real'. But, in an overly-nuanced world that many times seems all-too-short on common sense, that may be an asset.

As to whether or not anyone should bother to read what I say, I leave that up to you. Should you do so and decide to comment, feel free. I'm always interested in other people's opinions. I may or may not reply. Don't take offense if I don't. One thing I will not waste time on is arguing with leftists, regardless of their particular flavor – 'liberal', 'progressive', or 'socialist'. In years past I used to engage in lengthy debates with them since I believed many of them were (and still are) well-meaning. Although sometimes enjoyable, most of those debates ended up being a waste of time. 10 to 20 years ago that was an acceptable indulgence to me. In this late hour, however, when our country is on the precipice of social, economic, and political collapse, I simply don't have that kind of time and energy to waste. Those who don't understand by now that it was socialist ideology that brought America to the sorry state it's in aren't worth the effort anymore. Call it triage. Now is the time for us who wish to restore America to its traditional greatness to stand up, speak truth in the face of political correctness, and support and inspire other patriots – not argue with those who Lenin would have called 'useful idiots'.

That said, no doubt there will be commentary left by those vehemently opposed to the ideas presented in this blog – most likely those aforementioned leftists. Others who agree with the premises behind my arguments may wish to engage those who don't in debate. If you have the time and/or derive enjoyment from such a pastime, knock yourselves out. Even though this is my sandbox, I have no desire for it to be merely an echo chamber. However, I will use the power to delete comments when necessary, but will try to do so judiciously, and only then for obvious trolls or those whose comments descend into the gutter. (By my standards, of course.) I will not let my sandbox turn into a litter box.

This blog is dedicated to the idea that, in spite of her flaws, the America that existed pre-1960 was a good and decent place. The cultural revolution that caused the erosion and near-destruction of that America is what we must fight – to stop any further damage and to repair what we can. We must become counterrevolutionaries. We must fight because the world that will exist after the destruction of Traditional America is complete is a dystopian one unfit for any who value human freedom and dignity. It is certainly not a world I am willing to live in. That fight begins in our minds.

For too long we have let our enemies define what is acceptable thought and speech. We have allowed this for so long we now find ourselves in a society where one utterance or expression of belief deemed 'insensitive', 'intolerant', 'non-inclusive', 'hate speech', 'racist', or otherwise unacceptable to the PC priesthood can cost us our career, business, or even our physical freedom. In such a world, where we are constantly told what we must believe or else suffer the consequences, emphatically declaring what one does *not* believe can be more of a counterrevolutionary act than merely stating what one does believe.

The first part of my 'Declaration of Non-Belief' will be the subject of the next essay.

2 – I Will Not Drink the PC Kool-Aid – What I Do Not Believe, Part 1

First Published on May 31, 2015

This first part of my 'What I do not believe' series of essays focusses on the key philosophical issue in the struggle between us and our leftist enemies – moral relativism and the illusory 'tolerance' that results. In their attempts to deny us our innate moral compasses, our enemies seek to render themselves immune to ethical judgements.

By doing so, however, they introduce a fatal paradox – by divorcing the ethical question of what is correct behavior from any sense of a higher moral order in the Universe, they render all moral judgements mere opinion, including their own.

In such a world, all that remains to arbitrate different views as to what constitutes right conduct is force or, to put it another way, that 'might makes right'. This is why, at their core, leftists cannot help but be totalitarian.

***

In our current politically correct society, where the PC thought police and their agents in academia, the media, and government incessantly tell us what we must believe and extol the virtues of 'tolerance' for all except those who dissent with them, it can be more of a counterrevolutionary act to unequivocally declare what one does *not* believe. Here, then, is my 'Declaration of Non-Belief'.

I do not believe Traditional Americans should cede their cultural heritage to the Marxist 'progressives'. – The left in the West, whether they call themselves 'liberals', 'progressives', or 'socialists', loathe and are committed to the destruction of Western Civilization. For decades they have been waging a cultural cold war against Traditional Western values. Their primary weapons are the ideologies of moral relativism and 'multiculturalism', along with the complementary enforcement creed of political correctness. Until we treat this as a war, as they do, we will continue to lose.

I do not believe in moral relativism. – There are some actions that are inherently good and some that are inherently evil. Although cultural mores differ from place to place and from historical era to historical era, that affects behavior at the margin. At its core, the human spirit has an innate, God-given understanding of right conduct (i.e. a conscience). This innate understanding was summed up well by Christ's Golden Rule.

Most advanced religions and belief systems throughout history (with a few notable exceptions such as Islam) express some form of that Golden Rule, although they don't always live up to it in practice. That said, not all faiths or cultures are equally morally valid – some are clearly better than others. Some traditions encourage moral development in the people by emphasizing the universal spirit in all humanity while others do just the opposite.

Christianity and the Western Civilization it helped to form are an example of an uplifting faith and culture. Although Western Civilization, like all other cultures, had its dark chapters in history such as the practice of slavery, reformers could point to the words of Christ ('love your neighbor as thyself', 'love your enemy', the Parable of the Good Samaritan, etc.) to demonstrate such behavior was morally wrong.

Other traditions do not provide that. Islam is an example of a religion that does not. A Moslem of good-moral character is at a grave disadvantage to those within his culture who advocate the ISIS brand of Islam, with its barbaric blood-lust towards non-Moslems, for he cannot point to anything within the Koran or Islamic teaching to argue that the jihadist's behavior is wrong. In fact, the jihadi is more scripturally correct, for his savage behavior more accurately reflects Mohammed's teachings, which ordered good conduct towards Moslems only and slavery or death to non-believers.

Then there are cultures that are completely beyond the pale. The Aztecs were an example of one of those truly evil cultures. Their gods' demands for assembly-line human sacrifice shocked even the hardened Conquistadors, and made the Aztecs a scourge to neighboring tribes that was impossible to co-exist with in peace. Their evilness was their own undoing, however. One of the reasons Cortez and a few hundred Spaniards were able to conquer millions of

Aztecs was that those neighboring tribes, long oppressed by them, were more than willing to ally with the Conquistadors against their tormentors.

Some cultures are definitely more barbaric than others, while others are morally superior. Moral relativism seeks to deny this fact, and is one of the main weapons the enemies of Traditional Western culture have used to assault it. If, as the purveyors of political correctness claim, there are no legitimate grounds to declare one set of behaviors superior to another, it leaves defenders of traditional culture intellectually and philosophically disarmed in the face of evil. That has led to the moral and cultural rot that permeates our nation today and will eventually lead to our utter destruction if not vigorously repudiated and fought.

I do not believe 'tolerance' is a virtue in and of itself. – Tolerance of people of good character, who have honest differences of opinion, is a good thing. It allows us to enjoy the blessings of the marketplace of ideas while living in peace with good societies throughout the world who may be different from ourselves. However, tolerance of evil or behaviors destructive to our traditional culture, such as those espoused by the politically correct elite, is not virtuous. It is suicidal.

3 – Multiculturalism and Diversity – What I Do Not Believe, Part 2

First Published on June 1, 2015

Unfortunately, events that have transpired since I first wrote this essay have only further confirmed its central thesis.

Ethnic animosities have continued to grow until blatantly militant and racist movements such as the so-called "Black Lives Matter" group arose and incited a nationwide campaign of assassination against law enforcement officers.

Openly fascist and racist Mexican nationalist groups such as La Raza ('The Race') harassed, beat, and assaulted supporters of Donald Trump at his political rallies throughout the American Southwest while Hispanic-controlled police departments looked on and did nothing.

And, as I write this during President Trump's first month in office, there is a growing movement in Hispanic-dominated Southern California to secede from the United States and open commentary, from all sides of the political spectrum, that America is now in a state of cultural civil war. It is only a matter of time before that 'cold' civil war turns 'hot'.

***

I do not believe 'diversity' and 'multiculturalism' lead to a peaceful society. – One of the most Orwellian doctrines of the politically correct creed is that 'diversity is strength'. To voice the slightest doubt about this axiomatic statement immediately gets one labeled as a racist heretic.

But is it true in fact? History and an honest look at human nature quickly put the lie to that naïve assertion. Although other factors such as economic well-being also influence how stable a particular nation is, the correlation between high levels of ethnic diversity and correspondingly high levels of societal unrest in the form of ethnic tensions, race riots, secessionist movements, or even civil war is undeniable.

The root cause of this is that it is natural for human beings to identify themselves most with their tribe – that group of people with whom they share a common bond of blood, religion, language, and history. They also tend to chafe under rule by members of a different tribe. There is nothing inherently wrong with this – it is simply human nature.

Conflicts arise when the borders of a political unit don't match the ethnic makeup of the people within those borders. In modern history, this often happened in the wake of the collapse of an old empire, either when that empire was defeated in war or retreated as a result of imperial decline. Then foreigners with little knowledge or interest in the local tribal realities on the ground carved up the old imperium by haphazardly drawing lines on a map.

Following World War One, Allied diplomats created the unstable nation-states of Czechoslovakia and Yugoslavia from among the remnants of the Austro-Hungarian Empire. The Czechs and Slovaks were fortunate enough to be geographically segregated, so their eventual peaceful divorce was a simple matter of drawing a new border between them to form the Czech Republic and Slovakia. Yugoslavia wasn't so lucky, with a population consisting of historically antagonistic Serbs, Croats, and Moslems – a situation made worse when Marshal Tito forced those ethnic groups to integrate in an effort to make them identify themselves as Communist Yugoslavs rather than as members of their respective tribes. Unfortunately, it turned out that the only thing holding Yugoslavia together was the power of Tito's personality. Soon after his death the country disintegrated into civil war – the bloodiest conflict seen in Europe since World War Two.

Likewise, Allied diplomats dismembered the Ottoman Empire into numerous unstable nations, including Lebanon and Iraq. Lebanon succumbed to sectarian violence in the 1970s between Sunni Moslems, Shiite Moslems, and Maronite Christians. Iraq was held together by the iron fist of the Baath Party but, after the US deposed Saddam Hussein that country quickly dissolved into a civil war between Shiites, Sunnis, and Kurds that rages to this day.

Africa is home to some of the most tribally diverse nations in the world – fragments of the European Empires that once dominated the continent. Not surprisingly, it is also the most war-torn continent, with multi-tribal countries such as Rwanda, Sudan, and the Democratic Republic of the Congo the most recent to sink into genocidal civil wars that caused millions of deaths.

Although civil wars also occur in mono-ethnic nations, they tend to be religious in nature (such as the Catholic-Protestant wars in Europe) or have co-ethnics with radically different cultures (as occurred in the American Civil War). As a rule, however, mono-ethnic, mono-cultural nations are inherently more stable. The Czech Republic is stable even though Czechoslovakia was not. Nor are we likely to see much civil unrest in nations such as Norway or Japan.

Another source of instability to a nation is having a significant minority population with co-ethnics in a neighboring country, especially when that minority doesn't assimilate into the native population. Catholic Irishmen in Northern Ireland are one example of this, and that led to 'The Troubles' with the native Protestants that lasted for generations. The Kurds in Turkey have clashed with the government in Ankara for decades, and that will likely only increase with the formation of a de facto Kurdish state in northern Iraq. The Hispanic invasion of illegal aliens into the American Southwest promises to destabilize the United States.

But what about peaceful multi-ethnic nations such as Canada, Belgium, and Switzerland? Canada has come close to breaking up several times in the past couple of decades as a strong secessionist movement in Quebec barely lost referenda to separate from Ottawa. Belgium and Switzerland's secret to holding together as nations is that they allow great amounts of local autonomy to their various ethnic groups, with the central government only handling common issues such as national defense – in other words, they are true federal systems, like the United States used to be.

The take-away from all this is that multi-ethnic nations that don't allow significant local autonomy to their various ethnic groups run the risk of suffering ethnic civil wars. This risk is higher in societies that choose to emphasize the differences between those groups rather than a common national character.

Given its increasingly centralized government, growing multi-ethnic, multicultural character, and a politically correct elite that fans the flames of historical resentments between those ethnic groups, this bodes ill for the future of the United States of America.

4 – Democracy – What I Do Not Believe, Part 3

First Published on June 1, 2015

As I wrote in this essay, 'pure' or 'direct' democracy is nearly always the enemy of liberty and the friend of tyranny. And the timeless safeguards the Founding Fathers built into our constitutional system saved freedom once again during the Presidential Election of 2016.

The leftists in the Democratic party, as their name suggests, have long sought to expand 'direct' one-person, one-vote democracy to an ever-expanding universe of groups who are likely to vote for them – mainly by increasing the number of newly-arrived immigrants, legal and illegal, from the Third World looking to benefit from Democrat-sponsored entitlement programs.

And it is suspicious, to say the least, that the Democratic Party has been consistently and vehemently opposed to laws that require individuals to positively identify themselves as citizens prior to voting. Why do that unless they disproportionally benefit from illegal aliens voting, individuals repeatedly voting in multiple precincts, and/ or voting in the name of recently deceased citizens?

When President Obama went on television in the months prior to the 2016 election to reassure illegal aliens they did not have to fear deportation if they turned out to vote he did nothing to dispel that reasonable suspicion, regardless of repeated white-washing of the issue in the leftist mainstream media. (Ironically, the Left's strident and hysterical opposition to voter ID laws stands in stark contrast to the way they ran their 2016 Democratic National Convention in Philadelphia – there delegates were required to show their credentials before they could go onto the convention floor to vote. Confirming who votes obviously mattered more to the Democratic Party establishment when they were concerned folks might sneak in to vote against Clinton.)

The leftist media would have us believe that Hillary Clinton won the popular vote by 3 million. Just three states, New York, Illinois, and California, gave Clinton a net gain of 5 million votes. Since all three of those states have very strong Democratic Party machines and are "sanctuary states" that are extremely welcoming to illegal aliens, it's not out of the realm of possibility that a significant portion of that 5 million were invalid and/ or illegal votes. Even if the official numbers are accurate, however, that still means Trump won the other 47 states by approximately 2 million votes.

Either way, the genius of the Founding Fathers saved us from the tyranny of a second, far worse Clinton Presidency. The Electoral College was expressly designed to keep the interests of less-populous states, who would not have ratified the Constitution otherwise, from being steamrollered by the more-heavily populated ones. That's exactly what it did in this case – it protected us Traditional Americans in the heartland from four more years of domination by leftists in the three main elitist, Cultural Marxist power centers of New York City, Chicago, and Los Angeles.

***

I do not believe 'democracy' is a particularly good or stable form of government. – One of the most pervasive modern civic myths is that democracy is a superior form of government and universal suffrage is a basic human right that inevitably leads to good governance. But anyone who's ever seen one of those 'man in the street' interviews where would-be voters can't answer the most basic historical or civics questions like 'who is the vice-president?', 'what are the three branches of government?', or 'what country did the United States win its independence from?' knows the basic flaw of democracy – if 50% + 1 of the electorate are stupid, greedy, or immoral then that is the kind of government they will vote in.

The Founding Fathers were suspicious of democracy and were concerned that direct democracy of the 'one person, one vote' variety would lead to a tyranny of the majority. Instead they set up a limited constitutional republic with numerous checks and balances built in, one of which was protecting the liberty of the people from the voters themselves.

Nowhere is the word 'democracy' to be found in the Declaration of Independence, Constitution, or Bill of Rights. Of the major offices of government set up by the Constitution (The Presidency, Senate, House of Representatives, and Supreme Court) only the House of Representatives was directly elected by voters, and even then the franchise was usually limited to property owners. There were buffers between the voters and the other offices – the Electoral College selected the President, senators were selected by the legislatures of the states they represented, Supreme Court justices were nominated by the President and approved by the Senate. Two of the benefits of these safeguards was that they prevented the federal government from becoming too large and powerful vis-a-vis the states and helped keep the people from raiding the treasury.

This arrangement worked pretty well for the first 125 years or so of the Republic, but then early 'progressives' started chipping away at the checks and balances and the system began to morph into something entirely different. In 1913 (a year of evil that also inflicted on America Woodrow Wilson, the Federal Reserve, and the first permanent income tax) the Seventeenth Amendment was ratified and became part of the Constitution.

That amendment changed the way senators were selected – instead of being chosen by the state legislatures they would now be elected by popular vote. As a result, the state governments lost the only real leverage they had in Washington and it opened the door for the growth of the omnipotent federal leviathan we suffer under today, with the states relegated to mere administrative units of the national government.

Another change that has occurred since the founding of the Republic is the extension of the voting franchise to nearly anyone with a pulse (in some places like Chicago even a pulse is optional). Most of the original states limited voting rights to adult white male property owners. The expansion of the franchise to non-whites and women by later generations was necessary to fulfill the promise set forth in the Declaration of Independence that 'All Men are Created Equal'.

Dropping the property-owning requirement was problematic, however, as it brought voters into the system who had an incentive to use the government as a tool to redistribute property from one group of citizens to themselves. Ultimately, this led to our current sad state where approximately half the electorate takes more from the government than it pays in taxes. Of course they are going to vote for the candidate who promises to be the biggest Santa Claus, regardless of the fact the goodies are paid for with money stolen from the rest of society.

The Founding Fathers were also rightly concerned that direct democracy would lead to tyranny. In the absence of a strong constitutional framework protecting the political minority and a cultural tradition of respect for individual liberty, it nearly always does. When the Kaiser was deposed in Germany after World War One and democracy was foisted on that nation, it didn't take long for the German people to vote in Hitler. In Iraq after Hussein was overthrown, elections quickly brought to power pro-Iranian Shiites to the detriment of minority Sunnis and Kurds. Following the so-called 'Arab Spring' that deposed Mubarak in Egypt, the people quickly voted for the Muslim Brotherhood and theocracy.

And for people of European descent, whom the politically correct orthodoxy consider the source of all evil in the world, what happened to whites in nations where democracy completely removed them from the corridors of power is particularly illustrating.

After 'one man, one vote' was implemented in South Africa the African National Congress immediately came to power. It wasn't long before the crime rate soared and it was open season on whites, particularly white farmers.

In neighboring Rhodesia it was even worse, where Robert Mugabe and his henchmen launched a violent campaign against white farmers as part of a collectivist effort to expropriate their land and quickly turned a prosperous, peaceful nation, one that used to be called the 'breadbasket of Africa', into a starving, Marxist, tribal hellhole known as Zimbabwe.

As our constitutional protections in America continue to be eroded and respect for individual liberty is replaced by socialism, Americans run the increasing risk of having the same type of thing happen here.

5 – Race – What I Do Not Believe, Part 4

First Published on June 2, 2015

This essay examines the leftist article of faith that people of European descent are inherently racist as well as those issues that, when discussed rationally by Traditionalists, inevitably bring on slanderous charges of 'racism' by politically correct Cultural Marxists on the Left.

The issue of the disproportionally-high rate of crime among American blacks is discussed for the first time in this anthology, as is the need to secure America's borders and the existential threat Islam poses to the West. (Even though Islam is, of course, not a race.)

One month into Trump's Presidency these topics of discussion have thankfully become commonplace, but in mid-2015, at the height of political correctness, they were still considered radical and extreme. The idea of a Hispanic-dominated Southern California seceding from the United States would have been considered particularly outlandish, but is now being openly advocated by the Left.

***

I do not believe whites are inherently racist. – While every race has their idiots and bigots, to say that whites are inherently racist is absurd. Over the past 60 years, white America has bent over backwards to right the historical wrongs of slavery and post-Civil War institutional racism.

White America has thrown trillions of dollars towards the black community, beginning with the Great Society programs of the mid-1960s and continuing to this day. The fact that the money was unwisely spent and created more problems than it solved is irrelevant – a truly racist society wouldn't have spent it at all.

During the 1950s and 60s, white America also took steps, through legislation, to eliminate discriminatory practices such as segregation and Jim Crow laws and guarantee that blacks finally enjoyed the full benefits of citizenship.

In addition to rewriting the law to ensure civil rights for blacks, whites acquiesced to subjecting themselves to decades of truly discriminatory affirmative action policies. Finally, this allegedly racist nation voted in Obama as president twice even though blacks only make up 13.2% of the population.

If modern white America feels negativity towards American blacks, it is because it has become increasingly clear that equal opportunity is not enough for many, perhaps even most, of them – they demand perpetual preferential treatment and a free pass on uncivilized behavior. Every time racial pimps like Jesse Jackson and Al Sharpton shake down another company for protection money in the name of 'diversity' or play the 'race card' to justify black criminality, or when the Obama administration instigates yet another race riot a la Ferguson or Baltimore, 'white-guilt' fatigue grows.

I do not believe Traditional Americans can peacefully co-exist with the barbaric sub-culture of the black inner city. – Decades of 'entitlements' that subsidized the destruction of the traditional black family, along with politically correct excuse-making for black lawlessness, have created mini-Mordors at the heart of most American cities. This orc-like hedonistic subculture, glorified in rap and hip-hop, has declared de facto war on non-blacks and any black who tries to escape the poisonous environment that subculture creates. (Any black who tries to excel is condemned by other blacks for acting 'too white'.)

Whether this war is expressed by 'The Knock-Out Game', armed robbery, car-jacking, rape, or murder, the violence rate of blacks is outrageously higher than that of other races. According to Department of Justice data, blacks committed 52.5% of homicides in the US between 1980 and 2008 – four times their percentage of the population. Take out murders by blacks and the US would have a homicide rate somewhere between Liechtenstein and Luxembourg. Racial profiling isn't bigotry, it's just common-sense prudence. If non-black America ever decides it's fed up and begins to treat black thugs the same way they treat others it will be a bad day for the 'Boyz in the Hood'.

I do not believe securing America's borders is 'racist'. – To state the obvious, America is being invaded. The southern border, from

Tijuana to Brownsville, is wide open. Thousands, perhaps even tens of thousands, of illegal aliens enter our country every day – no one really knows the exact number. Many are people seeking a better life for themselves and their families, some work for the cartels to bring drugs into the country, while others enter meaning to do us more direct harm. In addition to those coming north from Latin America, there are increasing reports of Middle-Eastern Moslem terrorists infiltrating America as well.

Even without the terrorist risk, however, the unending flood of Latin American illegal aliens is an existential threat to Traditional America. Mexican nationalists have spoken for decades of a 'Reconquista' of the American Southwest, and the extreme demographic shift in places like Southern California practically guarantees this will eventually take place.

Mexico is reconquering the American Southwest the same way Anglos originally conquered Texas from Mexico – through illegal immigration and demographics. Once the 'Texians' significantly outnumbered the native Mexicans they rebelled and eventually won independence for the new Republic of Texas, and a short ten years later Texas joined the United States.

It is quite possible a similar dynamic will take place in reverse, with Hispanics becoming the dominant ethnic group in the American Southwest and eventually breaking away to form their own political unit. (Either a semi-autonomous region at first if it is a slow breakup or complete independence if it is sudden.) Mexican nationalists already have names for this future Mexican Southwest – 'Aztlan' or the 'Republica del Norte'. Should such an 'Aztlan' win its independence from the United States it probably wouldn't take long before it rejoined Mexico.

But illegal immigration can fundamentally change America long before anything as drastic as a secession of a Hispanic-majority Southwest takes place. The vast majority of recent immigrants, both legal and illegal, hail from nations and cultures that do not have a tradition of limited government. After they gain citizenship, they will be far more inclined to vote for the party of big government – i.e. the Democratic Party.

If current immigration trends continue, it won't be long before we see the death of the Republican Party at the national level unless it moves even more towards the left, and with it will go any vestigial hope traditional, tea-party conservatives have to retain influence in national politics. Some estimates have Texas becoming a 'blue' state within another decade or so. Around that time, Traditional Americans will no longer have the ballot box available to them as a meaningful tool to preserve their way of life.

That is why Obama is daring to take such blatantly unconstitutional measures as his recent executive order legalizing and eventually giving citizenship to up to 11 million illegal aliens – he knows final political victory against traditional, conservative America is within the grasp of the Cultural Marxists. That is why the PC priesthood decries any calls for tightened border security as 'racist', even though no other country in the world allows as porous a border as America's southern one. On the contrary, the idea of securing America's borders is not racist, it is merely advocating that America exercise its national sovereignty as any other country would.

Not securing the border is an act of cultural suicide.

I do not believe Islam is a 'religion of peace'. – The word 'Islam' does not mean peace, it means 'submission'. Islamic apologists say that it means submission to God, but it also reflects the worldview of Islam towards people of other faiths – namely that they should be forced to submit to Moslem dominance. When Moslems say Islam is a 'religion of peace', the 'peace' they refer to will only occur when the rest of the world submits to Sharia law and us infidels (*dhimmi*) are converted, or taxed and systematically degraded (via the *jizya*) – or simply killed outright.

Islam, as a doctrine, instills a moral code that clearly differentiates between proper treatment towards those 'in the club' (i.e. other Moslems) and utter savagery towards those 'outside the club' (non-believers) – a code more akin to that of an organized crime family or street gang rather than a peaceful religion teaching universal truths.

I do not believe the West can live in peace with Islam. – The jihadists have repeatedly declared war against us, have murderously acted upon that declaration countless times, and are increasingly calling the shots in the Moslem world. The wishful thinking of many in the West that there is not an ongoing millennia-long war with orthodox Islam, or seeks to minimize its threat to our way of life, is irrelevant. Since it takes two to keep the peace, but only one to perpetuate a war, there will be no peace with Islam – at least so long as there are those of us who refuse to 'submit' to it.

6 – The Rule of Law – What I Do Not Believe, Part 5

First Published on June 3, 2015

This essay examines the state of Law as it exists in modern America and identifies two main problems with it. The first is that the concept that all are equal before the law is now dead in the United States. This was dramatically confirmed for all to see a year after this essay was written when the Obama Justice Department brazenly refused to prosecute (or even investigate) Hillary Clinton for her myriad crimes and did everything in their power to shield her from accountability during her presidential campaign. (Now, in early 2017, those same leftists are calling for investigations of members of the incoming Trump Administration, with no credible evidence of wrongdoing and for nebulous alleged 'offenses' that pale in comparison to what the Clintons got away with.)

The second main problem is that there are now so many laws on the books that it is impossible to obey them all, making all people potential criminals and vulnerable to legal harassment and prosecution at any time. In such an environment, when what is 'legal' and what is morally right are not necessarily the same thing, the Law becomes weaponized and a means for those in power to oppress their political opponents. That is why the globalist Left have been so vicious in their efforts to retain the power of the Presidency and deny it to those who would oppose their totalitarian agenda – it has been transformed over the past century into the most potent law-wielding force on Earth, and all humanity is impacted, in one way or another, by the edicts issued from that imperial office.

***

"The two enemies of the people are criminals and government, so let us tie the second down with the chains of the Constitution so the second will not become the legalized version of the first."

-    *Thomas Jefferson*

I do not believe the rule of law exists anymore in the United States. – The rule of law is the concept that society should be governed by laws, not men and that 'no one is above the law'. By this criteria, it is clear that the rule of law doesn't exist anymore in America. One set of laws apply to us 'unwashed masses' in 'fly-over country' and another to the globalist bankster elites and their minions in the political class.

Make a mistake on an IRS form and see how fast the full weight of 'the law' comes down on you. But IRS employees themselves can 'willfully understate' their tax liabilities and underreport income and, instead of being punished like you and me, get promoted and receive bonuses.

Engage in retail theft or defraud someone and you can rightly expect to be prosecuted and most likely serve time if caught. But work for one of the 'too big to fail' international mega-banks and you can defraud the people of the world for tens of trillions of dollars with impunity. If you work as the Chairman of their cartel in the United States (known as the Federal Reserve) you are expected to systematically steal from the unwashed masses through financially repressive policies such as unending inflation and artificially-depressed interest rates – policies that crush savers and pensioners trying to live on fixed income to the benefit of borrowers, the largest of which is the US government itself. Then, after you retire as Fed Chairman, you can take a lucrative job with a high-flying hedge fund you used to 'regulate'. Ben Bernanke just did this exact thing. A blatant payoff in return for easy regulation while Fed chairman, you might ask? Nonsense. There's nothing to see here – move along, citizen.

If you are well-connected in today's America you can also illegally 'intermingle' customer assets with the operating capital of your failing hedge fund to cover losing bets in the market. That's what Jon Corzine, former head of Goldman Sachs, former Senator and then Governor of New Jersey, did in 2011 when he was CEO of MF Global in an unsuccessful effort to avoid having his company become the 8th largest bankruptcy in US history – to the tune of $1.6 billion of client funds stolen. Not only was Corzine not convicted of this crime, he wasn't even charged. It's good to have connections.

And who can forget that multi-decade, slow-motion train wreck of sleaze and venality that has polluted the American political landscape for so long, those poster children of all that is rotten and corrupt in this country – Bill and Hillary Clinton. Countless articles and books have been written about these vile people and their endless scandals and yet, in spite of all that, Hillary is still considered the front-runner for the Democratic Party's 2016 presidential nomination. The Clintons continually break the law with impunity but have never been held accountable for any of their crimes. Those two alone make it clear that the rule of law is dead in America.

These examples barely scratch the surface of the institutional corruption in modern America. But there is another problem with the law in today's United States. In an ethical society, laws should be synonymous with what is good and moral. They should be limited to only punishing behavior that is harmful to others. They should not be used to curtail citizens' freedom of choice or channel their behaviors into those that are desirable to government officials or special interests — as soon as that occurs the law is perverted into a tool of social engineering and a means to legally steal from one group of people on behalf of another. Roman Senator Tacitus, who lived after the Republic had morphed into the Empire and therefore knew something of corruption, summarized it well when he famously stated, *"Corruptissima re publica plurimae leges"* – The more corrupt the state, the more laws.

But that is exactly what has happened in this country. A very small percentage of laws and regulations in modern America actually protect citizens from harm. Most are arbitrary, unjust, and written by special interests and lobbyists for this group or that with a profit to be made or a social axe to grind. There are so many laws and regulations on the books it's impossible for citizens to know them all, let alone obey them. According to Charles Murray, author of a recent essay in the Wall Street Journal on this topic, there were about 4,450 federal crimes we could commit as of 2007 and, in 2013, the Code of Federal Regulations numbered over 175,000 pages. The laws are so convoluted that, if you obey some, you are bound to inadvertently violate other, contradictory ones. And that doesn't even include the myriad state and local laws on the books.

This guarantees that we are all criminals whether we know it or not, at the mercy of the next state agent or apparatchik whose radar screen we pop-up on for whatever reason. And the cost of violating these laws and regulations (or, in many cases, even being suspected of violating them) can be very high indeed – asset seizures, punitive fines, incarceration, and even death at the hands of their militarized agents.

Worse still, we can run afoul of government even if we break no law at all. Many non-criminals have been killed due to bureaucratic incompetence. It doesn't take much internet research to find numerous examples, some dating as far back as the 1980s, of law-abiding citizens being gunned down by agents of the state, either in the name of the 'War on Drugs', 'War on Gun Violence', or some other nonsense, when SWAT teams mistakenly raided the wrong addresses and the residents reflexively tried to defend themselves. It's become dangerous to be innocent in this country.

This state of affairs has been steadily growing for many decades under the political leadership of both major parties. But post-9/11 the power of the state over the citizenry has gone parabolic, with the passage of Patriot Acts 1 & 2 under the Bush Administration and the blatant wielding of governmental power by the Obama Administration against their political opponents in recent years. Worse yet, Bush, and now Obama, claim the President has the right to kill anyone in the world solely at his own discretion, including American citizens, if he declares them 'enemy combatants'. Under current law in the United States, whoever occupies the Oval Room in the White House is an elected, de facto dictator with more effective power at his fingertips than any Roman Caesar could have dreamed of.

Traditional Americans face a dilemma when dealing with this new reality. By our nature we tend to be moral and law-abiding. But what do we do when the law itself is no longer honorable or just? What do we do when the law is used as a weapon to empower the enemies of Traditional America and destroy those who would defend it? What do we do when the government itself becomes the greatest lawbreaker by routinely violating the highest law in the land – the Constitution?

The people of Germany faced the same dilemma 85 years ago. They failed when they allowed Hitler to use legal means to gain power and then pervert the law to authorize the Nazis to do all the evil that followed. *All of the atrocities committed by the Nazis were completely legal under German law of the time.*

The main thing for us to remember is that what is 'lawful' and what is morally right are not always the same thing, although the powers-that-be would have us believe so. And as the Nuremberg trials showed us, 'I was only following orders' or 'I was just obeying the law' won't get us off the hook, either with God or our posterity.

7 – Law Enforcement: 'To Protect and Serve' – What I Do Not Believe, Part 6

First published on June 5, 2015

In this essay I discuss what I believe to be one of the gravest threats to the liberties of the American people – the militarization of law enforcement agencies over the past 50 years.

The Founding Fathers, having been on the receiving end of heavy-handed enforcement of Parliament's edicts by British soldiers, were very leery of having military troops enforce Law except for extreme cases such as putting down insurrections. Fresh in their minds when they wrote our Constitution were memories of Royal Customs agents and companies of British soldiers, armed with general warrants authorizing broad search authority over entire neighborhoods, ransacking their homes and taking whatever they wished. To add insult to injury, the Colonists were required by law to house British troops in those very same homes.

As a result, the Founders included the Third, Fourth, Fifth, and Eighth Amendments to the Bill of Rights. They did not want the new federal government of the United States to ever have the power to violate citizens' homes and property rights the way the British did. That revulsion of having the military police citizens became part of America's republican character. This was reinforced a century later with the passage of the Posse Comitatus Act following the Union Army's occupation of the South during Reconstruction, which reconfirmed that federal troops should not be used to enforce domestic policies within the United States.

What the Founding Fathers could not have anticipated, however, was that police departments would morph into de facto military units as described in this essay. This is because police departments did not exist during the time of the Founders – they were not created until the late 1800s. However, I have no doubt they would have had much to say (and none of it good) about the militarization of law enforcement and the erosion of the Fourth and Fifth Amendments that has occurred in the past 50 years as a result of the so-called "War on Drugs" and now the "War on Terror".

In the two years that passed since this essay was written, leftist racist groups such *as the so-called 'Black Lives Matter' movement fomented a nation-wide campaign of targeted assassination of law enforcement officers that culminated with the massacre of five Dallas officers and three in Baton Rouge in July 2016.*

As a result, Traditional Americans have reflexively rallied around the police, and that is, for the most part, a good thing. The majority of police officers are decent people who are trying to do a very difficult job.

However, the danger is that we may allow that sentiment to become unquestioning support for the agencies – local, state, and federal – that employ those officers. We must always distrust the amassing of unchecked police power, no matter how noble the alleged reasons for that accumulation may sound.

As dangerous as our enemies may be, the threat to our liberty may be greatest from those who promise us safety and security – if only we give them just one more little bit of police power to spy on us, search us, regulate us, or further restrict our freedoms.

***

"Those who would give up essential Liberty, to purchase a little temporary Safety, deserve neither Liberty nor Safety."

- *Benjamin Franklin*

I do not believe law enforcement exists to 'protect and serve' the people. – In this era of lawlessness, the on-going threat of Islamic terrorist attacks, and racial civil unrest in places like Ferguson and Baltimore, this is a difficult topic for many defenders of Traditional America to grapple with but one that must be addressed. Again, Traditional Americans tend to be law-abiding and see members of law enforcement as decent, courageous protectors of their communities against the forces of criminality and chaos. Many officers are but, unfortunately, like any other group of people, there are those within their ranks who aren't. This is nothing new – there have been examples of good and bad cops for as long as there have been police departments.

What has changed is the culture of law enforcement itself. Long gone are the days of the beat cop who was an integral part of the community and who was on a first-name basis with everyone in the neighborhood. Also gone are the days when a TV program like 'Adam-12' was popular, a show that seems hopelessly quaint by today's standards. (Yes, kids, there actually was a time in living memory in this country when policemen served a warrant by knocking on your door and showing it to you rather than smashing the door down with a battering ram, throwing in flash-bangs, and shooting your dogs.) Reed and Malloy have been replaced by guys in Darth Vader suits. Peace Officers have morphed into LEOS – 'Law Enforcement Officers'.

This is an important semantic distinction. Police in any society reflect the culture they are drawn from, their members are informed by the prevailing zeitgeist, and they take their marching orders from the political authorities of the day. Originally, the first police forces created in the United States in the 19th century reflected the republican principals still prevalent in the country at that time and were local, autonomous from central authority, and generally served the interests of the citizenry by preserving the peace – hence the term 'peace officer'. Since the relatively few laws of the day were mostly in line with the constitutional goal to 'establish justice and provide domestic tranquility' and focused on crimes against citizens and their property, the peace officer of good moral character was fortunate in that working his profession and doing what was right were usually one and the same.

Unfortunately, the statist trends implemented by the Cultural Marxists to destroy Traditional America had its effect on the police as well. As previously discussed, as the Law was perverted into an instrument of social engineering and institutionalized theft government statutes and regulations became increasingly divorced from what was moral and right. The mission of the police evolved along with it. No longer were they merely required to 'keep the peace' or 'protect and serve' the public, they were now also the enforcers of state power. More of their targets were citizens accused of non-violent violations of civil law or regulatory edicts. Hence their eventual name change from 'peace officers' to the more accurate 'law enforcement officers'. Over time, police forces also became increasingly centralized and nationalized.

The first nascent national police force, the Bureau of Investigation (later to become the FBI), was formed in 1908 during the 'progressive' era of the early 20th century. (Its initial mission was to fight interstate trafficking of prostitutes.) Over the next century federal agencies sprouted like weeds until they now regulate nearly every aspect of American life. Most federal agencies, even those as seemingly innocuous as the Food and Drug Administration, the Agricultural Department, the Consumer Product Safety Commission, and even the Railroad Retirement Board have their own armed enforcement divisions and militarized SWAT teams.

State and local police departments were increasingly militarized and brought under a de facto federal umbrella as well. The 'War on Drugs' started during the late 1960's and greatly expanded during the 1980's gave statists the opportunity to start blurring the lines between the police and military as Posse Comitatus was eroded in the name of fighting the cartels. Asset forfeiture laws were enacted for the same supposed reason and introduced a profit motive for departments to seek out lucrative subjects to target, further corrupting the ethical foundation of policing.

Then came 9/11, the 'War on Terror', the creation of the fascist-sounding 'Department of Homeland Security', and what author Radley Balko calls 'The Rise of the Warrior Cop'. By 2015, for all practical purposes distinctions between local, state, and federal law enforcement agencies, along with the separation between civilian and military forces, had been erased. Police departments now use military equipment, employ tactics, and don uniforms virtually indistinguishable from soldiers. American law enforcement has become a de facto standing army of the kind the Founding Fathers feared would become destructive of liberty.

Their behavior is increasingly that of an occupying army trampling the rights of a subjugated people as well. Random DUI checkpoints and forced blood-draws of drivers on American highways, clear violations of fourth amendment protections, are increasingly common. Public sexual assault of motorists, in the form of roadside body-cavity searches, have occurred in Texas and New Mexico. And when interacting with citizens, modern law enforcement officers tend to escalate and overreact to the slightest hint of questioning or disagreement by those citizens, no matter how outrageous their own behavior. Even though their department's official policy may be that they should use the 'minimum force necessary to neutralize the threat' their actions increasingly display a martial ethos of 'when in doubt, empty your magazine' more appropriate to the battlefield than American streets.

In such a culture a sociopathic, controlling personality can be an asset. At the very least, it makes it harder to identify the truly bad cops, particularly when departments routinely whitewash poor behavior of their officers. The recent shooting in North Charleston, South Carolina is a good example of this. Initial local newspaper reports quoted the usual kind of bland, bureaucratic department-speak from the North Charleston PD – 'the officer employed lethal force to defend himself against an assailant who tried to use that officer's taser against him, blah, blah, blah...' (paraphrased) However, a couple of days later a video surfaced that put the lie to that press statement by showing that the LEO had actually fired eight shots at the back of an unarmed fleeing man, who clearly wasn't an 'imminent threat of death or serious bodily harm' to that officer, hitting him five times and killing him. Although there are times that criminal thugs and their supporters falsely accuse officers of using unnecessary force (as happened in Ferguson), I cannot help but wonder how many other bland press statements from departments around the country, that ostensibly clear officers of wrongdoing following 'internal investigations', are actually cover-ups of equally heinous crimes that the public automatically believes in the absence of any solid video evidence to the contrary.

Another disturbing trend that contributes to American police behaving like an occupying army is the type of indoctrination they now receive as to the nature of the threats facing them. In addition to obvious ones such as criminal gangs, cartels, and Islamic terrorists they are increasingly focused on people with Traditional American values as well.

Law enforcement officers have been taught over the past couple of decades that the Founding Fathers would be considered terrorists today because they 'used violence to achieve political goals', and label as 'potential terrorists' anyone who: is 'unduly' concerned with the Constitution and the Bill of Rights, especially gun rights; is suspicious of the federal government; opposes the Federal Reserve; is distrustful of the United Nations and other international organizations; or supports third-party candidates such as Ron Paul. In recent years the Obama administration has added veterans returning from the wars in Iraq and Afghanistan as 'potential terrorists' as well.

In essence, police today are being taught that anyone who might someday resist the encroachment of the omnipotent state is a potential threat. And the powers-that-be aren't just *talking* about Traditional Americans as a potential threat – they're prepping for a war with us. The billions of rounds of ammunition and thousands of armored vehicles procured by DHS in recent years isn't to suddenly secure the border or fight off an invasion – it's to use against you and me.

This state of affairs leaves defenders of Traditional American values in a quandary. On the one hand, conservative Americans want to support the police and see them as heroic men and women (the proverbial 'thin blue line') standing between their communities and anarchy. This is understandable since there really are criminal elements out there threatening our well-being and way of life, and any criticism of police is mistakenly taken to be support for thuggery. However, the PC powers-that-be who helped create those criminal forces as a means to destabilize and destroy Traditional American culture in the first place are also increasingly using law enforcement as a tool to do the exact same thing. Thus the law enforcement 'cure' offered is as potentially destructive to our nation and liberties as the criminal 'disease' itself – if not more so.

If current trends continue, the day will come when Americans will regret having so completely 'out-sourced' their personal responsibility to protect themselves, their families and their communities to the state. They will come to learn the hard way that law enforcement's main function is not to defend them but to 'protect and serve' their overlords, those who would destroy Traditional America. Americans will finally awaken to the real dilemma, summarized by the Roman poet Juvenal, *"Quis custodiet ipsos custodes?"* or "Who watches the watchmen?"

In modern America, who polices the police? More importantly, who polices their masters, the ones who have placed themselves above the law and trample upon our liberties? *We* must. We must, because there is no one else to do it for us. We must, because if we don't we will awaken one day to find ourselves and our children serfs on a 21st century high-tech plantation.

We must, because apathy and inaction will lead to the death of all we hold dear.

8 – Gun Prohibition – What I Do Not Believe, Part 7

First Published on June 10, 2015

This essay debunks the gun control argument and examines why private ownership of firearms is the essential precondition for individual liberty to exist.

Fortunately, this is one issue Traditional Americans were winning long before the political counterrevolution that swept Trump into the White House. Throughout the eight years of the Obama Presidency sales of firearms to private parties remained at record levels month after month. Following the Heller *(2008) and* McDonald *(2010) Supreme Court decisions, concealed-carry of firearms became legal in all 50 states. As of this writing in early 2017, 13 states (fully one-quarter) have now passed 'constitutional carry' into law, which recognizes the unabridged 2nd Amendment right of citizens to carry concealed handguns without any government permit or license.*

America has come a long way since the 1980s when most states prohibited the carrying of firearms by private citizens. Contrary to apocalyptic predictions by liberals that society would become 'The Wild West' and that 'blood would flow in the streets' the exact opposite happened – the level of violent crime plunged. Turns out criminals hesitate to attack people if they think they might get shot in the process.

Traditional Americans, more than any other people in the world, understand that allowing themselves to be rendered defenseless in the face of Evil does not make them safe. That is why we are the world's last bastion of freedom. Most of the gun-owners in the United States are among the approximately 62 million people who voted for President Trump. We are well-armed and trained, and a great many of us are veterans. We are the largest citizen army in the world. We are fed up with what the Cultural Marxists and globalists have done to our country and will not be cowed. And we're not going anywhere.

***

"Americans have the right and advantages of being armed – unlike the citizens of the countries whose governments are afraid to trust the people with arms."

-   *James Madison*

I do not believe laws restricting or prohibiting ownership of firearms make society safer. – I have saved discussion on the proper role of firearms in a free society to be the last of my 'what I do not believe' essays because it is the most important. The God-given right of the people to keep and bear arms is enshrined in the 2nd Amendment of the US Constitution, but it is the first in importance because it safeguards all the others.

Although the 2nd Amendment refers to the generic term 'arms', it is clear that the Founding Fathers intended that phrase to refer to the most effective weapons available in their time – firearms.

Those on the Left who would restrict the People's access to firearms profess to do so for the noblest of reasons. They claim that society would be safer if firearms were restricted to the police and military. After every mass-shooting at a movie theater, school, or other public place they shrilly argue that, 'if only guns weren't available those types of heinous crimes wouldn't be possible'. 'Gun control' proponents also point to the high levels of gun violence in places like Chicago and Baltimore as further proof of the need to restrict firearms.

As with all the politically-correct policies of the Left, the motives of those who advocate for gun prohibition range from the well-meaning, stupid naiveté of Lenin's 'useful idiots' to the nefarious intentions of the Cultural Marxists who manipulate them.

Let's deal with the stupidity of the 'useful idiots' first. Any of you who actually think banning guns lowers crime, I'm talking to you now. The rest of you who have common sense and already get this, please be patient while I attempt to reason with our logically-challenged liberal brothers and sisters. (As futile as that is.)

All your 'gun control' laws have one fatal flaw – criminals don't obey laws. If you look it up (go ahead, we'll wait for you) that's what the definition of a 'criminal' is. So, if a guy is evil or crazy enough to be willing to murder someone, he's probably not going to care if it's illegal for him to possess the gun he's using to shoot his victim. Shocking, but true. The thugs shooting up the inner cities also don't care that they're breaking gun laws. By the way, Chicago and Baltimore have some of the strictest gun laws in America – that's working real well, isn't it? Likewise, a whack-job doesn't care that the school he's shooting up has been declared a federal 'gun-free zone' or that the movie theater's owners have posted 'no guns allowed' signs on their property. That just makes it better for him because he knows there's likely no one in there who can effectively resist him. Your 'gun-free zones' are, in reality, 'victim-disarmament zones.' As Wayne LaPierre of the NRA correctly points out, "The only way to stop a bad guy with a gun is a good guy with a gun."

"But wait," I can hear the liberals protest, "I'm in favor of cops having guns. They're the good guys responsible for protecting us. They can stop the bad guys." Wrong answer. First of all, no one has the legal or moral right to out-source their responsibility for their own protection to others. The courts have repeatedly found that police do not have a legal obligation to protect citizens from crime. Even if they could, the police can't be everywhere all the time. As the old cliché goes, 'when seconds count, the police are only minutes away'. Unless you are very, very lucky and a cop happens to be around when a criminal's about to kill you, the only thing the police can do is bag and tag your body and process the crime scene. You're on your own until they arrive.

"Hold on a minute," the liberals will snivel, "If there are fewer guns on the street there'll be less of them for criminals to get their hands on and we'll all be safer." Wrong again. You still think you can control evil people's behavior with laws? You weren't paying attention earlier, were you? Do-gooders like you made alcohol illegal in the 1920s and that sure kept people from getting liquor, didn't it? Recreational drugs have been prohibited since the 1930s and that stopped drug abuse in its tracks, right? Of course not. So just how did booze and pot and coke get into the country when it was strictly *verboten*? Well, other bad people called 'smugglers' had the audacity to sneak across America's borders with the stuff.

I'm gonna go out on a limb here and guess that, since the bad people *inside* America will always want to use firearms to victimize the good people who obey gun laws, they will get their bad-people buddies *outside* America to sneak some guns into the country for them. I'm also betting that they won't have much trouble getting across the southern border the liberals have worked so hard to leave undefended.

And we really don't need our liberal friends, who most likely have never held or fired a gun in their lives and don't have the first clue what it takes to use one to effectively defend against an assailant – let alone 4 or 5 (predators tend to travel in packs) – to tell us we don't need a magazine that holds more than 10 rounds. We also don't need to hear those who wouldn't know the difference between a blunderbuss and a howitzer tell us we can't possess an AR-15 because it's a scary-looking, 'military-style' 'assault rifle' with no 'sporting use' like a deer rifle has. We shouldn't even *try* to explain to them that an AR-15 is just a semi-automatic that shoots no faster than a Ruger 10-22 (for you liberals, that's a small, inoffensive-looking rifle that fires equally small and inoffensive .22 caliber bullets) or that a .308 or 30-06 bullet from a deer rifle is actually far more deadly than the 5.56 mm round fired from an AR-15 because it strikes the target with more foot-pounds of energy – we know they didn't cover physics and numbers and all that science-y stuff in their Gender Studies course. Let's just say the 2nd Amendment ain't about shooting Bambi and leave it at that.

But let's humor the liberals for a moment, play make-believe and imagine that we could wave our magic wands and just make all those nasty guns go away for good. *(Poof!)* Ahhh, nice – isn't it? Look at that – a whole ecosphere free of those horrid, evil, death-dealing machines. Uh-oh – wait a minute. The place is starting to look like, well, 1200 A.D. or so – a savage world ruled by the strongest, biggest brutes swinging the sharpest blades.

Kinda like the two Moslem guys who ran down an unarmed British soldier named Lee Rigby on a London street outside his barracks back in 2013 with their car, then proceeded to carve off the young man's head with a meat cleaver and kitchen knives. Since Britons aren't allowed to possess firearms anymore (with very few exceptions) nobody on the street felt they could do anything to take the bastards out. The jihadis had nine minutes before **unarmed** police showed up (What's the point of that?) and set up a cordon, then five more before armed police finally arrived and engaged them with firearms. During this time they could have easily attacked other innocent people had they decided to. Fortunately, they didn't, and one chose instead to give a rambling, pro-Islamic monologue to a lady who bravely engaged him in conversation while another passerby filmed him.

Then there was another guy who also decided to use a knife to attack his victims in a 'gun-free' zone. He was a convert to Islam (I won't bother with his name either) who, last year, went to the place he used to work (a food distribution center in Moore, Oklahoma) and stabbed a 54 year-old lady named Colleen Hufford to death. He then proceeded to cut off her head. After that he attacked a second lady named Traci Johnson and slashed her throat before being shot by an off-duty reserve deputy named Mark Vaughan who also worked there. Fortunately, she survived her wounds. The deputy had to run out to his car 130 yards away in the parking lot and get an AR-15 from his trunk since company policy forbade employees from possessing handguns in the building, even if they were licensed to do so. Had somebody in that office been legally armed with a gun Mrs. Hufford might still be alive today.

These examples (and there are countless others) illustrate that the 'gun-free' world envisioned by liberals would not be the idyllic, pacifistic paradise they claim. Rather, it would be very much like the world was before firearms were invented – a place ruled by brute, physical force where anyone who wasn't strong enough to fight back was easily dominated. Back to a time when the mounted, armored knight was king (literally), and the elite 'nobles' were the equivalent of a medieval biker gang demanding continuous tribute from a helpless populace. It took a large investment of time and money (which most people didn't have), in the form of a lifetime of martial training and the astronomical cost of armor and horses, to be able to wield force effectively. Most folks ended up being serfs because going up against a guy in plate armor with a wooden pitchfork usually didn't work out very well.

The invention of firearms changed all that. Suddenly, a peasant could be armed with a relatively inexpensive musket, get trained in its use in a few days, and have the capability to punch a hole through the best armor. Feudalism was dead. As firearm technology improved and became more reliable it was the great equalizer. A 150 pound man could now easily defeat someone twice his size. A 100 pound woman could take out a would-be rapist. A 54 year-old grandmother could fight off a knife-wielding savage.

It's no coincidence that the concept of individual liberties didn't exist prior to the invention of firearms. Political theory always evolves to reflect changes in the balance of power between individuals and the State. That's where the ideas of the Founding Fathers and the 2nd Amendment come in – and why the Cultural Marxists so desperately want to disarm us.

Once firearms became affordable enough for the average man to purchase that man was no longer a subject – he was a citizen with the same effective military power at his disposal as any individual soldier. As long as he remained armed, he held the final veto in his hands against any oppressive actions others may have wished to inflict upon him. For the first time in history, the common man could stand up to tyranny. The Founding Fathers did just that and won America's independence.

The reason the Founding Fathers enshrined the right to keep and bear arms in the 2nd Amendment is that they knew full well that firearms in the hands of the people were 'necessary to the security of a free state'. Subsequent history, especially the murderous 20th century, proved over and over again that they were tragically right.

The single largest cause of premature death in the 20th century was government. Over 250 million people were killed by their own governments – more than were killed by foreign armies in all the wars of that bloody century. Whether it was the Turks killing a million Armenians in 1915, Stalin murdering tens of millions of Ukrainians in the 1930s, Hitler sending 6 million Jews and millions more '*untermenschen*' to the gas chambers, Mao slaughtering tens of millions of 'counterrevolutionaries' during the 'Cultural Revolution', Pol Pot doing the same in Cambodia in the 1970s, Idi Amin in Uganda…, Pinochet in Chile…, Marcos in the Philippines…, etc., etc., all those genocides had one thing in common – the targeted peoples had been disarmed by gun control laws first. Not one took place against a well-armed people who could fight back.

There are those who would say 'it can't happen here'. Don't bet on it. The most dangerous people in the world are utopian ideologues, for they can call on the certainty and hubris of a zealot to justify any evil they do in the name of 'The Cause'. To them, people are just means to an end, mere disposable 'human resources' to be swept aside if they stand in the way of 'Progress' towards the 'perfect' future.

The Cultural Marxists seizing control of America are just such utopian ideologues. Their gun control laws have already resulted in the deaths of innumerable innocent lives who were denied the inalienable right to effective self-defense against evil criminals employing freelance violence against them. When Americans are fully disarmed we will be completely at the mercy of those holding the levers of power. We will then be exposed to the possibility of increasing official governmental violence directed towards us – violence potentially genocidal in scope.

We cannot allow this. We must view with utmost suspicion any who would disarm us – for whatever supposed reason. We cannot trust in the good will of those in power – history shows the folly of that. We **must not** surrender our right to effective self-defense. We **must** keep our guns.

That is not negotiable.

9 – Homosexuality – Propaganda vs. Reality

First Published on June 14, 2015

In the Summer of 2015 the 'gay rights' propaganda blitzkrieg was in full swing in the months leading up to the Supreme Court ruling on homosexual marriage. Although I am personally indifferent towards homosexuality between consenting adults, in this essay I warned that those pushing the 'gay rights' agenda to normalize what was previously considered deviant sexual behavior are Cultural Marxists whose real objective is to destroy traditional Western culture.

This was born-out after the Supreme Court's landmark Obergefell ruling legalized homosexual marriage on June 26, 2015 – the 'LGBTQ'-activist crowd almost immediately began clamoring for legalization of 'transsexual' access to public restrooms of the opposite biological sex as the next great 'civil rights' struggle of the age.

As crazy as it may sound now, don't be surprised if their next demand is the normalization of pedophilia as merely another 'alternative' lifestyle, and when they argue that children have a 'right' to experience 'sexual discovery' with adults. If current trends continue, the leftist deployment of this new affront to sanity seems inevitable.

The Cultural Marxists will not stop their aggressive attacks against normalcy until the last shreds of our traditional culture are completely erased. One of the best ways to do that is to destroy the traditional family structure and eliminate cultural norms against destructive sexual behaviors.

They're well on their way to victory on that front in the Culture War.

***

In this day and age, one can't turn on the TV, go online, or (for many people) even go to work without being bombarded by the 'Gay Rights' propaganda machine. In just the last couple of months I've seen (in addition to the breathless news speculation about the upcoming Supreme Court decision on homosexual marriage)…a Wells Fargo commercial with two lesbians learning sign-language so they could adopt a deaf little girl (how nice —made me feel real warm

& fuzzy towards the 'too-big-to-fail' megabank); a Pentagon 'gay pride' ceremony where an Army Brigadier General publically introduced his 'husband' with the Secretary of Defense proudly looking on; an extremely effeminate dude with a lisp jauntily wearing a rose-covered 'fascinator' with the other ladies on the pre-race show for the Kentucky Derby (A 'fascinator' is a small & dainty type of women's hat. Yes, I had to look it up. Thanks NBC.); and, of course, the earth-stopping transmogrification of former testosterone-laden Olympian Bruce Jenner into 'Caitlyn', the new patron saint of trannies everywhere. (Sorry RuPaul, but you are soooo 90s…)

With that in mind, a rational person would assume our country is just bursting at the seams with *hordes* of homosexual folks. So it was with great surprise that I stumbled upon an interesting article from Bloomberg News the other day that compared the perception of the American people regarding the prevalence of homosexuality in their society with the actual number of Americans that self-identified as homosexual or bisexual.

According to the article, a new Gallup poll showed that Americans believe that 23% of their fellow citizens are homosexual. However, when asked to self-identify their own sexual preference the number that identified themselves as homosexual, bisexual, or 'transgender' was…*wait for it*….**less than 4%.**

Here's a link to the Bloomberg article:

http://www.bloomberg.com/politics/articles/2015-05-22/americans-vastly-overestimate-size-of-lgbt-population

"What's going on here?" I thought. "Why such a big disconnect?" I did a little more research and found a couple of other articles on the same topic – one from the *Washington Post* written in 2014 and another from *The Atlantic* written in 2012.

Here are the links to those two articles:

http://www.washingtonpost.com/national/health-science/health-survey-gives-government-its-first-large-scale-data-on-gay-bisexual-population/2014/07/14/2db9f4b0-092f-11e4-bbf1-cc51275e7f8f_story.html

The results quoted in these articles mirrored Gallup's recent poll – the *Post* quoted the Centers for Disease Control and Prevention's National Health Survey that showed 96.6% of Americans identified themselves as heterosexual while *The Atlantic* quoted two earlier Gallup polls that said:

> *"In surveys conducted in 2002 and 2011, pollsters at Gallup found that members of the American public massively overestimated how many people are gay or lesbian. In 2002, a quarter of those surveyed guessed upwards of a quarter of Americans were gay or lesbian (or "homosexual," the third option given). By 2011, that misperception had only grown, with more than a third of those surveyed now guessing that more than 25 percent of Americans are gay or lesbian. Women and young adults were most likely to provide high estimates, approximating that 30 percent of the population is gay. Overall, "U.S. adults, on average, estimate that 25 percent of Americans are gay or lesbian," Gallup found. Only 4 percent of all those surveyed in 2011 and about 8 percent of those surveyed in 2002 correctly guessed that fewer than 5 percent of Americans identify as gay or lesbian."*

As to the ramifications of such a gross misperception of the reality of the size of the homosexual population in America, all three articles adopt a 'nothing-to-see-here', politically-correct attitude towards the survey results and try to twist them into a positive for the homosexual-normalization crowd.

The *Post* avoided discussion of the implications of the results entirely, instead claiming that the fact the question was asked at all…

> *"…in an influential (CDC) survey used to guide government funding and research decisions was viewed as a major victory for the gay community, which has struggled with a dearth of data about its special health needs."*

You bet. Nice way for those champions of PC orthodoxy to spin it – as a 'health-care' issue.

The Atlantic, not surprisingly, wasn't much better. Its article focuses on the political ramifications of the misperception with regard to issues such as homosexual marriage. (And comes to erroneous conclusions, of course.) It said:

> *"Such a misunderstanding of the basic demographics of sexual behavior and identity in America has potentially profound implications for the acceptance of the gay-rights agenda. On the one hand, people who overestimate the percent of gay Americans by a factor of 12 seem likely to also wildly overestimate the cultural impact of same-sex marriage."*

We'll get to the cultural impact of same-sex marriage in a moment, but for now let's just point out that the *number* of homosexual marriages that are performed is irrelevant. Rather, the fact that such unions are legally sanctioned by the state ***at all*** is the essence of the attack on the traditional definition of marriage. *The Atlantic* author then continues:

> *"On the other hand, the extraordinary confusion over the percentage of gay people may reflect a triumph of the gay and lesbian movement's decades-long fight against invisibility and the closet."*

Substitute the words *'propaganda campaign'* for *'fight against invisibility and the closet'* and you have the first, albeit oblique, acknowledgement in these articles of the real cause for modern Americans' ignorance regarding homosexuality.

Finally, the Bloomberg article timidly punts the question as to the cause of the disparity, saying:

> *"It's unclear why people think there are six times as many lesbians and gays as there actually are."*

Then it bravely lets Gallup take the lead by quoting the polling company as it nervously tip-toes towards the truth:

> *"The overestimation [of the size of the gay and lesbian population] may also reflect prominent media portrayals of gay characters on television and in movies, even as far back as 2002, and perhaps the high visibility of activists who have pushed gay causes, particularly legalizing same-sex marriage."*

'Ding, ding, ding! We have a winner!' *(Finally!)*

The cause of the gross distortion of the American people's perception of the prevalence of homosexuals among them is – pro-homosexual propaganda in the media and the agitation of homosexual 'activists' over the past 60+ years.

Once Gallup broke the ice Bloomberg belatedly jumps on board and adds the following:

> *"Several gay, lesbian, bisexual, and even transgender characters have become prominent in recent years on TV shows such as 'Modern Family,' 'Scandal,' 'Degrassi,' and 'Glee,' as well as in movies including 'Brokeback Mountain' and the Academy Award-winning biopic 'The Imitation Game.'"*

I have to admit that I too was surprised at the miniscule number of Americans who self-identify as homosexuals – I had assumed the number was closer to 10 percent. Although I didn't realize it until I read *The Atlantic* article, the 'one-in-ten' number was the percentage most frequently reported by early 'sex researchers' such as Alfred Kinsey and quoted by paleo-homosexual agitators in the mid-20th century. I can only assume my own distortion of the real number by a factor of three came as the result of subsequent media saturation in the decades since.

In the interest of clarity, I will discuss my personal feelings towards homosexuals before addressing the impact of the normalization of homosexuality on Traditional American culture. First, I am not a 'homophobe' – I do not fear homosexuals any more or less than any other human being. I am also quite secure in my own sexuality as a 'straight' male. I really like females and, frankly, think the male body is pretty icky. That said, I also believe that whatever **consenting adults** do behind closed doors is their business – in a truly free country with individual liberty that is the way it has to be. So long as they don't hurt anyone else, their sexual practices are a matter between them and God.

In my personal dealings, I do not let a person's homosexuality stand in the way of a normal relationship. I have known many over the years, and the vast majority I've met seem to exhibit the same asshole-to-decent folk ratio as the rest of the human race. I also have family members who are homosexual and I love them dearly. That is what I define as real 'tolerance'.

What I do not appreciate and do *not* tolerate, however, is having someone else's sexuality shoved in my face. I am proudly old-fashioned in that I believe one's sexual practices should not be trumpeted about in polite society – to do otherwise demonstrates a boorish lack of manners and poor upbringing. This applies equally to heterosexuals as well as homosexuals. I find a straight man who brags and goes on and on about his many conquests just as 'slutty' as a woman who behaves the same way. I find Miley Cyrus shaking her ass half-naked every time she's on stage (Stick that damn tongue back in your mouth, girl!) or Janet Jackson popping out her tit during a nationally-televised Super Bowl halftime show in front of millions of children just as crass as two homosexuals sucking-face in public.

To those of us with any sense, a person's sexuality doesn't confer on them any special virtue. It certainly shouldn't give a person special legal status. That said, nobody should be physically assaulted or harassed because of their sexuality and neither should homosexuals. However, freedom is a two-way street. A homosexual's right to be free of harassment does not mean they should be allowed to violate a Christian's equally-important rights to free association or religious freedom by insisting that a Christian bakery has the legal obligation to serve their homosexual wedding ceremony. They don't. (I couldn't help but notice the homosexual agitators in this case didn't try their publicity stunt at a Moslem bakery, an ethnic group who murderously despises homosexuality – I'm sure they didn't want to confuse their politically correct comrades by forcing them to choose between two 'protected' classes.) To all who are homosexual – you are not a victim. Get over yourselves.

The bottom line is, we don't care about your sexuality one way or the other, so long as you don't infringe upon our right to be left alone or pollute our culture.

This whole, '***Look at me!*** – I'm sexually hyper-promiscuous and that makes me uber-cool...' BS meme is just a worn-out relic of the 'sexual revolution' the Boomer Generation was misled into by their Cultural Marxist mentors in the 1960s. Since then, we've lived in the detritus that 'revolution' has left behind – frighteningly high rates of children born out of wedlock, with 'baby-daddies and mommies' replacing traditional mothers and fathers; increasing uncivilized behavior of youth raised in non-traditional homes; more and more single mothers becoming dependent on 'entitlements' as government increasingly takes on the traditional economic role of father; untold tens of millions of human beings killed by abortion in a silent genocide on-going since 1973; widespread sexually-transmitted diseases crippling and killing millions more.

This was all by design. Without delving too deeply into the history and evolution of Cultural Marxism (I'll save that for another post), for now let's just say a group of Marxist intellectuals broke with their Communist brethren after the First World War and came to the conclusion that Western societies would not fall to Marxist revolution so long as they had a strong middle-class inoculating them against the specter of class warfare. They determined the best way to destroy that middle class (along with waging economic warfare against them through onerous taxation and, later, outsourcing of manufacturing jobs to the Third World) was to attack the underlying traditional culture that supported it, and they figured the best way to do *that* was to undermine traditional mores and the family structure that transmitted those middle-class values to succeeding generations. The normalization of homosexuality is one of the methods used by the Cultural Marxists to degrade both traditional mores and families by eroding the perceived importance of the traditional family structure among the people.

There have always been homosexuals in human societies. Although different cultures throughout history have approached homosexuality differently, I am not aware of any society where homosexuals were celebrated or considered completely equal to heterosexuals, and none where they were dominant. (Any Gay Studies majors out there, feel free to point out any example you think I might have missed.)

A civilization that did so wouldn't last long. Societies have no evolutionary incentive to encourage homosexuality – homosexuals do nothing to contribute to the propagation of the next generation and can only confuse children as to their traditional gender roles within that culture, a division-of-labor settled upon, not arbitrarily, but after countless generations of trial-and-error.

Even in those societies where, at first glance, homosexuality appears to have been condoned, there are often nuances that complicate a simple assertion that it was lauded. Ancient Greece and Rome are often pointed to as examples of societies that were accepting of homosexuality. However, even in those cultures there were limits. Although the Greeks and Romans asserted that it was natural for a person to be moved by beauty in the physical form of either sex, it was expected that all sex, whether hetero- or homosexual, be practiced in moderation and with decorum. Also, for males, it was understood that the individual receiving the 'erotic attention' of the other should be the inferior one in the power relationship, such as a slave.

Later cultures in the Western tradition adopted less-accepting standards towards homosexuals. Although against the law in most places, in practice homosexuals were not usually targeted unless they were indiscreet. With the Victorians, for example, there was a tacit understanding between the overwhelmingly heterosexual society and the tiny homosexual population of 'you be discreet, and we'll pretend not to notice'.

Again, the Cultural Marxists changed all that. Anything that supported traditional culture was to be reviled and anything damaging to that culture was to be encouraged. Homosexuality was thus to be publically promoted, first through demanding 'tolerance' for homosexuals, then 'equality', then finally legal supremacy.

A subversive political agenda is the best explanation for the ruthless urgency the 'gay rights' propaganda machine is now exhibiting in their ever-increasing assault on our culture. A traditionalist would rightly question the wisdom of rushing to redefine an institution as ancient as marriage, formed through thousands of generations of human trial-and-error, as something other than between one man and one woman. We should also question the rationale for tampering with something so basic to our way of life just to satisfy the desires of a mere 3.4% of the population.

The politically correct Left in the West believe they have already won the war on this issue, and all that is left for them to do is marginalize and mop-up the last pockets of resistance. We still in opposition to the radical homosexual agenda must take this fight seriously and have the courage to stand up, speak up, and be willing to face politically correct reprisals for espousing traditional beliefs. For, although this may not be as immediate an existential threat to our survival as the issues covered in my earlier posts, the radical normalization of homosexuality certainly poses a long-term threat to our traditional culture.

We must not be afraid to fight for our traditional values regarding homosexuality. If homosexuals are indeed genetically 'hard-wired' to be 'gay', as homosexual activists continually assert, then we are equally 'hard-wired' to be 'straight'.

We have nothing to be ashamed of.

10 – A Tragedy, 'Gun Control' Revisited, and the Specter of More 'Blowback'

First Published on June 18, 2015

This essay was written in the immediate aftermath of the massacre of nine black Christians at the Emanuel African Methodist Episcopal Church in Charleston, South Carolina by a young white man named Dylan Roof.

The fact that President Obama and the Left used the shooting as an opportunity to immediately call for more gun control came as no surprise. Neither was the Left's demonization of all whites and anything of European (and especially Southern) heritage after the first pictures of Roof were made public – images showing him wearing a jacket with patches of the old flags of white-ruled South Africa and Rhodesia on it while holding a Confederate battle flag.

Finally, I pointed out that racially-motivated attacks were to be expected in light of the toxic Cultural Marxist obsession with group identity politics and division along racial lines that has been injected into our nation's culture over the past half-century.

Unfortunately, this assertion proved all too true in the years since, with the most notorious examples being the targeted assassinations of mostly white law enforcement officers by "Black Lives Matter" sympathizers throughout 2016 and the systematic black and Hispanic assaults against predominantly white Trump supporters during the presidential campaign of that same year.

The Charleston massacre was an anomaly in one sense, however – most racially-motivated attacks in America are usually committed by minorities against whites, though they are usually reported as run-of-the-mill assaults and murders rather than 'hate crimes'.

As of this writing, all-out race war hasn't erupted in the United States yet, but the country remains a powder keg of racial distrust and hostility ready to explode at any moment.

***

It is 2 PM Eastern Time, June 18, 2015 as I sit down to write this –

approximately 17 hours since a 21 year-old white man shot and killed 9 members of the Emanuel African Methodist Episcopal Church in Charleston, South Carolina.

Details are still coming in. The good news is that the shooter was quickly identified and arrested. The rest of what has been reported so far is, to say the least, not good.

It is difficult to speak so early after such a tragedy about its ramifications. I would not normally do so as it is unseemly to comment before people have had a chance to come to grips with the shock and horror an event like this brings.

Unfortunately, not everyone has the same sense of decorum. President Obama wasted no time to use his first remarks on the tragedy as an opportunity to push for more 'gun control' measures. (More on that in a minute.) That, along with other disturbing details of this case, compel me to share a few thoughts as a rebuttal.

First, the particulars of this attack as it is being reported right now: The alleged shooter (I won't use his name – I do not believe in giving this type of evil person the attention they crave.) entered the church around 8 PM last night local time and sat in the back as a prayer service was taking place. It does not appear that his presence alarmed the parishioners, since survivors reported that they invited him to join them. Approximately an hour later the individual opened fire at point-blank range, killing 6 women and 3 men, one of whom was the church's pastor, the Reverend Clementa Pinckney.

I didn't know anything about Reverend Pinckney, so I did some quick internet research and was doubly saddened to realize that last night Traditional America lost an ally and brother in the struggle to restore values to our culture.

I came upon a three-minute compilation of remarks given by Reverend Pinckney a few short weeks ago on the floor of the South Carolina Senate. (He was a respected state senator in addition to being a minister.) He was speaking on behalf of a bill that would require law enforcement officers to wear body cameras (an excellent idea) introduced in the days following the murder of Walter Scott, the unarmed man shot five times in the back by a North Charleston police officer as he attempted to flee.

I was immediately struck by several things about this man. First, even while he spoke about a racially-charged police brutality case such as the killing of Walter Scott, I didn't hear any of the incendiary, bombastic rhetoric of an Al Sharpton or the simplistic sloganeering of the 'Black Lives Matter' crowd.

Instead, I heard a calm, reasoned man making his points in a dignified, methodical way. I heard a Christian man reference the story of the Apostle Thomas, who wouldn't believe Jesus had returned until he put his hands in Christ's wounds, as an example of how his community felt when confronted by the news of the murder of Walter Scott – incredulity that a police officer would do such a thing but having no choice but to acknowledge the fact when confronted by video proof.

I heard a man who brought tears to my eyes as he concluded his remarks by saying, *"Our hearts go out to the Scott family; our hearts go out to the Slager family* (the family of the police officer); *because Jesus called on us to love all..."* I heard a Christian man speak who epitomized my assertion in an earlier post that Christianity is an uplifting faith that gives good people of every ethnicity or culture the moral ammunition to moderate the more hateful influences in their community. I heard a man who I believe would have said that not only do black lives matter – *all* lives matter.

Now *our* hearts go out to the Pinckney family, the families of the eight other people slain last night, and yes, even the family of the young man who committed this heinous act – ***"...because Jesus called on us to love all..."***

As soon as I saw the photo of the young man who police say murdered Reverend Pinckney and the other eight members of his flock I quickly realized that the aftermath of this particular massacre has the potential to become very, very ugly. I knew that a large quantity of gasoline had just been poured on a fire that already had the risk of exploding into a conflagration. In addition to the typical surly expression of the type of young person who would commit a massacre like Columbine or Sandy Hook – a troubled, angry youth who spent far too much time playing *Call of Duty* in his parent's basement – the first thing that jumped out at me were the two patches on the right side of his jacket. They are the flags of pre-ANC-ruled South Africa and the flag of independent Rhodesia prior to the takeover by Mugabe and the subsequent change into Zimbabwe. I immediately thought, "Oh, boy – here we go."

Those flags, in addition to comments the shooter allegedly made prior to firing that were something to the effect of, "You rape our women and you're taking over our country – you have to go," strongly indicate that this young man was probably (at least partially) influenced by what most likely will be characterized as 'white nationalist' thought.

The former white-dominated governments of South Africa and Rhodesia are universally reviled in politically correct orthodoxy. However, like most things, there are three sides to every story – this group's, that group's, and the truth, which is somewhere in the middle. Those white governments, though far from perfect, were nowhere near as evil as they are portrayed and *all* people in those two nations, both black and white, suffered from the collapse of society and the economy that followed when those governments were replaced by black Marxist regimes.

Not all people who point out these historical facts are neo-Nazis or white supremacists. I referenced these facts myself in my earlier post on 'Democracy' (When I warned of the danger to white populations when they find themselves minorities in a society dominated by people of other tribes – especially tribes who don't share the same Western cultural traditions of constitutional restraint on government or respect for individual liberty.), and I am most certainly *not* a neo-Nazi or white supremacist. Although I believe certain judgements can be made about cultures as a whole, I also strongly believe in taking each person one-by-one and giving them the chance, whenever possible, to prove whether they fit the stereotypes about their particular group or not.

Unfortunately, I don't expect the same courtesy to be extended to white defenders of Traditional American and Western values. Last night, immediately after news of the shooting came out, the social media universe exploded with calls from many on the Left to gut the

2nd Amendment and from many others to just disarm 'crazy white people'. Others called, once again, for the National Rifle Association to be declared a 'terrorist organization'.

President Obama didn't help matters when he took the podium this morning, adopted his best 'stern' tone and demeanor that one would use on an intransigent child, and scolded (right-wing) America for standing in the way of implementing comprehensive 'gun control'. He also said that America has far more of these gun massacres than other countries, then immediately amended that statement by saying, "more often". I will not get into the merits of the arguments for or against gun-prohibition laws here (since I covered that topic in detail in a recent post) other than to mention that the same tools that allow the weak to stand up to the strong and preserve liberty also allows, unfortunately, evil weaklings to prey on undefended victims.

However, I will say that, as usual, the President is being disingenuous by ignoring numerous overseas massacres in lands with strong 'gun-control' laws. I can think of several just off the top of my head that took place in recent years where the assailants used firearms against their victims – the Luxor massacre of 62 tourists by orthodox Moslems in Egypt in 1997; the Moslem terror attacks on numerous targets in Mumbai, India in 2008 that lasted three days and left 164 dead; the Moslem attack on a shopping mall in Nairobi, Kenya in 2013 that killed 67; and of course the 'Charlie Hebdo' attacks that took place earlier this year in Paris. I would include the all-too-frequent massacres committed by ISIS and their affiliates across the world, but I'm sure the President doesn't consider those to be examples of 'gun violence' since most of their victims were merely beheaded by knives or burned alive.

I hope I'm wrong, but I strongly suspect that the same President who couldn't bring himself to even identify the two gunmen in the Charlie Hebdo attacks as 'Islamic' and refused to travel to Paris to show his solidarity against Moslem terror with other world leaders, and who insists to this day that the Fort Hood massacre was an act of 'workplace violence' and not Moslem terrorism, will not hesitate to have his administration hammer on the fact that the shooter in this case was white and appeared to have racial animus towards his black victims. We shouldn't expect reasoned, balanced thinking from the

Left.

What we *should* expect, however, is for these types of attacks, motivated by ethnic hatred, to increase in frequency in the years to come. Consider it 'blowback' – the consequences of the decades-long, politically correct campaign the Cultural Marxists have waged to inflame racial hatreds and divisions in this country. We should not be surprised that unhinged members of racial groups – whether the young white man in this particular case, or American black converts to Islam plotting to abduct and behead police officers, or others yet unknown – are acting on the virulent message of racial identity politics peddled by the PC elite.

Historically, a multi-ethnic, multi-cultural nation that emphasizes the differences and historical animosities between its constituent groups eventually breaks apart – usually violently. For America, the only thing standing in the way of that horrible fate are Godly men like Reverend Pinckney who are willing to be peacemakers and reach across in fellowship to other groups.

May God grant that we continue to have enough good men like him to hold the specter of racial civil war at bay.

11 – Aftermath – Christians in Charleston Grieve With Grace and Love While the PC Left Spews Racial Hatred, Anti-Gun Hysteria, and Other Moronic Drivel

First published on June 22, 2015

In the aftermath of the Charleston massacre, the Left enthusiastically followed Rahm Emanuel's infamous dictum of 'never let a good crisis go to waste'. They smeared whites, conservatives, and gun owners in a vain attempt to paint them as inherently racist, dangerous, and the source of all evil in the country.

In spite of the Left's best efforts, the good people of Charleston refused to burn their city down like the idiots in Ferguson and Baltimore did. Unfortunately, in the years to come they would find multitudes of minorities who would eagerly lap up the poison of identity politics and racial hate the Cultural Marxists are always so willing to dish out.

The Left never lets the truth get in the way of a pet theory or narrative they're peddling, and the delusional foam-at-the-mouth hypocrisy, outright lies, and hate they spewed during the Summer of 2015 on the subject of race was, unfortunately, merely the prelude to the complete meltdown into full-blown insanity they indulged in following the election of Donald Trump.

At the time I wrote this essay I still believed it was worthwhile to make the effort to refute their lies. In it, in addition to calling attention to some of the most egregious examples of the Left's hypocrisy, I debunked the myth of widespread violent white racism.

***

God bless the people of Charleston. Once again they have shown true grace and dignity in the face of circumstances that would have caused other cities to explode into racial violence. (The first time was their similar calm response to the police murder of Walter Scott.) The families of the fallen set the tone early with an inspiring display of Christian love and forgiveness that took the wind out of the sails of racial hate peddlers like Al Sharpton.

There is nothing I, nor anyone else, can say that will add to the heartfelt eloquence their faith gave them as they spoke to their loved ones' killer, so I won't even try. I will only make the observation that their words, and the effect they had in uniting the people of Charleston, are an excellent example of the power of traditional Christian values and how they can triumph over the forces of evil and balkanization.

We need those traditional values more than ever, as those politically correct purveyors of lies on the Left have outdone themselves following this latest tragedy. They have spewed their stupidity non-stop since Wednesday night and it shows no sign of diminishing any time soon. Most of what they say would be laughable if their attacks on our safety, freedoms, and way of life didn't potentially have such dire consequences.

They have disgorged their idiocy at such a prodigious rate it is impossible to keep up with it all. It is exhausting to try and sickening to listen to. Instead, I will just comment on a few of the more egregious examples.

First, let's start with the Sophist-in-Chief. Not content with merely launching arrogant, specious attacks on supporters of the 2nd Amendment before the bodies of the victims were even cold, President Obama has spent the days since (when he wasn't golfing on a lush course in drought-stricken California) lecturing white America on how racism runs deep in our DNA and in trying to establish edgy 'street cred' with 'progressives' by daringly uttering the 'N-Word-That-Must-Not-Be-Uttered' on a socialist podcast. Very helpful, Barry. Now the word is he's going to give the eulogy at Reverend Pinckney's funeral this week, so he'll have his chance to insult conservative whites some more and try to whip up tensions in Charleston. Maybe he can succeed where Sharpton failed, but I doubt it.

Then there's the hypocrisy of Hillary Clinton. (Of course, using the words 'hypocrisy' and 'Hillary' in the same sentence is redundantly-repetitive.) The Anointed-One-Who-Would-be-Barry's-Successor couldn't 'let a good crisis go to waste' and quickly started spitting fire on the campaign trail, attacking gun owners and scolding white

America by saying, *"We have to face hard decisions about race, guns, violence, and division."* She also lamented that white Americans need to *"question our assumptions about race and privilege"* and that *"for a lot of well-meaning, open-minded white people, the sight of a young black man in a hoodie still evokes a twinge of fear."*

This coming from a woman who epitomizes 'white privilege' – one who lives in an upscale, lily-white neighborhood and doesn't have to live with the multiculturalism she preaches (Think she's interested in establishing low-income housing in her neighborhood?); has never worked a day in her life in the private sector yet has over $100 million in the bank; runs a bribery factory called 'The Clinton Foundation' that sends only a small percentage of the graft it harvests to needy minorities (or anybody else, for that matter); and who need never worry about owning a gun to protect herself from a would-be mugger in a hoodie because she is surrounded by taxpayer-funded Secret Service minions.

And if she really wants to find those spreading hate and division, Hillary should look first at socialist so-called 'comedian' Bill Maher. Speaking about the Charleston shooter he said, *"We can never know why someone snaps, but I bet you I know where he got his news,"* blaming The Drudge Report and Fox News for the massacre. The libtard went on to spew, *"I wouldn't say we should be droning Fox News, but we did drone Anwar al-Awlaki because he inspired people. He didn't do any terrorist acts, but he did inspire people."*

Good move, Maher. By your 'logic', if some leftist nut now takes your words to heart and firebombs Fox News or assassinates Matt Drudge it's on your head, Slick. You might want to think twice before you open *that* can of worms.

Even so-called 'conservatives' couldn't resist getting in on the act. Karl Rove, Bush 43's political wunderkind, said, *"...basically, the only way we can guarantee that we will dramatically reduce acts of violence involving guns is to basically remove guns from society, and until somebody gets enough 'oomph' to repeal the Second Amendment, that's not going to happen."* With neo-con 'friends' like that, who needs leftists?

Finally, there was the church shooter's alleged 'manifesto' that supposedly allowed us to peer inside his drugged-out, deranged mind and ascertain just what 'hate speech' on the internet made him slaughter those innocent people. It turns out the main thing he was upset about was that he discovered the PC media was distorting the facts of the Trayvon Martin case and that they grossly underreport black on white crime on a routine basis.

Unfortunately, he may have been a whack-job, but he was right about that. Blacks are far more likely to commit violent crimes against white persons than vice versa. In addition to extensive DOJ and FBI crime statistics, there are many, many examples that illustrate this. Perhaps someday I will try to compile some of those examples but there are many other websites that have already done so. However, since the release of the church shooter's 'manifesto', if you point out that obvious fact you can expect to be accused of being a racist (no surprise there) but even worse, a possible white-supremacist terrorist just looking for a black church to shoot up.

Now, law-abiding black Americans are not responsible for black criminals' bad behavior. But neither are most whites, who are also decent and law-abiding, responsible for other whites who are racist killers.

And speaking of that alleged horde of white-supremacist killers the PC elite would have us believe are sweeping America, can you remember the last time a white person killed a black person in a high-profile 'hate crime' in this country? You know the PC media would fall all over themselves to extensively cover such an atrocity. Some friends and I were trying to remember and the most recent one we could come up with was the black guy (James Byrd, Jr.) that was killed by two neo-Nazi losers in Texas back in 1998. (They chained him to their truck and dragged him for three miles on a gravel road.) If you can think of any other high-profile white-on-black murders since then please comment and let me know.

As heinous as that crime was, it was **seventeen years ago.** Not exactly an epidemic of hate.

The church shooter himself may have inadvertently destroyed the politically correct argument that there is rampant white terrorism against blacks in America. In his 'manifesto', he lamented that, "*We have no skinheads, no real KKK, no one doing anything but talking on the internet,"* and that's why he had to launch an attack himself.

In other words, he couldn't find any white racist – *in South Carolina, birthplace of the Confederacy* – willing to help him attack a black church.

'Nuff said.

12 – Hey, Amazon – Do You Really Want to Stand Against Murderous Hate Speech? Then Stop Selling the Koran

First published on June 26, 2015

In the days following the Charleston massacre the Left falsely claimed Dylan Roof was inspired to mass murder by a pervasive culture of white hate and began a purge of anything that could be identified as 'white culture' that continues to this day.

*Conveniently ignored by those self-proclaimed arbiters of what does and what does not constitute 'hate speech' is a culture that really **does** have hatred at the core of its belief system – Islam.*

In this essay I refute, using passages from the Koran itself, the politically correct leftist article of faith that 'Islam is a religion of peace'. Nothing could be further from the truth. I also call out those cowardly hypocrites who would have us believe such a dangerous lie.

Political correctness kills – no more so than in the soft-peddling of the existential threat Islam poses to the West. It saps our will to resist and emboldens our enemies.

It is the ideology of traitors.

***

Although the news has been largely drowned out in the PC media by rapturous celebrations of the US Supreme Court's invention of a constitutional right to homosexual marriage and the ongoing cultural purge of all things Confederate, murderous orthodox Moslem jihadis pulled off a hat-trick of slaughter today.

First, an Islamic State suicide bomber blew up a Shiite mosque in Kuwait City, killing at least 25, in the latest round of the ancient civil war within Islam between the Sunni and Shia wings of that religion. Just another day in the neighborhood in that part of the world.

Second, near Lyon, France, a Moslem, apparently disgruntled with his employer, cut off the man's head, wrote Arabic slogans on it and impaled it on a factory fence, then dumped the rest of the man's body 30 feet away. He stuck two homemade jihadi flags in the ground next to the head, then got in his vehicle and crashed through the gates of the factory (which produces pressurized gas products). He drove into several gas tanks and caused some relatively minor explosions, injuring two workers, in an apparent attempt to cause a larger secondary explosion in the factory itself.

The murderer was taken into custody by French police and claimed he was acting on behalf of the Islamic State. His wife, before she was also taken into custody, told a radio station (according to a report from the Daily Mail online):

> *'I don't know what happened, he left to go to work as normal,' she said.*
>
> *She said he was a delivery driver who left, as normal at 7am. 'My heart stopped when I heard he was a suspect,' she added. 'He went to work this morning at 7am. He does deliveries. He did not return between noon and two, I expected him this afternoon.*
>
> *'My sister said turn on the television. She was crying... I know my husband. We have a normal family life. He goes to work, he comes back...We are normal Muslims. We do Ramadan. We have three children and a normal family life.'*

They were 'normal Muslims', the killer's wife said. Unfortunately, that's probably true, but not in the way she meant it.

Finally, in Tunisia, two jihadis armed with Kalashnikovs walked onto a beach frequented by Western tourists and gunned down at least 37 innocent people who were sunbathing on the shores of the Mediterranean. The attackers no doubt knew that most of the people on the beach would be non-Moslem, since the faithful would most likely stay away during Ramadan.

It was quite a day, and a hell of a way to cap off a week filled with even more Moslem carnage. Yesterday ISIS fighters attacked the northern Syrian town of Kobani and indiscriminately massacred at least 145 Kurds, including elderly, women and children.

On Tuesday it was reported that ISIS had released yet another recruiting snuff film, this time of 16 supposed 'spies' being murdered by the group. Obviously looking for more 'dramatic' and 'creative' ways to kill 'infidels' and 'apostates', the first four victims were put in a car which was then blown up by an RPG; five more were put in a cage (similar to the one the Jordanian pilot was burned alive in earlier in the year) and lowered into a swimming pool to drown (all while being videoed by cameras affixed to the cage); and the *piece-de-resistance*, when the remaining seven were forced to kneel, had detonation cord wrapped around their necks and exploded – killing all seven and decapitating several.

So how does the politically correct elite and media in the West respond to these ongoing, never-ending, jihadist atrocities? In their usual neutered way. So-called 'Conservative' British Prime Minister David Cameron said this today following the massacre of Britons and other Europeans on that Tunisian beach:

> *"The people who do these things, they sometimes claim to do it in the name of Islam," Cameron said. "They don't. Islam is a religion of peace." He said the attackers acted from "a twisted and perverted ideology we have to confront with everything we have".*

Once again we hear, without any scriptural references to back it up, the politically correct nonsense that 'Islam is a religion of peace'. It would be easier to 'confront (the attackers) with everything we have' if the politically correct elite were honest and accurately identified the ideology motivating Moslem murderers.

Cameron was correct to say that the attackers acted from 'a twisted and perverted ideology'. However, it is **orthodox Islam itself** that is the twisted and perverted ideology – not some fringe interpretation of it.

The politically correct Left reflexively dismisses this reading of Islam as 'racist', 'bigoted' or 'hateful'. Let's go directly to the source and find out from the words of Mohammed himself, as recorded in the Koran, as to just how 'peaceful' Islam is:

> *"Against them make ready your strength to the utmost of your power, including steeds of war, to strike terror into the hearts of the enemies, of*

Allah and your enemies, and others besides, whom ye may not know, but whom Allah doth know." **Sura 8:60**

"Oh ye who believe! Take not the Jews and the Christians for your friends and to each other. And he amongst you that turns to them (for friendship) is of them." **Sura 5:51**

"Prophet, make war on the unbelievers and the hypocrites and deal rigorously with them. Hell shall be their home: an evil fate." **Sura 9:73**

"Slay the idolaters wherever ye find them, and take them captive, and besiege them, and prepare for them each ambush. But if they repent and establish worship and pay the poor-due, then leave their way free. Lo! Allah is Forgiving, Merciful." **Sura 9:5** (This is one of the most infamous Koranic passages known as 'The Verse of the Sword', often quoted by jihadis.)

"Therefore, when ye meet the unbelievers in fight, smite at their necks; at length, when ye have thoroughly subdued them, bind a bond firmly on them." **Sura 47:4**

"Fight those who believe not in Allah or the Last Day, nor hold that forbidden which hath been forbidden by Allah and His Messenger, nor acknowledge the religion of Truth, (even if they are) of the People of the Book (Jews and Christians), *until they pay the Jizya* (a tax inflicted on non-believers) *with willing submission, and feel themselves subdued."* **Sura 9:29**

Strong stuff – and quite clear. According to the Koran, there will only be 'peace' when the entire world converts to Islam or 'feel themselves subdued' 'with willing submission'. The jihadist who murders those he considers 'infidels' or 'apostates' is just following the commands of his 'holy book'.

As for those apologists who would claim that I am just 'cherry-picking' the worst verses I could find in the Koran to cast Islam in a bad light, the unfortunate truth is that I am not – there is nothing in the Koran to abrogate these verses, nor has any subsequent interpretive tradition arisen within Islam to dilute their virulence. Instead of being 'extremist', these passages are taught in mainstream Islam throughout the Moslem world.

But what about Moslems we've met who are decent and peaceful? In every faith tradition there are many members who are not particularly meticulous in following the strict teachings of their religion – such as Catholics who support contraception and abortion or secular Jews who don't follow a kosher diet. Likewise, there are many Moslems who are born into Islamic cultures who don't strictly adhere to scriptural commands as adamantly as their more orthodox co-religionists. Most of those 'moderate Moslem' people will never turn to jihad against others.

But they will also not turn Islam into a true 'religion of peace'. When faced with the preaching of orthodox imams who command jihad as a requirement of authentic Islam the Moslem of good-will towards other faiths is at a fatal disadvantage – there is simply nothing in the Islamic tradition he can point to as a means to moderate the traditional Koranic passages. (i.e. he is scripturally-incorrect) That is one of the main reasons ISIS and other jihadi groups are growing so fast in the Moslem world. The poisonous message of jihad rings true to more and more Moslems, particularly young ones.

In the West, the politically correct elite and their minions in the media ignore, deliberately distort, and cover up these truths about Islam – all while hypocritically exaggerating the (minimal) threat of violence from politically incorrect groups. (Especially those of European descent who support and defend traditional Western values.)

A week ago a crazed young white man shot and killed nine churchgoers in the first really heinous white-on-black crime seen in America in nearly two decades. The politically correct elite insisted that there had to be some underlying message of hate inherent in white American culture that led the gunman to commit such a horrific act – ignoring the obvious explanation that he was a mentally-ill person whacked out on psychotropic drugs known to cause homicidal thoughts as one of their side-effects.

Yet, since photos were discovered of the gunman posing with Confederate battle flags, the politically correct left insisted that *must* be the source of his murderous motivation. They immediately demanded that all traces of Southern history or anything that might be a source of cultural pride for white Americans – whether historic flags, Confederate war memorials, or statues of Confederate war leaders – be eradicated from public spaces.

The Purge has reached levels of the absurd. Wal-Mart, Amazon, and other retailers have removed Confederate flags from their inventory. (Although Amazon continues to sell Nazi and Communist memorabilia.) Amazon has also ordered the authors of books that have the Confederate flag on their covers to either change those covers or the company says it will remove them from their site. Commemorative license plates issued to members of the group 'Sons of Confederate Veterans', which has a Confederate battle flag on it, will no longer be issued in Georgia.

Perhaps most ridiculous of all – Apple has removed an app of a computer game about the Battle of Gettysburg because it has a Confederate battle flag in it. Perhaps the idiots at Apple aren't aware that the Confederates were one of the two armies that fought there.

Where the hell will this lunacy end? Perhaps the day will soon come when we'll see the explosive detonation, Taliban-style, of the bas-relief of Jefferson Davis, Robert E. Lee, and Stonewall Jackson carved on Stone Mountain, Georgia. Rush Limbaugh predicted the next flag the politically correct leftists will go after as 'a symbol of white privilege and oppression' is the United States flag itself. As absurd as that sounds, with the current collapse of our culture we can't rule anything out.

All this because of the murder of nine people. Just today alone, the three Jihadi attacks killed at least 63. Where is the outrage? Where are the calls that we must understand the ideology of hate that motivated these Moslems to perpetrate such heinous slaughters?

There won't be any. Can't offend the Moslems. Don't expect President Obama, who found time to rhapsodize extensively about the Supreme Court ruling on homosexual marriage in the morning and once again attacked the 2nd Amendment during his eulogy of Reverend Pinckney in the afternoon, to say much about these Islamic atrocities. Even if he does, you can expect him to ignore the fact that the terrorists were Moslem at all.

As for Amazon, if they had any courage and *really* wanted to stand against murderous hate speech they would stop selling copies of the Koran.

Don't hold your breath.

13 – The Death of the Republic?

First published on June 29, 2015

The end of June 2015 was a dark time for Traditionalist defenders of the old Republic. First came the Charleston massacre, which forced Traditionalists to defend themselves against an all-out leftist media onslaught that slanderously alleged they and their culture were to blame for the killings.

With American patriots distracted by the non-stop, 24-hour 'mainstream' propaganda stream breathlessly pushing the narrative that White America was inherently racist and evil, the globalist quislings known as the Republican congressional leadership quietly snuck through a vote granting President Obama Trade Promotion Authority to 'fast-track' a deal to establish the Trans-Pacific Partnership. The Trans-Pacific Partnership was to be the largest globalist trade deal to date, NAFTA and GATT on steroids, designed to destroy what little remained of American sovereignty and transfer the remnants of its economic base to Asia.

Then came two of the worst days in Supreme Court history since the infamous Roe v. Wade *decision of 1973. On June 25th, nominally-conservative Chief Justice John Roberts joined the liberal wing of the court and engineered a convoluted legal argument to remove the final constitutional barriers to the implementation of the disastrous Obamacare government takeover of America's health care system.*

Then, the following day, the court decreed in the landmark Obergefell *decision that homosexual marriage was a 'constitutional right' guaranteed by the 14th Amendment and would now be the law of the land in all 50 states.*

The Left was absolutely giddy following this amazing string of victories. They could not contain their hubris and loudly proclaimed themselves victors of the decades-long Culture Wars and declared Traditional America vanquished.

They were so confident in their total victory they simply couldn't resist rubbing Traditional America's collective faces in the pile of cultural shit they'd so proudly created. On the night of the Supreme Court decision legalizing homosexual marriage, Obama ordered the White House to be lit up in rainbow colors to publicly celebrate the great victory. Fox News anchor Megyn Kelly berated former

Arkansas Governor Mike Huckabee on her prime-time program for stating that he would resist the tyrannical 'imperial court' just as the Founding Fathers had resisted a tyrannical monarchy. Time Magazine *called for churches to be stripped of their tax-exempt status and declared that "Orthodox Christians must now learn to live as exiles in (their) own country".*

By the end of June 2015, I despaired for the future of America. Deep in my heart I had come to believe that all hope to peacefully restore our nation to its former glory was lost for good. But, as the old saying goes, things are always darkest before the dawn.

In retrospect, June 2015 was the high-water mark for the globalist, Cultural Marxist Left in America. It turned out that their giddy hubris was matched by a simmering, sullen awakening of the sleeping giant that was Traditional America. For tens of millions of Traditionalists these were the final straws that broke what was left of their good will, and a creeping awareness began to spread among them that a counterrevolution against the Cultural Marxist tyrants was necessary. The Left's subsequent aggressive, arrogant overreach in pushing for ever-more extreme demands, such as forcing the 'acceptance' of transsexual men into their daughters' bathrooms, only solidified Traditional America's resolve and further fueled the pre-counterrevolutionary tinderbox.

Fortunately, at least so far, that counterrevolutionary impulse has found a peaceful political outlet in the form of the tsunami of popular discontent that propelled Donald Trump to the White House. However, this Traditionalist backlash has only just begun, and those on the Left who are now foolishly trying to resist it do so at their peril. They pushed the political pendulum so far to the left over the past half-century it is now inevitable it will swing back equally hard towards the right.

The Left has yet to see the full pent-up righteous fury of Traditional America, but they soon will if they continue with their insurrectionist attempts to render America ungovernable that they began in the wake of President Trump's election.

When the Day finally arrives and they reap the whirlwind they've sown for so long, I, for one, will shed no tears for those traitorous bastards.

***

The last two weeks have been terrible for Traditional America and her defenders. It began with the massacre in Charleston that the politically correct Cultural Marxists capitalized on to launch an all-out offensive on the 2nd Amendment, slander White America by declaring them complicit in those murders, and advocate, Soviet-style, the air-brushing from American history anything they deem culturally-offensive.

While America was distracted by all the media noise and static over the Confederate battle flag, the US Congress quietly voted to give President Obama Trade Promotion Authority (TPA) to negotiate a treaty on the Trans-Pacific Partnership (TPP). The TPA, also known as the 'fast track' on trade deals, sets limits on Congress as to how they can address the final treaty that results from the President's negotiations – they can offer no amendments, cannot filibuster, the time for debate is limited, and there must be a simple up or down vote within 90 days.

The body that those negotiations seek to establish, the Trans-Pacific Partnership, is problematic, to say the least. Though it is advertised as a benevolent organization that will facilitate 'free trade' and economic growth to countries along the Pacific Rim, the current draft of its charter supposedly has 24 chapters and runs approximately 800 pages (according to Senator Rand Paul), covering and promising to extensively regulate such wide-ranging aspects of the economy as: agriculture; industry; copyright law (It purportedly seeks to criminalize minor infringements such as unauthorized downloads, while other clauses will benefit big pharmaceutical companies by delaying the appearance of cheaper generic drugs on the market.); telecommunications; increased regulation and surveillance of the internet (Some reports say it would 'encourage' ISPs to institute a 'three-strikes-and-you're-out' provision barring individuals access to the internet for violating its regulations – see http://tppinfo.org/ – an effective way to kill free speech on the net.); financial services; government procurement; customs; the environment; labor relations; a section describing the treaty as 'a living agreement' (Subject to on-going 'evolution' without congressional approval or oversight?); and much, much more.

It is also said to include the establishment of supra-national, un-elected tribunals to arbitrate disputes between the signatory nation-states. Each nation would get equal representation in these bodies, so if the United States gets to send a representative to act as an arbitrator the Sultan of Brunei gets to send one as well.

Worse yet, under this treaty, multinational corporations get equal standing with nation-states before those trade dispute tribunals, and are empowered to sue countries for damages if they feel a nation's laws have hurt them financially – up to and including demanding payment for 'potential profits' they might have lost.

So if, for example, the U.S. Congress passed a law saying that government agencies could only procure equipment manufactured in the U.S. (not that America actually *makes* anything anymore) a company based in Vietnam could sue and receive damages from U.S. taxpayers for the amount of the cost of the equipment the U.S. Government didn't buy from them. (Not to mention the fact that any other foreign company that makes the same product could theoretically sue as well.)

Likewise, should the U.S. Government pass a law forbidding the Federal Reserve from bailing out an overseas-based, too-big-to-fail multinational megabank such as HSBC (like they did in the aftermath of the 2008 financial crisis), but then went ahead and bailed out a U.S. one like Citibank or Wells Fargo instead, the foreign bank would theoretically be able to sue U.S. taxpayers for the amount the Fed gave the U.S.-based bank.

In other words, what little we know about this treaty is that it is a fascist (using Mussolini's definition of 'fascist' as 'the merger of state and corporate power') corporatist's wet-dream – it absolutely destroys what little is left of national sovereignty and provides even more avenues for the 'vampire-squid' multinationals of the world to suck even more wealth from hapless taxpayers.

No one is really sure what the proposed treaty contains exactly, except for the government apparatchiks negotiating it and some 'stakeholders' – representatives of large multinational corporations who are also included in 'advisory committees' to the negotiators. It's classified, you see. (Just like Obamacare was before it was passed.) The public isn't allowed to know what's in it – apparently we're not 'stakeholders'. (Republican Congressman and 2012 Vice-Presidential candidate Paul Ryan, in a truly Nancy Pelosi-esque moment, said we'd be 'allowed to see it after it's passed.')

Even U.S. senators and congressmen are restricted from knowing much about what they're voting for – lawmakers are only 'allowed' to go into a secure room in the Capitol and examine a copy of the draft bill, are watched while they read it to make sure they don't make any notes or copies, and are forbidden from speaking publicly about what they've read.

The treaty will be the largest trade agreement in history, affecting nearly 800 million people, and is expected to impact 40% of all U.S. foreign trade and cede American sovereignty in many egregious ways, only one of which I touched on earlier. It is yet another globalist threat to the freedom and economic security of the American people – just as NAFTA was.

'Free trade' is a lovely libertarian theory – that prosperity rises as borders are eliminated and no longer stand in the way of the free movement of goods and people – so long as all the parties involved are playing by the same rules on a level field. However, in practice, eliminating protective tariffs in prior so-called 'free trade' agreements has been disastrous for America – especially when the countries we're trading with pay their people sweatshop wages and their governments heavily subsidize their so-called 'private' companies. If you thought Ross Perot's 'giant sucking sound' of good American jobs leaving our shores for third-world nations was loud before, just wait until this monster is passed.

It's interesting that Obama, that staunch 'progressive', has joined with the Republican leadership (who would sign any sheet of paper so long as its title included the words 'free trade') to strongly advocate for this treaty – just as Democratic President Bill Clinton and then-First Lady Hillary pushed through NAFTA in the 1990s.

Of course the Clintons were handsomely rewarded for their support, and Bill is now the ex-president with the highest net worth – well over $100 million. I'm guessing Barry was offered the promise of getting his very own 'Obama Foundation', heavily funded by the powers-that-be after his departure from the White House, if he agreed to play ball – and was no doubt threatened with something *very bad* if he didn't. (Can you say 'Dealey Plaza'?)

If there was any doubt before, we now know who Obama *really* works for – the globalist banksters behind this hellish deal. You know – the same ones who are funding the politically correct Cultural Marxists destroying our culture.

I can't help but also find interesting the timing of the Charleston massacre. It couldn't have been more perfect for the globalists and their Cultural Marxist minions. On June 12th the House of Representatives voted down TPA for the TPP.

On June 17th the church shootings happened.

While the American people were distracted by the overblown, politically correct, media shit-storm over the Confederate flag, Congress quietly re-voted on TPP on June 22nd and passed it this time with very little fanfare.

Well-played, Global Fascists…well-played indeed. The attacks on the 2nd Amendment and the instigation of a potential race war in America were just icing on the cake in line with their overall plan of conquest. Their standard *modus operandi* is – disarm, divide…then conquer.

Now, I don't know if the Charleston church shooter was an asset of an updated, 21st century version of an MK-ULTRA-type secret mind-control program or not, but the timing couldn't be more perfect. The massacre, and the subsequent distractive media culture-war brouhaha, has all the trappings of a false-flag psy-op. It's happened many times before.

Then, to continue the two weeks from hell, on June 25th the U.S. Supreme Court handed down its second ruling on Obamacare, and once again Chief Justice Roberts pirouetted through linguistic hoops to save the disastrous law, saying that Congress didn't *really* mean the individual states should set up health-care exchanges, they meant 'The State' (i.e. the federal government). In other words, the way is now clear for a single-payer health care system paid for by the federal government – what the socialists (and their masters in the insurance industry) wanted all along.

The next day, June 26th, the Court handed down their ruling in favor of homosexual marriage, making it 'the law of the land' in all 50 states. It was a death-blow to what remains of traditional Judeo-Christian cultural and religious mores in this country and, as the vast legal apparatus against 'discrimination' is now turned on defenders of Traditional American values, there is nothing the Cultural Marxists in control of the levers of power won't do to crush them.

There are already calls to remove tax-exempt status from churches. Time Magazine is one of first to do so:

http://time.com/3939143/nows-the-time-to-end-tax-exemptions-for-religious-institutions/

And contrary to the assurances of Justice Kennedy (Reagan must be spinning in his grave now), there will be nothing to stop the persecution of religious individuals and businesses who don't jump on board the 'diversity-celebration' bandwagon.

(Ironically, Chief Justice Roberts railed against the majority in the ruling on homosexual marriage for 'legislating from the bench' and 'creating law out of thin air' that 'had nothing to do with the constitution' – the exact same thing *he himself* did the day before in his ruling on Obamacare. The man is either unhinged, bought-off with a *lot* of money, or the NSA has dug up some *really* good dirt on him.)

There are many Americans, who are our allies on most issues, that are indifferent to the ruling on homosexual marriage. I have anarcho-capitalist, libertarian friends who have told me, 'I don't care what gays do, as long as I don't have to pay for it.' They say they are 'fiscally conservative, but socially liberal'.

I'm afraid it doesn't work that way. Societies and cultures are exceedingly complex systems, like the weather. Change one variable and many unintended consequences can (and usually do) result. (i.e. the famous 'Butterfly Effect') Our Western, Judeo-Christian traditions are what eventually evolved into the political philosophy of the Founders that underlies all the freedoms we take for granted – including our economic freedoms. Take away that underlying philosophy and that gives the Cultural Marxists the opening to inflict economic Marxism on the country as well as destroy the culture.

I believe the assumption that religious traditions, along with the self-discipline those religious beliefs instill in the citizenry, can be removed from our culture without causing severe practical dislocations in our society and daily lives is mistaken. The Founding Fathers were clear that the system they set up would not work for people who would not govern themselves or their passions. If you don't have God in your society you will never have enough cops. Modern America, with its prevailing 'do-whatever-feels-good-whenever-you-want-and-damn-the-consequences' ethos, seems determined to put the Founders' assertion to the test.

I started writing this blog a couple of months ago with the hope that *something* could be done to help Traditional Americans regain influence through the political process and reform our country – that perhaps there was still time to turn this thing around. I've always tried to be an optimist. Therefore, it pains me deeply to have to say that, after the events of the past two weeks, I'm no longer sure that's possible. I fear the politically correct enemies of Traditional America have injected their poison too deeply into her body politic.

Their cultural coup d'état is nearly complete. The Cultural Marxists and their globalist masters are firmly in control of the levers of power in Washington. Our old republican system of limited government, long on life-support, now appears completely dead.

The Presidency became infused with imperial power long ago, far supplanting the other federal governmental branches in supremacy. That office is now occupied by a man who, through his words and deeds, has shown nothing but contempt for Traditional America and support for her enemies, both foreign and domestic. In light of an electorate that is increasingly brainwashed by political correctness and pulled ever further left by uncontrolled immigration, it is doubtful that a traditional conservative can ever be elected President in America again.

The Supreme Court, though still ostensibly 5-4 in favor of justices nominated by Republican presidents, has shown by their two decisions last week that they have shifted as far to the Left as they've been since Roe v. Wade. We can expect no restoration of traditional values from that quarter – if anything, they're more likely to continue to erode them.

And the Congress, dominated by the invertebrate Republican leadership since their party's landslide mid-term election victory in 2014, have repeatedly shown that they will do nothing meaningful to stop or reverse the abuses of power of the other two branches.

The Cultural Marxists sense victory is close at hand and are arrogantly rubbing it in the noses of Traditional Americans. If flying the Confederate battle flag on the grounds of the South Carolina capitol is a slap in the face of black Americans, as the politically correct elite and media assert, then they know full well that the illumination of the White House – the 'People's House' – in rainbow hues on the night of the Supreme Court's homosexual marriage decision sends the message to Traditional Americans, loud and clear, that they have lost the Culture War and there is no place for them or their beliefs in the New Order (which is truly an *Obama-nation*).

One of the few vocal defenders of traditional values left in the political realm at the national level, former Arkansas governor Mike Huckabee, released a statement in response to the Supreme Court's homosexual marriage ruling that, *"I will not acquiesce to an imperial court any more than our Founders acquiesced to an imperial British monarch. We must resist and reject tyranny, not retreat."*

Fox News host Megyn Kelly had the governor on her show that night:

http://www.mediaite.com/tv/megyn-kelly-grills-huckabee-about-rejecting-scotus-like-it-or-not-they-get-final-say/

Seemingly incredulous at that comment, she read Huckabee's statement about the court's ruling and said, *"What does that mean…you **have** to accept the ruling, right? Are you planning on **not** accepting the ruling in some way?"*

Huckabee replied, *"Well, how do we accept something that, on its face, is unconstitutional? Has the Congress yet acted…has it said…?"*

Kelly cut him off, saying, *"How do you **not** accept it? It's the Supreme Court's job to interpret the Constitution and tell us what it means and* (her eyes widened in exasperation) ***like it or not***, *they **do** get the final say unless the people decide to pass a constitutional amendment…"*

Although I found her tone pretty condescending to Governor Huckabee and her apparent bafflement at the suggestion that there should be *any* kind of resistance to tyranny quite telling, Kelly makes a valid observation, up to a point. There *are* limits, within the current system, to what Traditional Americans can do about judicial and governmental encroachments on their way of life or abuses of their liberties.

In addition to the idea of constitutional amendments, Senator Ted Cruz raised the possibility of an Article V constitutional convention of the states to re-form (in the literal sense) the government. Given the lack of spine of most in the Republican Party, however, both ideas are effectively non-starters.

But there *are* other options available to Traditional Americans, even if it turns out that real reform is impossible.

We can admit defeat and surrender to 'the inevitable'. Or, we can admit defeat and flee the country, as many wealthy Americans are already doing. Or, we can admit defeat, withdraw from public life, mentally and spiritually isolate ourselves from the 'mainstream' culture (like the Amish) and accept a life of 'internal exile' in our own country, as suggested by this essay in Time Magazine:

http://time.com/3938050/orthodox-christians-must-now-learn-to-live-as-exiles-in-our-own-country/

The politically correct Cultural Marxists that run Time Magazine would just *love* it if we took that defeatist message to heart. We should all just go away, shut up, and lie down next to our dish in some remote rural corner of 'flyover country'.

But there are still other options available to Traditional Americans, ones the politically correct Cultural Marxists and their globalist masters *wouldn't* like.

One unpleasant truth for them is that Traditional Americans, being far more productive than those that support the Left, pay the vast majority of the bills in this country. Someday, those people may finally get fed up with being abused by those who survive off their largesse, pull a 'John Galt', and go on strike, withdrawing their consent and support for the current irredeemably corrupt and evil system.

And there is one final option that is always available to Traditional Americans, one bequeathed to us by the wisdom of our Founding Fathers. It is an option *we* have not forgotten, even if Megyn Kelly has.

With July 4th swiftly approaching, many of us may decide the time has come to pull out our nation's birth announcement, dust it off, and see how the words in it apply to modern, 21st century America.

"When, in the Course of human events..."

14 – We Hold These Truths to Be Self-Evident…

First published on July 3, 2015

In this essay I raised the possibility that the irreconcilable differences between the "seething, mutually-loathing camps" the American people had divided into might someday reach the point where secession and partition of the United States becomes the only way to peacefully resolve them. More than two years later I still hold to that belief – but it seems no one is inclined to seek peaceful solutions any longer anyway.

In this reimagining of how future patriots could use the original Declaration of Independence as inspiration to create their own Declaration, I focused on all the myriad areas which the Federal Government and the globalist minions that run it have usurped power from 'We the People'. I was amazed at how long of a list I was able to quickly come up with.

This essay may turn out to be not be as far-fetched as it seemed when I first wrote it…

***

There is a storm coming.

You can feel it in the air. The tension is palpable.

Though they may not always be able to tell you exactly why, most Traditional Americans know something is terribly wrong with their country. Financially, spiritually, and culturally, America is coming apart.

Financially, the nation is still reeling from 'The Great Recession' that began in 2008 and has the potential to slip into 'The Greatest Depression' at any moment as the monetary financial heroin injected into the system by the Federal Reserve to keep the economy from collapsing wears off.

The federal government is nearly 19 trillion dollars in debt, and isn't even pretending to try and balance their budget anymore as 'entitlements' grow exponentially. Productive Americans find themselves doubly squeezed as real wages, adjusted for inflation, have steadily declined since 1971 while their tax burden has increased to roughly half of their income after federal, state and local taxes are levied against them. To add insult to injury, they increasingly see those taxes used to fund agencies and programs that attack their liberties and way of life.

Spiritually, the country is being increasingly secularized, and the concept of a divine creator has been largely removed from public discourse. As a result, ethics have eroded in both in the public and private spheres and have been replaced by a socially-corrosive attitude of 'anything goes'. Liberty has also suffered as the concept of unalienable rights, derived from Nature's God, is replaced by mere privileges granted (and just as easily revoked by) the laws of men.

Culturally, the politically correct Cultural Marxists have mercilessly attacked Traditional America and successfully divided the People along racial, religious, class, and gender lines into seething, mutually-loathing camps. As tensions rise, the threat of violence increasingly hangs over our heads.

Many Americans have decided to leave the country while they still can. Many others say they would consider doing so. A recent poll showed that 35% of native-born Americans would consider leaving the United States to live in another country. The percentage is even higher among millennials, between the ages of 18 to 34, at 55%. Here is the link to a story about those poll results:

http://www.cnbc.com/id/102799503

Though many say they would emigrate to seek greater economic opportunity, I'm sure many others are leaving because they sense the upcoming collapse of the United States of America as we know it.

Then there are those of us who will stay, come what may, because America is our home – the land of our forefathers. I am one of those persons. I do not believe in surrendering my home to those who seek to destroy it. If and when circumstances in America get so bad that people feel the need to flee for their safety, I would much rather stay and help my like-minded countrymen work to form new, albeit smaller, nations out of the wreckage of the old – nations rededicated to the old American virtues and traditions of our Founders.

I believe the time will come (perhaps sooner rather than later), when Traditional, 'red-state' Americans will begin to question the logic of continuing to subsidize the alien, hostile, Marxist culture prevalent in the 'blue-states'. How long before a state like Texas recognizes the fact that it would be far better off economically if it didn't have to support the socialist idiocracy of California? How long will people in Montana tolerate politicians from Illinois and New York telling them what constitutional freedoms they may continue to exercise and which must be sacrificed on the altar of political correctness?

What cultural bonds would hold the United States of America together at that point? A common history? No – that's being purged by the Cultural Marxists. A common language? No – armies of unassimilated aliens have turned America's old 'melting pot' into a combustible 'salad bowl-of-Babel'. A common philosophy or religion? Not a chance – Traditional Americans and modern leftists are in diametric, vehement opposition on nearly every meaningful issue. Can it really be said that, deep down in their hearts and minds, people from those opposing camps even consider each other countrymen at all anymore? It's becoming more and more difficult to do so.

Of course, if wasn't always this way in America. When the United States still had a federalist system, the rights guaranteed to 'the states respectively, or to the people' in the 10th Amendment of the Constitution made each state a 'laboratory of democracy' empowered to experiment with different policy solutions to common problems. Using this equality of opportunity, some states would enact better solutions than others and enjoy the benefits of better results. Others who didn't fare as well but were wise enough to emulate the more successful examples could become successful themselves, while those states too stubborn to change the error of their ways would soon find their people 'voting with their feet' to move to the better states. This dynamic can still be seen, even today, by the large number of people moving from 'blue' states to more economically successful ones like Texas.

On cultural issues, federalism provided an essential safety valve for society. If someone didn't like their state's stand on, say, abortion or homosexual marriage, or felt safer with or without prohibitions on firearms, they could usually find a state whose official policy more closely matched their personal beliefs and move there.

The Cultural Marxists, of course, changed all that. As power was increasingly centralized in the federal government at the expense of the states, 'one-size-fits-all' became the new law of the land. If the Supreme Court magically discovered a constitutional right to abortion or homosexual marriage and decreed that all 300+ million people in the United States must obey their diktat or else suffer the consequences, but 40+% of those people vehemently disagree, there is now no recourse for that political minority. Alienating at least 4 out of 10 Americans over core beliefs is not a good way to increase domestic tranquility.

Multiply that dissatisfaction by 10,000 times for each arbitrary and corrupt law or regulation on the books the people suffer under and you have a recipe for disaster. Good people will only suffer so much abuse before they cry, "Enough!" There is an old saying that applies to the current state of affairs in America – 'When real reform becomes impossible, revolution becomes inevitable.'

As disgust and distrust between the Marxist Left and Traditional Americans hardens into hatred, physical separation may very well be our only long-term hope for peace. Like a person trapped in a bad marriage with a co-dependent, abusive spouse, Traditional Americans have endured on-going systematic abuse from the very people who depend on them for financial support and believe themselves 'entitled' to such largess from those who actually create things and work for a living. (Of course, the parasitical powers-that-be in control of the federal government and their dependents who drank the PC Kool-Aid will likely not let their 'golden geese' go peacefully, but that's a conversation for another post.)

As we celebrate this Fourth of July, and with those ideas in mind, it may be useful for us to reexamine *The Declaration of Independence* and reflect on how it might be adapted for our circumstances in the future:

85

IN ASSEMBLY, July 4, 20??

The unanimous Declaration of the Constitutional States of America,

When in the Course of human events, it becomes necessary for one people to dissolve the political bands which have connected them with another, and to assume among the powers of the earth, the separate and equal station to which the Laws of Nature and of Nature's God entitle them, a decent respect to the opinions of mankind requires that they should declare the causes which impel them to the separation.

We hold these truths to be self-evident, that all men are created equal, that they are endowed by their Creator with certain unalienable rights, that among these are Life, Liberty and the pursuit of Happiness.

That to secure these rights, Governments are instituted among Men, deriving their just powers from the consent of the governed.

That whenever any Form of Government becomes destructive of these ends, it is the Right of the People to alter or to abolish it, and to institute new Government, laying its foundation on such principles and organizing its powers in such form, as to them shall seem most likely to effect their Safety and Happiness.

Prudence, indeed, will dictate that Governments long established should not be changed for light and transient causes; and accordingly all experience has shown, that mankind are more disposed to suffer, while evils are sufferable, then to right themselves by abolishing the forms to which they are accustomed.

But when a long train of abuses and usurpations, pushing invariably the same Object evinces a design to reduce them under absolute Despotism, it is their right, it is their duty, to throw off such Government, and to provide new Guards for their future security.

Such has been the patient sufferance of these states; and such is now the necessity which constrains them to alter their former Systems of Government.

The history of the present Federal Government of the political entity known as the 'United States of America' is a history of repeated injuries and usurpations, all having in direct object the establishment of an absolute Tyranny over these Constitutional States. To prove this, let Facts be submitted to a candid world.

- *They have betrayed the People by imposing a hostile, alien political philosophy upon them, and have implemented all ten planks of the Communist Manifesto; including a graduated income tax, seizure of inheritances, and indoctrination of our children in government schools.*
- *They have combined with others, through their abuse of the power to make treaties, to subject us to jurisdictions foreign to our Constitution, and unacknowledged by our laws; giving their Assent to their acts of pretended Legislation.*
- *Through specious use of 'The Interstate Commerce Clause', They have inserted themselves into and regulated every aspect of the lives of the People, no matter how minute, unconstitutionally usurping powers reserved to the States or the People.*
- *They have erected a multitude of New Agencies, and sent hither swarms of Agents to harass our people, and destroy their prosperity.*
- *They have created a Secret, parallel government and military-industrial complex unaccountable to the People and destructive of their Liberties.*
- *They have entangled the Nation in a series of unceasing, unconstitutional wars and alliances contrary to the People's interests.*
- *On the pretext of securing the People, They have established Standing Armies of armed Agents in our midst, and have protected them, by mock trials, from punishment for murders they have committed, including the immolation of a church along with all of its parishioners.*
- *Meanwhile, they have rendered our borders defenseless, allowing vast hordes of aliens hostile to our Traditions to freely invade our nation.*
- *They have claimed the power to assassinate Citizens, without Due Process, or to seize and detain them in military prisons indefinitely, without trial, at the sole discretion of the occupant of the Office of the Presidency.*
- *They have embraced torture as an implement of official policy, a practice repugnant to all Civilized People.*
- *They have endeavored to disarm the People and render them defenseless against criminal predation and the Agents of Despotism.*
- *They have unconstitutionally ceded authority over the Nation's economy to an unelected cabal of private banks known as 'The Federal Reserve', and have allowed them to abolish real, constitutional money in favor of the false weights and measures of a fiat currency, enslaving the People in perpetual Debt Bondage.*

- *They have mortgaged the future of the People by draining the Treasury and assuming unsustainable obligations.*
- *They have enticed vast numbers of the People into dependency by redistributing to them largess stolen from their fellow Citizens.*
- *They have systematically stolen from Citizens, who were innocent of any crimes, through the criminal misapplication of 'asset forfeiture laws'.*
- *They have repeatedly infringed upon the People's right to the free use of their own lands and property through the imposition of onerous regulations.*
- *They routinely violate the right of the People to be secure in their persons, data, and effects by subjecting them to extensive surveillance of every aspect of their Lives, unconstitutionally maintaining dossiers on them, and destroying any vestige of their Privacy or Liberty.*
- *They have violated the rights of the People to free religious association by wielding the Power of Law to compel Citizens to participate in practices they find morally repugnant.*
- *They have unconstitutionally abridged the rights of the People to free speech and assembly, and to seek redress of grievances, by restricting the exercise of those rights to limited, out-of-the-way areas the government has dubbed 'First Amendment Zones'.*

In every stage of these Oppressions We have Petitioned for Redress in the most humble terms: Our repeated Petitions have been answered only by repeated injury. A Government whose character is thus marked by every act which may define a Tyrant, is unfit to rule a free people.

Nor have We been wanting in attentions to our supposed representatives in the Federal Government. We have warned them repeatedly when their actions exceeded the limits on their power as set forth in the Constitution. We have appealed to their native justice and magnanimity, and we have conjured them by the ties of our common history to disavow these usurpations, which, would inevitably interrupt our connections and Union.

They have denied our common history, choosing instead to sow discord among the People and to be deaf to the voice of Justice and Tradition.

We must, therefore, acquiesce in the necessity, which denounces our Separation, and hold them, as we hold the rest of mankind, Enemies in War, in Peace Friends.

We, therefore, the Representatives of the Constitutional States of America, in General Assembly, appealing to the Supreme Judge of the world for the rectitude of our intentions, do, in the Name, and by Authority of the good People of these States, solemnly publish and declare, That these Constitutional States are, and of Right ought to be, Free and Independent; that they are Absolved from all Allegiance to the Federal Government of the political entity known as the 'United States of America', and that all political connection between them is and ought to be totally dissolved; and that as Free and Independent States, they have the full Power to levy War, conclude Peace, contract Alliances, establish Commerce, and to do all other Acts and Things which Independent States may of right do.

And for the support of this Declaration, with a firm reliance on the protection of divine Providence, we mutually pledge to each other our Lives, our Fortunes and our sacred Honor.

On this Fourth of July weekend, in addition to enjoying time with family and friends, cook-outs and fireworks, take a few moments and reflect on the bravery and audacity of our Forefathers who risked all to win, against seemingly insurmountable odds, the freedoms they then bequeathed to us.

May God Bless all of you and may He grant us the fortitude to be worthy successors to their legacy.

15 – Clinton's Trump Card – How 'The Donald' Can Clear Hillary's Road to the White House

First Published on July 12, 2015

This is the first of many essays I wrote about the 2016 presidential election. On June 16, 2015, Donald Trump announced his candidacy. As you will be able to easily tell from this essay I was not initially impressed nor did I trust him.

I quickly identified some of the traits that opponents of Trump cite to this day as reasons to not like him – his tendency to speak in sweeping, rambling generalities and platitudes when not reading from a prepared statement; his propensity to 'jump in the gutter' and engage in childish-sounding name-calling against opponents; and most importantly, a history of flip-flopping on issues to the point where many times it's difficult to know what his positions truly are.

The first problem, Trump's tendency to ramble and go on tangents while speaking, became much less of a problem as the campaign progressed. He stuck to his prepared remarks more often and, with practice, greatly improved at giving policy speeches.

The second issue, his propensity to engage in Jerry Springer-like, lowest common denominator discourse with his opponents, turned out to be one of his greatest assets, particularly when dealing with crass and dishonest enemies on the politically correct Left. For decades the Cultural Marxists had easily cowed Republicans into submission on issue after issue by taking advantage of the latter's excessive Traditionalist sense of decorum and dignified reserve.

No one has ever accused Trump of having excessive decorum and dignified reserve. He is a rhetorical street fighter who responds to all insults and attacks with many times the incoming venom. The globalist establishment, mainstream media, and both Democratic and Republican opponents had no idea how to deal with him – he simply refused to follow the usual politically correct script.

When they called him a racist after he made uncontrolled borders and illegal immigration the keystone of his campaign, removed his shows off network television, and boycotted his products he didn't crawl away with his tail between his legs like nearly everyone else had previously done – he aggressively counterattacked and escalated his rhetoric on the subject.

So it's been ever since on issue after issue. When the leftist mainstream media produced a decade old, off-the-record video tape late in the campaign of Trump engaging in 'locker room talk' and bragging about supposed sexual conquests of women, they accused him of being a misogynist. That quickly blew up in their faces when he correctly and incessantly pointed out that the hypocrites had no credibility on the subject after decades of defending serial rapist Bill Clinton and his enabler Hillary.

Following his victory, when the Left desperately tried to pin the hoax of 'Russian collusion' onto him, he stood resolutely against the false charges and correctly and repeatedly called out the mainstream media for being the purveyors of fake news that they are until finally, as of this writing, it appears that false narrative is finally starting to crumble in the wake of Comey's testimony to the U.S. Senate confirming there is no evidence to support it.

Even if President Trump had accomplished nothing more than exposing political correctness for the paper tiger it has always been, he still would have done America a great service and earned her eternal gratitude. Political correctness can only work when people surrender to it in foolish fear that others will believe the Cultural Marxists' accusations against them. As with any other bully, once they are stood up to their aura of invincibility vanishes and their power over others disappears.

Tens of millions of Traditional Americans quickly followed Trump's lead, asserting themselves against leftist thought-tyranny like never before and gleefully telling liberals/socialists/communists, wherever they found them, ever-more creative variants of 'shut the fuck up and pound sand, commie'. Watching the resulting meltdown of the Left throughout the world as their heads explode with collective butthurt has been a truly beautiful sight to behold.

From the start, Trump was the long-hoped-for knight who finally arrived to slay the dragon of political correctness. That was never a problem with him in my mind – in fact that was his greatest selling point. The deal-breaking problem for me was the last issue I raised in this essay – his apparent lack of a consistent political philosophy and dependability on what I consider fundamental issues. Particularly troubling to me was that, on his signature issue of immigration, he was on record, three short years prior to launching his bid for the Presidency, criticizing 2012 Republican nominee Mitt Romney for losing the election because of alienating Asian, Latino, and other 'people of color' by proposing an immigration policy far more tepid than Trump's 2015 rhetoric.

I understand that politicians, even those allied with Traditional America, will 'adjust' their position on an issue from time to time for pragmatic reasons. That's realpolitik and I get it. But for this drastic a flip-flop, on so fundamental an issue, I felt compelled to throw the bullshit flag on one whom, at the time, I considered to be little more than a celebrity media persona known as 'The Donald'. Add to that my initial belief, shared with the vast majority across the political spectrum, that he had only a snowball's chance in Hell of winning the election, and my greatest fear began to take shape in my mind — that, deliberately or inadvertently, he would run as an independent after failing to secure the Republican nomination, split the opposition to the Democrats, and ensure a second, even more disastrous Clinton Administration.

I thank God every day that I completely miscalculated President Trump's chances of winning. But I didn't understand at the time what Trump's exact motivation for seeking the Presidency was. I knew it wasn't to get rich — he already had a net worth of billions of dollars. It wasn't fame — he was a household name across the nation and many parts of the world. Some said it was for power but, even though he is clearly one of the greatest examples of a Type A personality to be found and certainly has a healthy dose of narcissism, his history doesn't seem to indicate a personality who feels the need to dominate others. In fact, nearly all of his former and current employees I've heard speak seem to love him and say he treated them well, and they wouldn't say that about a sociopathic asshole.

Which left a couple of other possible explanations. The first one that made the most sense to me was pointed out by a friend in early 2016. He'd stumbled upon a YouTube video of the 2011 White House Correspondents' Dinner, where President Obama went out of his way to publicly humiliate Trump, and in the most visible manner possible, in retaliation for comments Trump had made questioning Obama's citizenship. Obama didn't merely quickly roast Trump in the traditional good-natured way and move on — he verbally beat on him like a court jester for what seemed like an eternity.

A 2016 clip on the subject from the PBS documentary 'Frontline' examines some very interesting background information on this incident and is definitely worth watching for those who wish to understand Trump's motivation for seeking the Presidency. To find it, go to YouTube and search for "Inside the Night President Obama Took On Donald Trump | The Choice 2016 | FRONTLINE".

As the documentary shows, Obama's over-the-top verbal assault on Trump was an unexpected ambush. Trump was initially surprised and delighted to be invited to the prestigious event — delight which quickly turned to embarrassed mortification.

In that moment, when the young, hubristic Obama, supremely confident in his superiority and power, looked down his nose at Donald Trump and decided to 'put him in his place', it is eminently clear from Trump's expression and body language that Obama foolishly made an eternal enemy that day. It was like watching a scene from 'The Godfather'. To a proud man like Trump, this ultimate public humiliation could never be forgiven nor forgotten.

I have no doubt now this was a pivotal moment in American history. I believe it was in that moment Trump decided he was going to show the entire world just what he was capable of and rub the noses of all who ever doubted him in their own shit. That gloating, overconfident moment is when Obama destroyed any hope for his pathetic excuse of a 'legacy'. It was a sublimely powerful illustration of Psalm 16:18 — "Pride goeth before destruction, and a haughty spirit before a fall."

Looking back on that moment now, I cannot help but view Trump as a sympathetic figure. Furthermore, it makes the motivation for all of Trump's subsequent actions crystal-clear. Putting the media in their place for being the leftist, lap-dog sycophants they are and gleefully cheering while Obama berated Trump — check. Telling the White House Correspondents' Dinner to go fuck themselves when it came time to hold the first one during his Presidency — check. Doing everything in his power to dismantle every aspect of Obama's, and by extension, the Left's agenda — check. Destroying the nefarious plans of Obama's globalist puppet masters — check.

*Revenge is a motive I can understand, and yes, **respect**. There is no man with a shred of pride who would not do the same thing in Trump's shoes if he were able to do so.*

There are those who say, deep-down, that Trump has always been an America-First nationalist — a sort of 'sleeper-cell patriot' who mingled with members of the globalist Left by necessity and only until the opportunity came to hoist the Jolly Roger and move in to destroy them. Some comments from old interviews Trump gave as far back as the 1980s, along with many of his actions during the first four months of his young Presidency (such as pulling America out of the sovereignty and economy-killing Trans-Pacific Partnership and the Paris Accord on so-called 'climate change') supports this opinion.

For me, at the end of the day, whether Trump is really motivated by a sense of

93

pure patriotism, a thirst for revenge, or some combination of the two is irrelevant. In our particular circumstances, revenge will do – since those who Trump seeks vengeance against are the very same God-less, Marxist globalists who seek our destruction and the destruction of all we hold dear. His enemies are our enemies, and that's good enough.

As soon as I saw the clip of Obama's performance at the 2011 White House Correspondents' Dinner I resolved to vote for Trump because I instantly recognized he was the only candidate with the drive and (perhaps foolhardy) courage to defy the odds, take on what amounted to a suicide mission against the globalist cabal that had already anointed Hillary Clinton their next Minion-in-Chief, and actually have a chance to prevail.

History is replete with examples whereby Providence used imperfect men to accomplish His will. I believe the election of Donald Trump may very well be another instance. If so, in spite of his human imperfections, he will be the answer to the prayers of Traditional America and of good people everywhere.

***

The news cycle of the past month has been a churning pot of utter chaos. The Middle East descended further into anarchy as the Obama administration continued 'negotiating' in its on-going efforts to ensure Iran gets nukes while Moslem terrorism continued its unabated steady expansion across the world. The global economy teetered on the brink of collapse as one of history's greatest bubbles popped in China and the Eurozone experiment began to unravel, threatening to bring down the rest of the world in a tsunami of unpayable derivatives. Here in the United States the Culture Wars ratcheted up exponentially as politically correct assaults on Traditional Americans escalated across the board following the massacre in Charleston and the twin Supreme Court decisions on Obamacare and homosexual marriage. Finally, all of this took place against the opening acts of the Circus of the Absurd known as the 2016 presidential race.

Any one of these important stories would have dominated the news all by itself in normal times…but these aren't normal times. The dissolution of 'the world as we know it' has sped up so fast in the past few weeks it's become nearly impossible to keep up with it all.

In mid-June the subject of illegal immigration briefly bubbled up to the top of the cauldron. On June 16 Donald Trump announced he was entering the race for the Republican presidential nomination. During a long, apparently ad-libbed, bombastic (and mostly disorganized) announcement speech that seemed to touch on every talking point that would appeal to conservative Americans – from ISIS and Iran to Obamacare to China to fixing the economy, etc., etc., etc. – Trump uttered these now infamous words:

When do we beat Mexico at the border? They're laughing at us, at our stupidity. And now they are beating us economically. They are not our friend, believe me. But they're killing us economically.

The U.S. has become a dumping ground for everybody else's problems.

(Applause)

Thank you. It's true, and these are the best and the finest. When Mexico sends its people, they're not sending their best. They're not sending you. They're not sending you. They're sending people that have lots of problems, and they're bringing those problems with us. They're bringing drugs. They're bringing crime. They're rapists. And some, I assume, are good people.

But I speak to border guards and they tell us what we're getting. And it only makes common sense. It only makes common sense. They're sending us not the right people.

It's coming from more than Mexico. It's coming from all over South and Latin America, and it's coming probably— probably— from the Middle East. But we don't know. Because we have no protection and we have no competence, we don't know what's happening. And it's got to stop and it's got to stop fast...

Then, as he was summarizing the main points of his speech, he said:

I would build a great wall, and nobody builds walls better than me, believe me, and I'll build them very inexpensively, I will build a great,

great wall on our southern border. And I will have Mexico pay for that wall.

Mark my words.

Here's a link to the text of the whole 45 minute, 24 second speech: http://www.washingtonpost.com/blogs/post-politics/wp/2015/06/16/full-text-donald-trump-announces-a-presidential-bid/ (Yes, unfortunately I was masochistic enough to read the whole thing...)

Now, there are many reasons not to like Donald Trump as a presidential candidate but, to paraphrase the old saying, even a broken clock can sound right twice a day – especially when cynically pandering to frustrated, Traditional Americans desperate to hear, *just once*, a public figure have the nerve to say *something* – **anything** – politically incorrect.

Trump was right about several things in his comments on illegal immigration. America *has* become a 'dumping ground' for many other countries' social problems. Mexico, a failed state by most measures, has used the United States for decades as a social safety valve by sending its excess poor population north of the border.

By definition, most of the people making the trip north are going to be the least successful in Mexican society – if they were part of the upper classes they would have no reason to leave. The people illegally sneaking into America *do* tend to have more problems than those they left behind in their home countries and are thus a greater strain on our social services. There are also many violent criminals that come across the border along with illegal drugs.

Trump is also right that the United States government has absolutely no control and little knowledge of what is crossing the border, but we *do* know they include illegal aliens from many countries in addition to Mexico and probably Moslem terrorists from the Middle East as well. Finally, he is correct when he says the border needs to be physically secured.

Predictably, the politically correct elite and media had a fit. Leftist wailing and gnashing of teeth filled the airwaves. Trump was 'hateful', they said, 'mean-spirited' and 'disrespectful' to Latinos everywhere – a disgrace to our modern multicultural, inclusive, compassionate society.

The next day the Charleston massacre knocked the furor over Trump's immigration comments off the front pages for a couple of weeks. Then came the senseless murder on July 1st of 32 year-old Kathryn Steinle on a San Francisco pier by an illegal alien who had seven felony convictions and who'd been deported five times.

Illegal immigration was back at the top of the news. Trump doubled-down on his earlier comments and correctly cited Steinle's death as an example of the type of violent crime illegal aliens bring with them.

Liberal pundits from coast to coast lambasted him as a racist. Networks dropped his shows from their programming. Retailers stopped selling his products. Most of the other Republican candidates (with the exception of Cruz and Carson) denounced him and treated him like he had political plague.

So what could any right-thinking conservative supporter of Traditional American values *not* like about this man? Finally, here was someone with the guts to tell the politically incorrect truth – and who had the deep pockets and will to be able to weather the inevitable PC backlash. Who better to set this country straight than 'The Donald' – a man who's just proven he's willing to pay a large financial price for his convictions?

Absolutely nothing – as long as Trump is *really* who he appears to be. Unfortunately, even a cursory internet search reveals that his current, apparently strong 'convictions' on illegal immigration do not match statements he made on the subject as recently as three years ago.

During the 2012 presidential campaign Mitt Romney, not exactly what most Traditional Americans would consider a staunch conservative, advocated a fairly tepid 'immigration plan' that included the idea of making sure employers could not hire illegals, thus denying them the ability to earn a living, eventually forcing them to have to give up being in America and freely returning to their home countries. This concept was derisively dubbed 'self-deportation' by his political opponents – an idea later defended by Romney himself as a more 'compassionate approach' to the problem than arrest and forced deportation.

Shortly after Romney's defeat, Donald Trump gave this post-mortem on the Republican nominee's campaign in an interview with Newsmax:

> *The Republican Party will continue to lose presidential elections if it comes across as mean-spirited and unwelcoming toward people of color, Donald Trump tells Newsmax.*
>
> *Whether intended or not, comments and policies of Mitt Romney and other Republican candidates during this election were seen by Hispanics and Asians as hostile to them, Trump says.*
>
> *"Republicans didn't have anything going for them with respect to Latinos and with respect to Asians," the billionaire developer says.*
>
> *"The Democrats didn't have a policy for dealing with illegal immigrants, but what they did have going for them is they weren't mean-spirited about it," Trump says. "They didn't know what the policy was, but what they were is they were kind."*
>
> *Romney's solution of "self deportation" for illegal aliens made no sense and suggested that Republicans do not care about Hispanics in general, Trump says.*
>
> *"He had a crazy policy of self deportation which was maniacal," Trump says. "It sounded as bad as it was, and he lost all of the Latino vote," Trump notes. "He lost the Asian vote. He lost everybody who is inspired to come into this country."*
>
> *The GOP has to develop a comprehensive policy "to take care of this incredible problem that we have with respect to immigration, with respect*

to people wanting to be wonderful productive citizens of this country,"
Trump says.

Check out the article for yourself here:

http://www.newsmax.com/Newsfront/Donald-Trump-Ronald-Kessler/2012/11/26/id/465363/

Wow – that sure is a far cry from today's would-be builder of a 'great, great wall' (nobody builds a wall better or cheaper than 'The Donald', after all) dedicated to saving America's future by keeping illegals out. On the contrary, Trump in 2012 sounds *exactly* like one of those politically-correct idiots now criticizing his anti-illegal immigration comments in 2015.

Trump thought Romney's weak 'self-deportation' idea was 'maniacal' and 'mean-spirited towards people of color' and that 'the Democrats didn't have a policy on illegal immigration....but what they were is they were *kind*'!? (emphasis added)

Really????

What the hell's up with Trump, anyway? That's as big a flip-flop as Obama's 2008 opposition to homosexual marriage magically morphing into 'Rainbow Barry' becoming the Champion of the so-called 'LGBT' Cause by 2012.

If Trump believed three years ago that a 'mean-spirited GOP will not win presidential elections', why is he doing *that exact same thing* as a supposed Republican presidential candidate in 2015? Is he nuts? Did he just 'forget' what he said about immigration in 2012? Or does he have something else in mind?

It gets better…

Trump gave over $100,000 to the Clinton Foundation slush-fund and made numerous other donations to some of the most liberal Democratic politicians over the years – including Hillary's Senate campaign.

See this link:

http://www.washingtonpost.com/politics/trumps-donation-history-shows-democratic-favoritism/2011/04/25/AFDUddtE_story.html

To be fair, he also donated to Republican candidates as well, though not as much. It could be argued that, as a prudent businessman, he was hedging his bets by apolitically donating to both parties – a normal practice in our current corrupt system of buying influence using lobbyists and legal bribery known as 'campaign finance'.

It can also be argued, however, that a true defender of Traditional America would rather be caught dead before giving a dime to the vile Clintons and others of the same Marxist ilk such as Schumer, Lautenberg, Ted Kennedy, Reid, Rangel, et al.

So, we have in Trump a Republican candidate who has donated heavily to some of the most liberal politicians in America over the past couple decades or so. A man who suddenly does a complete 180 on illegal immigration sometime during the last three years. Why the change?

Then I came across this story and the pieces of the puzzle fell into place:

http://www.washingtonpost.com/politics/trump-vows-long-campaign-wont-commit-to-backing-gop-nominee/2015/07/09/8f75a5b8-264e-11e5-b72c-2b7d516e1e0e_story.html

There's one very simple explanation for the apparent contradiction that has to be considered. Maybe there's no contradiction at all. Maybe, deep down, Donald Trump is just another rich liberal – only one that knows how to spout conservative rhetoric.

Since he's currently doing something he previously said would keep Republicans from winning future presidential elections (i.e. saying things that 'come across as mean-spirited and unwelcoming to people of color', Latinos, and Asians) then it's possible that's *exactly* what he means to do – sabotage Republican chances of winning the 2016 election. Perhaps he's only pretending to be Republican in order to infiltrate the party's primary process and disrupt it from within – the ultimate RINO (Republican in name only).

Although he has brought some much needed attention to the issue of illegal immigration (a topic mainstream Republicans usually run from) he's also, at least for now, sucked all the oxygen out of the room and grabbed most of the media attention, to the detriment of the other candidates. With his Jerry Springer-style soundbites cluttering the airwaves, don't expect much deep analysis on any issue in the near future.

Even worse, although Trump says in the article that he believes the best chance for him to defeat the Democrats is for him to 'win as a Republican because I don't want to be splitting up votes" he doesn't rule out running as a third-party candidate if he doesn't win the nomination.

If he *does* decide to run as an independent in the general election we'll know the fix is in and the *real* reason for his candidacy will become clear, since he has to know he doesn't have a realistic chance to win.

I believe it's a reasonable theory that the Cultural Marxist 'powers-that-be' have their eye on Hillary Clinton to be their next presidential minion in the White House – based on the extraordinary free passes she's getting from law enforcement officials and the media regarding her many scandals (Clinton Foundation bribery, classified info on illegal unsecured e-mail servers, Benghazi, etc.) and her outrageous behavior on the campaign trail (almost no access to media, near total refusal to answer questions or give interviews, completely staged 'spontaneous campaign events', 'roping-off' reporters to deny them access to Her Majesty, etc.).

If this theory is true, the 'powers-that-be' would prefer that Hillary be able to win the election with a minimum of direct manipulation in order to preserve the illusion that American elections are a fair and open process.

There's one big problem with that plan, however. In spite of the fact that the Cultural Marxists' decades-long 'open borders' policy has stacked the demographic electoral deck so far to the left that it's nearly impossible for a true conservative to win the Presidency any more, Hillary Clinton is such a blatantly repulsive human being that there is no guarantee she will be able to generate enough turnout to win, even among the half of the American people that are so brain-dead they would vote for Satan himself so long as he had a Democrat jackass logo after his name.

Enter 'Plan B' – Donald Trump. Just as her husband's road to the White House back in the elections of 1992 and 1996 was cleared by another bombastic, eccentric billionaire businessman named Ross Perot, Hillary's path can be cleared by Trump.

Without Ross Perot taking crucial votes from Bush 41, America would not have had to endure the 25 years of sleaze and venality the Clintons brought to the country's public life. With Trump's help, the Clintons can once again be installed in the highest office in the land, and the public would never suspect 'the-powers-that-be' had any hand in it. Instead, disgruntled Republicans will blame 'that whacko' Trump for Hillary's victory – just as they blamed Perot for Bill's. (Pay no attention to the men behind the curtain…)

Trump currently leads the GOP field in a recent poll with 16%, slightly ahead of Jeb Bush. If he decides to run in the general election as an independent, it's a reasonable assumption that he could take *at least* that amount of would-be Republican voters with him. In the current electoral reality, where the Republicans must have everything go their way to even have a shot at keeping close to the Democratic nominee, that would be fatal.

I hope I'm wrong about Trump. I hope he miraculously experienced, sometime during the last three years, a sincere 'Saul-on-the-road-to-Damascus' moment, is now a genuine conservative ready to fight for Traditional American values, and isn't just spewing bullshit.

Because if he *is* deceiving Traditional Americans and gets Hillary Rodham Clinton elected the next President, and she gets four more years to complete the cultural, economic, and political destruction wrought during the eight years of Barack Hussein Obama, you can stick a fork in the United States of America.

It will be done.

16 – War on Our Doorstep – Why We Must *All* Become Minutemen Now

First Published on July 20, 2015

This essay was written in the immediate aftermath of a jihadist attack on a military recruiting station and Navy Reserve facility in Chattanooga, Tennessee that killed five American servicemen. Although a large part of the essay breaks down the potential scope of the orthodox Moslem terror threat in America, it also points out that other domestic enemies of Traditional America, such as radicalized minorities and leftists, have the potential to pose a terroristic threat as well.

A year after this essay was written, this prediction was borne-out by the 'Black Lives Matter' inspired military-style ambush that killed five Dallas police officers in July 2016. It was proven correct yet again nearly a year later when, in June 2017, a 66-year-old white male supporter of Bernie Sanders, spurred by the incessant wave of violent, bellicose rhetoric spewed by the Left in the wake of President Trump's election, used a military-style rifle in the attempted mass assassination of members of the Republican congressional baseball team practicing at a public park in Arlington, Virginia.

In this essay I called upon my fellow Traditional Americans to stop viewing this type of violence as random acts of crime and recognize it for what it is – nascent attacks against us in a new War of Cultures – a war pitting Marxists against champions of individual liberty, secularists against defenders of Traditional Judeo-Christian values, racial tribalists against those of other tribes, orthodox Moslems against everyone else.

Regardless of how much members of the 'respectable' establishment try to deny the fact, the many enemies of Traditional America long ago initiated a de facto 4th generation war against us – a fight-to-the-death Clash of Civilizations that will only end when one side is completely subjugated by the other.

In light of this new reality, I further called upon my fellow Traditional Americans to become 21st century, 4th generation Minutemen prepared to defend themselves and their communities against our self-proclaimed enemies. I also went into some detail as to how each citizen could arm and train themselves to repel the types of surprise terror attacks our enemies have typically used against us.

Had there been such armed and trained citizens present, some of the attacks against the West that have occurred in the two years since this essay was written might very well have been mitigated, or at least the death tolls might have been reduced.

Here is a partial list of those attacks: The November 2015 Paris attacks on a concert and soccer stadium that killed 137; the December 2015 San Bernardino attack that killed 14; the June 2016 attack on the Orlando nightclub that killed 49; the Bastille Day 2016 attack in Nice, France where 87 people were shot to death or crushed by a Moslem driving a truck; later in July 2016, the murder and decapitation of a French priest on the altar of his church while saying Mass; a November 2016 car and knife attack by a Somali refugee at Ohio State University that wounded 11; a December 2016 attack in Berlin where 12 people shopping at a Christmas market were crushed to death by a Moslem driving a truck; another truck attack, this one in Sweden in April 2017 that killed 5; and finally, the June 2017 van and knife attack on London Bridge that killed 7.

I left out bombing attacks such as the March 2016 twin bombings at the Brussels Airport and Metro that killed 35 and the May 2017 bombing at a concert in Manchester that killed 22 (mostly young girls), since it can be argued that an armed citizen would not usually be able to prevent such attacks.

As dire as the Islamic threat is, however, the long-term danger to Traditional Americans posed by radicalized leftists and minority groups may prove to be even greater as the United States continues its slide towards a Second American Civil War. After all, there are a lot more of them in America than there are Moslems.

Prepare yourself accordingly.

***

War has come to America. Not your grandfather's war, fought an ocean away in Europe or Asia while the American people, safe at home, followed the progress of battle watching newsreels or black-and-white TV – but a type of warfare not seen on American soil since Indians clashed with Whites on the western frontier.

This type of war is a War of Cultures, a Clash of Civilizations – in many ways the most vicious and intractable type of warfare there is. This war has snuck up on us slowly, over many decades, like the proverbial 'thief in the night'. The seeds were sown long ago – here at home by Cultural Marxist 'progressives' who have worked tirelessly to fray our social fabric by pushing hate-generating group-identity grievance politics over the principles of individual achievement and universal human rights our nation was founded on; and in the Middle East by a 'prophet' of evil and hatred who commanded his acolytes to go forth and wage endless war in the name of Allah against the 'unbelievers' until the entire world submits to his wicked creed.

The first shots of this war looked like, and were mostly labeled as, random acts of crime. Generations of minorities in this country have been taught that they are victims of white 'racism' and white 'privilege', and that the society they live in is inherently hostile to them. They have been taught that 'hate crimes' are violent acts committed by whites against minorities, but not by minorities against whites because, by the politically correct definition, only white people can be racists.

It should come as no surprise, then, that many minorities have decided to prey on whites. The Charleston church massacre notwithstanding, blacks in America are far more likely to commit crimes against whites than vice-versa – eight times more likely. Violence committed by (mostly Hispanic) illegal aliens against native-born Americans is on the rise as well, as was illustrated by the well-publicized murder of 32-year-old Kathryn Steinle by one of those aliens (who had previously been convicted of seven felonies and deported five times) while strolling with her father along a San Francisco pier.

Less well-publicized and well-known was the murder, five days later, of 30-year-old Carrie Jean Melvin. She was walking with her boyfriend in the touristy Hollywood neighborhood where they lived, just blocks from the theater where the Academy Awards are presented, when a black man, described as being 'in his mid-20s, approximately 6-feet tall, wearing dark clothes including a dark 'hoodie' (naturally) came up behind the couple, who turned at the last second to see who it was. The gunman pointed a shotgun at Carrie's head and fired, killing her instantly – all without saying a word to her or her boyfriend. Then the still-unidentified black man calmly got into a black sedan, which then drove off.

Here's a link to one of the stories I found about this case:

http://www.cnn.com/2015/07/09/us/hollywood-murder-mystery-carrie-jean-melvin/index.html

Police are baffled by the murder – there is no evidence it was a botched robbery as nothing was said by the killer and no demands were made. Ms. Melvin had no known enemies and there is no apparent motive even though the murder has the appearance of a targeted killing.

Perhaps this was some sort of gang initiation requiring the new 'banger' to commit a random killing to demonstrate his 'manliness', or maybe the black thug in this case just felt like killing a white woman for the hell of it. We may never know. What we do know is that, for the second time in less than a week, an innocent young white woman was gunned down in cold blood by a puke of color on the streets of the Great State of California.

As a mental exercise, just imagine the politically correct righteous outrage that would ensue if two black women had been gunned down in cold blood by white men. Marches would be organized by Jesse Jackson and Al Sharpton. Cities would go up in flames. Obama would appear on TV to lament that the victims 'could have been his daughters' and would send his Attorney General to 'investigate' the pervasiveness of 'white hate' in the nation. Washington and Jefferson would be dynamited off Mount Rushmore in a grand ceremony of triumphant 'diversity' because they were slave-holders and symbols of our nation's 'racist DNA'.

By comparison, what was the reaction of the so-called 'president' to these two murders of white women by minorities? Utter, total, cricket-inducing silence.

As tragic as the murders of Kathryn Steinle and Carrie Jean Melvin are, they are only two of the most recent examples of a very, very long pattern of violence by minorities against whites in this country. In recent years the high rate of minority violence against individuals

107

(especially when compared to their relatively low percentage of the population), along with their acts of collective violence such as 'flash mob' looting and race riots, has begun to cross the (admittedly inexact) line between run-of-the-mill 'crime' and the violence phase of what military theorists refer to as 'low-intensity conflict' or '4ᵗʰ generation warfare'.

'Low-intensity conflict' is defined by the US Army as:

> ...*a political-military confrontation between contending states or groups below conventional war and above the routine, peaceful competition among states. It **frequently involves protracted struggles of competing principles and ideologies.*** (emphasis added) *Low-intensity conflict ranges from subversion to the use of the armed forces. It is waged by a combination of means, employing political, economic, informational, and military instruments.*

https://en.wikipedia.org/wiki/Low_intensity_conflict

'4ᵗʰ generation warfare' is a concept along the same lines, but one that emphasizes non-state actors and non-traditional, 'outside-the-box' means of conflict that includes many tactics that would have been considered 'unorthodox' or 'unacceptable' during earlier wars in the modern era.

For a cursory view of a fairly complex and innovative military theory, I will refer again to what Wikipedia has to say on the subject:

> **Fourth-generation warfare** *(4GW) is conflict characterized by a blurring of the lines between war and politics, combatants and civilians.*
>
> *The term was first used in 1989 by a team of American analysts, including William S. Lind, to describe warfare's return to a decentralized form. In terms of generational modern warfare, the fourth generation signifies the nation states' loss of their near-monopoly on combat forces, returning to modes of conflict common in pre-modern times.*
>
> *The simplest definition includes any war in which one of the major*

participants is not a state but rather a violent non-state actor. Classical examples, such as the slave uprising under Spartacus, predate the modern concept of warfare and are examples of this type of conflict…

…Fourth-generation warfare is normally characterized by a violent non-state actor (VNSA) fighting a state. This fighting can be physically done, such as by modern examples Hezbollah or the Liberation Tigers of Tamil Eelam (LTTE). In this realm, the VNSA uses all three levels of fourth generation warfare. These are the physical (actual combat; it is considered the least important), mental (the will to fight, belief in victory, etc.,) and moral (the most important, this includes cultural norms, etc.) levels.

A 4GW enemy has the following characteristics: lack of hierarchical authority, lack of formal structure, patience and flexibility, ability to keep a low profile when needed, and small size. A 4GW adversary might use the tactics of an insurgent, terrorist, or guerrilla in order to wage war against a nation's infrastructure. Fourth generation warfare takes place on all fronts: economic, political, the media, military, and civilian.

https://en.wikipedia.org/wiki/Fourth-generation_warfare

4th generation warfare, unlike the first three generations of warfare (which were fought nearly exclusively between the militaries of nation-states) is characterized by participants who are non-state actors who give their primary allegiance to something other than the state – their perceived ethnic identity, racial or tribal group, religious or ideological beliefs, or even organized crime groups such as gangs, rather than what country they happen to be living in.

4th generation warriors come in many forms. The Cultural Marxists who launched the decades-long verbal, legal, and political Culture Wars against Traditional American values have thus far been engaged in the early, preparatory phases of 4th generation warfare against us. The violent leftist and racial groups that arose in the wake of the chaos they've created – whether the Nation of Islam or the Crips, Bloods, and Gangster Disciples; MEChA or the Latin Kings, La Raza Nation, and MS-13; or even the tree-spiking fanatics of the Earth

Liberation Front – will all provide willing foot soldiers in the upcoming violent phase of the war against us.

As bad as that is for Traditional Americans, the-powers-that-be have encouraged and fomented another, even more dangerous threat to us – Moslem jihad. Non-state groups such as Hezbollah, Hamas, Al Qaeda, and now especially ISIS have mastered 4th generation warfare in the 21st century. They have utilized new technologies such as social media to reach out and market their virulent, orthodox brand of Islam to Moslems around the globe, calling on them to come to Syria and Iraq to fight for the new 'caliphate' if they can or, if that's not feasible, to launch attacks against whatever enemy targets are near them with whatever means are at hand.

And those Moslems have done just that throughout the world, killing innocent 'infidels' and 'apostates' wherever and whenever they can. They will continue to do so.

The recent attack on the military facilities in Chattanooga, Tennessee that killed five servicemen is just the latest in a long string of Moslem attacks on Americans. Moslems have been killing Americans for over 40 years – most of my adult life. Nor is this the first time the leadership of the US Military left its troops defenseless in the face of this enemy.

In Beirut, Lebanon, on October 23, 1983, an Iranian suicide bomber drove a truck bomb into a barracks housing US members of a peacekeeping force, mostly Marines, killing 241. The gate sentries were given restrictive rules of engagement – they were not allowed to have a round chambered in their rifles and even had to have their magazines removed. It was later determined that only one Marine was able to load a magazine and chamber a round prior to the blast – but by then it was too late.

Over the decades this paternalistic attitude of the upper brass and the distrust they display towards their troops regarding firearms has only gotten worse. The Fort Hood massacre in 2009 that killed 13 soldiers could have been mitigated and the death toll much reduced if the troops had been allowed to carry sidearms to protect themselves. Yet even after that tragic event DOD policy did not change – soldiers are still defenseless on military installations to this day.

Then there were the reports in recent years that the current 'president' has raised this disdain and distrust towards the troops to an unprecedented level. Marines who marched in Obama's second inaugural parade in 2013 had the bolts removed from their rifles before they were allowed to approach him, rendering them incapable of firing…you know, just in case…

http://townhall.com/tipsheet/katiepavlich/2013/02/11/obama-disarmed-marines-for-inaguration-parade-n1509511

Previously, during a 2012 visit to Afghanistan by then-Secretary of Defense Leon Panetta, a unit of 200 Marines was forced to leave the tent where he was speaking and lay down their personal weapons (M-16s, M-4s, and M-9s) before they were allowed to return to the venue. It was later reported that a Major General in that unit's chain of command had made the decision to do so.

http://www.nytimes.com/2012/03/15/world/asia/panetta-visits-afghanistan-following-massacre.html?_r=5&ref=elisabethbumiller&

No matter who gave that order, disarming American soldiers in a war zone is unconscionable and clearly reflects this administration's dim view towards military personnel – a view echoed by the Department of Homeland Security's warning that returning veterans are a terror threat while continuously asserting that Moslems aren't.

The fact that a Commander-in-Chief feels he cannot trust his troops speaks volumes about the sorry state of our nation – and the true character of the man occupying the White House.

This past Friday, one day after the Chattanooga massacre, the current Army Chief of Staff said there would be no immediate change to the Army's policy of having recruiters exposed in undefended strip malls – the recruiters would not be armed and no armed security would be assigned to those facilities. He stated the 'safety risk of accidental firearms discharges' outweighed any potential benefit of servicemen being able to defend themselves. He did say, however, that the policy would be 'reviewed'. How proactive of him – and a perfect example of the type of risk-averse, bureaucratic, political hack that rises to flag rank in America's military today.

Although nearly three times as many American servicemen were killed in Fort Hood six years ago than in Chattanooga, in one way this most recent massacre is more ominous for America's future.

The Moslem US Army major who murdered his fellow soldiers in Fort Hood had given numerous warning signs to others of his increasing Islamic militancy prior to the massacre. Those warnings were repeatedly ignored due to rampant political correctness – but at least they were there.

The killer in Chattanooga, in contrast, was described by most of his former classmates and the residents of his neighborhood as 'likeable', 'friendly', 'helpful', and 'just a guy' – a regular American who just happened to be Islamic.

In other words, the gunman, prior to the launching of his attack, was a model Moslem immigrant – just the kind that multiculturalists like Obama point to as an example of how Moslem immigration is a good thing that adds to the 'mosaic of diversity' in our society and enriches America.

But this begs the question – if a Moslem like the Chattanooga shooter can go 'jihadi' with no warning, how many others within the estimated 3 million-strong Moslem community in America are ready to do the same thing?

A 2013 Pew poll asked American Moslems, "are attacks, such as suicide bombings, on civilians ever justified in defense of Islam?" 81% said 'no' – 9 percentage points higher than the survey's global average of 72%.

http://www.csmonitor.com/USA/Society/2013/0501/How-US-Muslims-are-different-Pew-poll-sheds-light-on-global-contrasts

The politically correct American media trumpeted these poll results as vindication of their repeated assertions that Moslem immigrants to this country 'are no different' than other groups that preceded them and present no threat to America. But they're missing a couple of important points.

First, the poll results assume the respondents were all telling the pollsters the truth.

Second, and more important – if 81% of Moslems in America say attacks against civilians to defend Islam are never justified, then **_19% believe they are_**, at least under some circumstances.

That 19% is no doubt potentially receptive to the type of jihadist propaganda ISIS has been beaming around the world via social media. That 19% number also confirms the Traditional American's standard retort to the politically correct 'kumbaya' bullshit that 'not all Moslems are a terror threat' – 'No, not all Moslems are terrorists, but nearly all modern terrorists are Moslem.'

For comparison, someone should take a similar poll of Christians in America and ask if they would support attacks on civilians to 'defend Christianity'. I guarantee you well over 99% of the respondents would ask the pollster, 'Are you nuts?'

19% of 3 million is 570,000 – over half a million Moslems in America sympathetic to the idea that civilian massacres to 'defend Islam' can be justified. If only 3% of *that* number (the rule-of-thumb, standard estimate of the percentage of people, in any population, who will take up arms and fight for a cause they believe in) are actually willing to pull the trigger on Americans they consider 'infidels', that gives us a number of 17,100.

The Pew poll also found that 1% of the Moslems in America polled responded that "attacks on civilians 'in defense of Islam' are **_often_** justified. 1% of 3 million is 30,000, and the percentage of *that* sub-group who would be willing to pull triggers on 'infidels' is no doubt *much* higher than the 3% we assumed for the larger, less militant, group who said that violence was only 'sometimes' justified.

I believe it's within the realm of possibility that, after exposure to orthodox Moslem propaganda from ISIS and other affiliated groups on social media, half of those 30,000 hard-core American Moslems would be willing to violently act on the militant beliefs they self-reported to the pollsters, placing our 'best guess' around 15,000 – a number in the same ballpark as our earlier estimate of 17,100.

In other words, *there are probably 15,000 potential jihadis, and possibly more, already embedded in American society and open to the idea of murdering American civilians in this country 'to defend Islam'.*

That's roughly the equivalent of three Army infantry divisions' worth of shooters (assuming an average division size of 15,000 and a shooter to support troop ratio of 1:2)

Already here in America.

Inclined to fight and die a martyr's death for Allah.

That's 300 for every state. According to the US Geologic Survey, there are 3,141 counties or county equivalents (boroughs in Alaska; parishes in Louisiana, etc.) in the United States.

http://gallery.usgs.gov/audios/124#.Vasv2mxRHIU

That means, by our estimate, there are potentially 4.76 jihadis for every county in the United States. How much damage could four to five ISIS sympathizers do in your county?

And that doesn't even count the jihadis sneaking across our undefended southern border or the ones flying into our country in comfort with student, work, or tourist visas the Obama State Department rubber stamps and hands out like candy.

Consider those numbers for a moment – and think long and hard about what it means for your future safety and the safety of your family. For *you* are the target in this new, seemingly unending war –

you and your children, your loved ones, and all of your friends and neighbors.

Jihadis, in their countless attacks on innocent people around the world over the past 50 years, in addition to targeting soldiers, have also killed civilians while – shopping in malls; sunbathing on beaches; working at the office; riding on buses and subways; studying in schools; eating in restaurants; flying on planes; worshiping at churches, synagogues, and temples; sailing on cruise ships; staying in hotels; watching or running in a marathon; partying at nightclubs; shopping at grocery stores; gassing up their cars (Remember the DC snipers? Moslem converts.); driving down highways; hiding in their homes; etc., etc., etc., ad nauseum...

Given the chance, jihadis in the United States would eagerly do to us Americans what ISIS is inflicting on its victims in Iraq – they would crucify our children, take our daughters as sex-slaves, rape and kill our wives in front of us and then, finally, have us star in one of their sick snuff films as they have little brainwashed Moslem jihad-lings carve off our heads with knives or some other twisted bullshit.

Here's a link to pictures from a recent ISIS video showing the beheading of an alleged member of Assad's regime forces who'd supposedly been captured at an ISIS checkpoint. The evil little prick doing the carving is one of what the 'Islamic State' calls their 'Caliphate Cubs'. Just another way for those 'creative' jihadi propagandists to titillate their Moslem fans worldwide...

http://www.dailymail.co.uk/news/article-3164999/ISIS-film-CHILD-carrying-beheading-time-Cub-Caliphate-seen-executing-prisoner-decapitation-terror-group-increasingly-use-boys-kill.html

Fortunately for us, Moslems don't control any substantial geographic area in the United States (yet), so they don't have the latitude to murder us in such entertaining, leisurely fashions and instead have to content themselves with merely shooting us or blowing us up.

Unfortunately, as the devastated families of the four Marines and one Sailor who died in Chattanooga can attest, that's bad enough. And things are about to get much, much worse as this type of attack becomes more prevalent.

So who will defend us from this utterly evil, implacable enemy who is determined to wage jihad against us in our streets?

The military? They're not even willing to protect their own soldiers – how can we count on them to protect us?

The Feds? They spend far too much of their time and energy jumping through hoops trying to deny that terror committed by Moslems in America is actually inspired by their sick 'religion'.

State and local law enforcement? They're just as likely to try to disarm us as protect us.

Politicians? Yeah, right. The Democrats, especially Obama, are actively complicit in infiltrating this enemy into our country and are doing everything possible to disarm us, while the Republicans talk a good game but never seem to do much about the problem. Nobody is even willing to cut the rate of Moslem immigration *into* America, let alone making the hard, politically-incorrect choice to deport the ones who are already here. For at least the immediate future (i.e. the next few years), they are here to stay.

There is only one protection we can count on – **ourselves**. Only **we** have a vested interest in our own safety and that of our loved ones.

Each one of us must become a modern day, 4th generation warfare Minuteman – ready to fight any and all attackers at a moment's notice. (Actually, we should practice to get our weapons out and on target within a couple of seconds, but you know what I mean…)

If a jihadi appears in our midst to inflict death upon our people we must be prepared to swiftly give him the martyrdom he claims to seek and send him to Hell where his 'prophet' awaits him.

If some gang-banger initiate 'wanna-be' closes in on us with the aim of killing our wife or girlfriend to get 'street-cred' with his 'peeps' we must immediately take the bastard out before he can empty his shotgun into her head.

What does this mean as a practical matter? It means you **must** have the tools on you, *at all times*, to do the job. That means firearms and enough ammunition to effectively engage and neutralize the probable expected threat(s). It also means being able to consistently put rounds on target at the distances you are most likely to encounter those threats.

What are the most probable threats we face? In the past, it was sufficient for most armed citizens, most of the time, to prepare to repel common thuggery such as armed robbers, carjackers, home invaders and attackers in the workplace. Most of these types of assailants could be expected to wield close-range weaponry such as handguns and shotguns, knives, or blunt-force weapons such as bats or pry-bars.

When facing such a relatively 'mundane' criminal threat, the armed citizen should, *at a minimum*, be prepared to fight off 1 to 4 such assailants. (Thugs tend to travel in packs.) The vast majority of these types of encounters will occur at close range.

Thus, to deal with the 'normal' types of criminal threats, the prepared armed citizen should train to smoothly draw from concealment and immediately engage the target(s) at anywhere from contact range to at least 10 yards out. They should carry the largest caliber they can comfortably and accurately shoot along with 4 to 5 rounds per expected assailant. That means, *at a minimum*, a semi-auto pistol with a spare magazine or a revolver with three speed-loaders. (Loaded with high-quality defensive ammunition – don't skimp!)

Preparing to face an armed jihadi, however, is a much more daunting task. In the event the Moslem terrorist(s) bring explosives to the party there's only so much the typical citizen can do other than to be aware of the threat, remain vigilant, and clear the area if suspicious items are spotted. Most of us will have to rely on law enforcement and military bomb disposal teams to safely clear any explosive devices.

Fortunately, explosives improvisation is a fairly technical endeavor most young jihadis will not resort to. The jihadis most Americans are likely to encounter will probably follow the MO of the recent 2015 attacks on the Charlie Hebdo offices in Paris, the sunbathers on the Tunisian beach, the art gallery in Garland, Texas, and the military facilities in Chattanooga – one to two men, armed with AK or AR-style 'assault rifles' with 200 to 300 rounds of ammunition each and, in at least some cases, wearing body armor.

When engaging such a threat it would be best if the armed citizen also had a rifle at his disposal. However, as a practical matter this is not likely to be the case. Carrying around a long gun and what soon begins to feel like a short-ton of ammo is simply impractical for most people going about their daily business – it's too cumbersome and indiscreet for most environments the average citizen spends time in. However, having one accessible in the trunk of one's vehicle is very reasonable. Although it may not always be feasible during an attack to retrieve that rifle it's good to have the option should the opportunity present itself.

Unfortunately, the sad truth is that most of us armed citizens who are forced to engage a jihadi terrorist will have to do so with handguns. Going up against a rifle with a pistol is normally *not* a good thing to do. The rifle has several key advantages – it has higher firepower (ammo capacity), *much* greater stopping power, and most importantly, a far longer effective range.

The good news is that these advantages can be at least partially mitigated with proper training. Another fortunate thing for us is that, at least in attacks so far, jihadis have displayed a tendency to close to very short range before opening up on their victims, thus negating their main tactical advantage. (Like the attacks in Tunisia, Garland, and Chattanooga.)

They apparently either haven't thought their tactics through enough or typically don't expect resistance from their initial targets. Either way, although we can't always count on them following that same pattern in the future, if they *do* engage us at close range it works to our advantage – the cop in Garland was quickly able to dispatch two rifle-wielding terrorists because they were dumb enough to pull their car right up to him, well within the effective range of his handgun.

If, however, you find yourself up against jihadis who are smart enough to snipe at you from longer range, or you hear a massacre going down on the other side of the mall or Wal-Mart you're in and decide you have to help your fellow citizens neutralize the threat, you are going to have to do something counterintuitive to prevail – you are going to have to run *towards* the danger and quickly close the gap between you and them, using cover as much as possible, until you are within *your* effective range with your pistol.

This is where training is key. Obviously, the farther away from the terrorists you can remain and effectively engage them, the better off you'll be. ***At a bare minimum***, you must train to be able to consistently hit a man-sized target with your pistol at 50 yards. 100 yards would be much better. That is the distance I usually train at for my long-distance shots. Although that may sound difficult it is actually quite doable with practice. A longer barrel, with its higher muzzle velocity and flatter trajectory, will help, so get a concealment rig that allows you to carry a full-sized pistol.

At ranges of 10 yards and closer, practice the following 'failure drill' to learn how to defeat an assailant wearing body armor – fire two quick shots center-of-mass into the torso and follow-up with an aimed shot to the head – targeting an imaginary 'triangle' drawn between the eyes and nose. If you hit that so-called 'Golden Triangle' you can immediately shut down his nervous system, neutralizing the threat.

Alternately, the follow-up shot can be aimed at the pelvis, with the goal of shattering a hip bone or severing a femoral artery – not quite as immediately effective as a head-shot, but it will immobilize him and give him something to worry about as he's bleeding out through his groin.

After you fire your third shot at the head or pelvis, practice glancing over each shoulder quickly to scan for other threats before you return your attention to your primary target. This will develop 'muscle-memory' to help your body break its natural inclination under stress to focus tightly on the main threat with a 'tunnel-vision' effect to the exclusion of everything else, effectively blinding you to what is going on in other parts of the battlefield. When under stress you will fight how you train, so practice good habits.

Also, you must carry much more ammunition to overcome a jihadi with a rifle and a couple of hundred rounds than you would in a typical encounter with street thugs.

The engagement with the thugs is likely to take place at close range and resolve very quickly (usually less than a minute) with relatively few shots fired.

On the other hand, the battle with the rifle-toting jihadi could easily turn into a longer, ammo-burning firefight, especially if he's at a greater distance, and could last minutes. (Which will no doubt seem like an eternity at the time.) Get into the habit of carrying as many magazines as you feasibly can – you can never have too much ammunition in such a fight.

Finally, and most important, seek out and get training from a qualified defensive firearms instructor – no matter your current skill level. We can always learn a new technique or tactic we hadn't thought of before. A little money and time spent now can save your life later.

To many reading this, this all might seem like overkill. But we live in a very different world today than existed even just a few years ago. The threats we once faced have evolved into something far worse than they used to be, and the savagery that is now routine is off the charts.

I know taking the steps described above is inconvenient. I know carrying a firearm and ammunition on your person all the time can be uncomfortable. I know changing the way you dress so you can conceal a full-sized pistol can be a pain in the ass. I know acquiring the proper weapons, gear, and training to be able to effectively fight off our enemies takes a significant investment of your time, money, and attention.

Do it anyway.

Being an armed citizen is no longer a lifestyle choice. It is a duty. Like it or not, accept it or not, we are at war. Our hometowns are now the battlefields of that war. We all have a decision to make – we can become active, prepared, and alert citizen-soldiers who take our place on the front lines of that struggle, doing our part to defend our nation, or we can be passive on-lookers meekly waiting for ourselves and our loved ones to become 'collateral damage'.

We Americans are blessed in that we are among the few people left in the world who can legally possess firearms, the most effective tools of self-defense available – thanks to the wisdom of our Forefathers who enumerated that God-given right in our founding documents.

It's a damned shame so many Americans are too complacent, lazy, or distracted by frivolity to exercise that right and duty – especially when it would only cost a relatively small amount of their time and disposable income.

It's hard to imagine a more horrible feeling than what you would experience while holding your daughter, wife or sweetheart in your arms as she gasps out her last breath – all while tortured by the knowledge you didn't do everything you could have done to protect her.

Don't be that guy.

Protect yourself.

Protect your family.

Protect your friends.

Protect your community.

If we all do this together we will end up protecting our nation.

This war is going to be a long one. Clashes of Civilizations always are. Our enemies, both foreign and domestic, are many, they loathe us, and the worst of them believe their 'god' commands them to kill us. There will be times in the days and years ahead 'that try men's souls', and we may come to wonder if there will ever be peace again.

But the Spirit of our Forefathers isn't dead in us yet. We will persevere – and we will dispatch every criminal and terrorist that tries to harm us like the vermin they are. We will not stand by and let Evil spread unchallenged.

With the blessing and help of Almighty God we will win this Just War – no matter the sacrifice, no matter how long it takes.

We Will Prevail.

17 – Three Months Gone – Status Update

First Published on October 17, 2015

Unlike most of my essays, this one wasn't about a single topic but was instead a summary of thoughts regarding multiple issues that streamed across the newswires in the late Summer and early Fall of 2015. It was a busy season.

The spectacle of Secretary of State John Kerry groveling to the Iranians on behalf of his 'lead from behind' 'Commander-in-Chief' to secure a nuclear deal was one of the lowlights of August 2015. Predictably, Iranian behavior did not improve after Obama's appeasement.

In January 2016 they captured two U.S. Navy patrol boats and their crews in the Persian Gulf and didn't release them until 15 hours later – but only after they'd gained wonderful propaganda footage of the 10 surrendered American sailors held at gunpoint, kneeling with their hands behind their heads, and later, of a female sailor forced to cover her head with a hijab while in captivity.

In addition, in January 2016, Obama paid a 1.7 billion dollar ransom to the mullahs in Tehran, $400 million of which were shipped over in bundles on wooden pallets, in an unmarked plane, in the dead of night, to secure the release of four Americans who were being held hostage by Iran. Pathetic.

However, the Iranians have been mostly silent and non-provocative since Trump became president. Imagine that.

The other big news story of August 2015 was the exposure, on hidden camera, of abortionists at Planned Parenthood bragging about selling body parts from murdered and dismembered unborn children on the open market. Ironically, the only people to get prosecuted for that episode were those who captured the footage – the profiteering abortionists got a free pass. Few other issues illustrate the irreconcilable divide between Traditional America and the Culture of Death espoused by the morally-bankrupt Left more than abortion.

In September 2015 Russia intervened in the Syrian Civil War at the request of the Assad regime in Damascus. In this essay I pointed out the fact that, under international law, Russia did nothing wrong in coming to the aid of a long-time ally in their fight against (mostly jihadist) rebels, and that it would be wise for

Russia, China, and the United States to ally against the common threat presented by orthodox Islam. No doubt any leftists reading this will cite that as proof that I am really a secret agent of Vladimir Putin.

I then compare and contrast the outcomes of two different attacks by gunmen on unarmed people – one that took place in August 2015 when a jihadist with an AK attempted to slaughter passengers on a French train but was disarmed and beaten unconscious by a couple of American servicemen and three other would-be victims; and the other a massacre of 9 people at a community college in Oregon in October 2015 where most of the victims reportedly tried to 'reason' with the gunman or begged for their lives to no avail.

Not surprisingly, leftist politicians and the media downplayed the fact both attacks occurred in supposedly 'gun-free zones' and used the massacre in Oregon as yet another excuse to push for more ineffectual 'gun control' laws. Then presidential candidate Ben Carson was attacked by the Left for correctly pointing out that would-be victims of gun violence, even unarmed ones, are far more likely to survive if they fight back rather than surrender.

The gun issue is one that Traditional America was winning long before the political counterrevolution that swept Trump to power, but the Left insists on beating the same old 'victims must be disarmed' drum that's been a loser for them for decades. Just can't fix stupid.

Finally, I commented on the state of the presidential election race as it stood in the Fall of 2015. At that point I was still unimpressed by Trump, remained dubious of his motivation for running, and considered him merely a potential spoiler who was likely to hand Clinton the White House.

Fortunately, I, like most people, had greatly underestimated him…

***

Hello everybody. Other commitments, and then a hand injury, have kept me from the keyboard for the past three months or so. Though it is still physically painful to type I will give it a go and see what happens.

Though I haven't been able to write, I've continued to watch as our world continues to disintegrate into evil and chaos. Unfortunately, there's been no shortage of things to write about.

August was relatively quiet as the summer wound down, with the main news being Obama's channeling of the ghost of Neville Chamberlain as he declared nuclear 'peace in our time' following his capitulation to the Iranian mullahs in their quest to get the bomb. Last I heard the agreement requires a veto-proof majority in the Congress to *reject* it, which turns the Constitution's language that requires treaties to receive a two-thirds majority *approval* to ratify them on its head, thanks to past and current Congresses abdicating their authority to the Executive branch through such mechanisms as the so-called 'fast track authority'. I have no doubt Obama will be able to muster up the one-third of Congress-critters (mostly Democrats, of course) necessary to ram this sick joke through.

As dangerous as a nuclear Iran will be, however, August also brought us a story that illustrates an even more existential threat to our traditional way of life and shows just how entrenched and accepted evil has become in our society – the exposure of Planned Parenthood and the Culture of Death they represent. The same Cultural Marxists and their idiot minions who went apoplectic over the killing of two lions in Africa (as bad and unnecessary as that type of so-called 'trophy hunting' is) were utterly silent at the confirmation that their abortionist heroes are cynically running a meat market selling organs from God-knows-how-many murdered babies.

Predictably, anyone 'insensitive' enough to point out that hawking baby parts on the open market is a bad thing found themselves immediately castigated by the Left as a monster out to deny free mammograms and birth control to underprivileged and minority women. You can't make this stuff up. Behavior that would have been considered too over-the-top for a dystopian sci-fi novel circa 1965 is now accepted and commonplace 50 years later.

The speed of news events picked back up again in September and continues into October unabated:

The relentless, slow-motion deflationary collapse of the global economy continued as central bankers impotently slapped financial Band-Aids on the problem in an effort to prevent the inevitable mother-of-all debt implosions. Since it was the central banks' 50-year orgy of Keynesian monetary recklessness that brought us this problem in the first place, one shouldn't be too hopeful they will be able to fix it.

On the Clash of Civilizations front, there finally appears to be a backlash and pushback brewing among native Europeans against the ongoing invasion of Moslems into their continent, as they belatedly realize that inviting in millions of unassimilable aliens hostile to their culture and very existence is probably a bad idea. It remains to be seen whether this realization comes too late or if enough native Europeans have the courage to act in the face of political correctness to make any difference.

At least one European has demonstrated he is immune to political correctness, is unapologetically nationalistic, and is willing to take the fight to orthodox Moslem jihadists such as ISIS – Vladimir Putin. He's quickly moved to fill the power vacuum in the Middle East left by an Obama administration exposed to the world as the real 'JV Team' when it comes to international affairs. Russian jets and cruise missiles did more in a week to cripple ISIS than Obama's year-long 'air campaign' against them. Apparently, the secret to a successful air offensive is to launch more than one or two sorties a day; actually drop bombs during those missions; and to strike targets housing command-and-control centers and munitions storage areas rather than empty buildings. (Who knew?)

Putin's intervention in Syria has been decried by both the socialist Obama administration and Republican neo-cons in Washington as support for Assad's regime in Damascus. We're supposed to be upset by this because Assad is an authoritarian dictator who should be overthrown so freedom and democracy can bloom in Syria. You know, just like it did in Iraq after Bush invaded and deposed Hussein or in Egypt and Libya after Obama fomented the 'Arab Spring' that toppled Mubarak and Gaddafi. Those worked out well.

Then there's the inconvenient fact that the Russians were actually invited into Syria by the established government there, one that has been in power and recognized by the international community since 1971. At least they didn't invade the place like the US has done to other countries in recent years under what later turned out to be dubious or outright false pretexts. As for providing support for ruthless dictators, the United States wouldn't do such a reprehensible thing, right? Just forget about the Shah in Iran; Diem in South Vietnam; Marcos in the Philippines; Battista in Cuba; Pinochet in Chile; Hussein in Iraq (before he went off the reservation and invaded Kuwait); etc., etc., ad nauseum. And this current president, who is so hell-bent-for-leather at removing Assad, has no problem whatsoever in turning a blind eye to the brutality of his Marxist hero Castro in Cuba and allowing a rapprochement with our old Cold War nemesis. When it comes to the supposed immorality of supporting dictators, it just depends on which way the wind is blowing that day.

Now, it can be argued that US support for all those dictators (except Castro, of course) were an effort to prevent something worse from coming to power and not just merely a cynical exercise in *realpolitik*. That may have been true in some of those cases. But the same thing can be argued about Putin's intervention in the Syrian Civil War now. Is he trying to expand Russia's strategic sphere of influence? Absolutely. Is he also preventing the spread of something far worse? I would say yes.

Now don't take me wrong – I am not a fan of authoritarian dictators of any political persuasion, and am certainly not an apologist for either Putin or Assad. I have no doubt that both are cold-blooded, right old bastards. But in the real world most times it comes down to a matter of degree. I'm not aware of any ISIS-style genocide against Christians occurring in Assad's secular Syria. Please correct me if I'm wrong. And whether you love him or hate him, there can be no doubt that any orthodox jihadist Moslem incursions into Russia will be vigorously and mercilessly repelled by Putin.

I believe the gravest long-term grand strategic threat to the survival of Western Civilization is the spread of Islam. All the other threats, even from geo-political rivals such as Russia and China, pale in comparison. Ironically, Russia and China share this same threat as well. It would make strategic sense for the West, Russia and China to all ally against this common enemy before it is too late. They can always fight each other later if they want to, but an Islamic-dominated world would make any other differences moot, since jihadists don't tolerate any non-Moslem entities or thoughts to exist.

Enough geopolitical discussion for now, but speaking of jihadists on a more micro level, one of them tried to massacre the occupants of a French train in late August but was subdued by five brave men – three Americans, one Briton, and a Frenchman. As discussed in my previous blog post in late July regarding the need to defend ourselves against violent attacks, this particular Jihadi, though armed with an AK, foolishly decided to attack at very close quarters and thus negated the tactical advantage of his long-range weapon. This allowed his unarmed, would-be victims to overcome him. These heroic people were lucky to have survived this attack in 'gun-free' France, but it does reinforce the necessity of resisting gunmen bent on mass murder by any and all means, even if one is unarmed. A murderous gunman, whether motivated by political, religious, or psychopathic reasons, will most likely kill you anyway, so you might as well go down fighting. And maybe, just maybe, you might successfully defend yourself like those men on the train did.

While on the subject of what is the proper response to a violent attack, contrast the assault on the French train with the recent mass shooting in Oregon at the beginning of October (on a college campus also designated as a 'gun-free' zone) that left 10 dead and many others wounded. By all accounts, the victims in this attack (with the exception of one Army vet who bravely contained the gunman to one classroom and saved many lives as a result even though he'd been shot five times) passively accepted their fate and allowed the gunman to kill them without resistance.

After he'd shot the instructor, he ordered the cowering students to stand up if they were Christian. To those who did he said, "Good, because you're a Christian, you're going to see God in just about one second," then shot them. Worse yet, he then called over an 18-year-old student and told him he was the 'lucky one', and that he would let that student live if he took an envelope and gave it to the police for him. First, however, the gunman ordered the student to sit in the back of the classroom and watch while he methodically murdered the rest of that student's classmates execution-style. The young man took the envelope and obeyed the gunman, who surprisingly kept his word and spared the young man's life.

In the aftermath of the shooting, presidential candidate Ben Carson pointed out that it would be better for people to resist in such circumstances, even against long odds. He said the following, *"Not only would I probably not cooperate with him, I would not just stand there and let him shoot me. I would say, 'Hey guys, everybody attack him. He may shoot me, but he can't get us all.'"*

The 18-year-old who survived by cooperating with the gunman took umbrage to Carson's statement and sent the following comment to CNN via Facebook, *"I'm fairly upset he said that. Nobody could truly understand what actions they would take like that in a situation unless they lived it."*

CNN wasted no time trumpeting the kid's comment in a damning story titled, **"Oregon shooting survivor offended by Ben Carson's remarks:"**

http://www.cnn.com/2015/10/07/politics/oregon-shooting-ben-carson-survivor/index.html

After all, there are no greater sins in this politically correct society, which would leave all of us neutered in the face of evil if it had its way, than to defend oneself or 'offend' somebody.

The 18-year-old survivor of this tragedy is right about one thing – nobody can know for sure how they will react when facing a life-threatening situation – especially with no warning and no time to mentally prepare. I could be wrong, but I'm guessing that prior to the shooting most of the victims spent little to no time considering what their options might be in such a situation. I also suspect that, like all too many other people in today's America, they were conditioned to think like a victim and to assume that anyone who has a gun in their hand is omnipotent. And that a person, when shot, clutches at themselves, goes *'Arrggg!!!'*, and then falls over dead instantly like on TV or in the movies, with no chance to respond. That firearms make gunmen unassailable. They're not.

I also know that the most 'normal' reaction of a human being when facing such a threat is to cower in fear or freeze like the proverbial 'deer in headlights'. When I was 18 I probably would have done the same thing. For most people, it takes education and training to overcome that natural inclination – training that most in our society never receive. Even with such training, however, there's no guarantee an individual will be able to rise to the occasion in a life-or-death situation. A person who performs with the bravery of an Audie Murphy in one fight may have his courage fail him in the next or vice versa.

I'm not faulting any of the victims in the Oregon shooting for what they did or did not do – I'm just stating facts. So was Ben Carson. He was merely stating that resisting criminal violence is a better option than surrender. He's right. Only a fool would argue that there's no difference between the results of the attack on the French train and the one that took place in that Oregon classroom. There is, and the difference is that unarmed would-be victims on the train resisted while those in the classroom did not. Whether anyone feels offended or not, the collective inaction of those in that Oregon classroom resulted in a far worse outcome, with greater loss of innocent life, than what occurred when the attacker of the French train was met with resistance.

Enough about that, and I won't even comment on the idiots pushing for more gun control in the wake of this tragedy – I covered the arguments for and against gun control extensively in an earlier post.

Ben Carson was right to speak up about the Oregon shooting. And speaking of candidates, the presidential reality show to determine who the next Figurehead-in-Chief will be has, of course, mercilessly plodded on during the past three months. Trump's poll ratings have declined from the high twenties to the mid-twenties and the level of support for the one who I fear could be the greatest RINO of all time may have peaked. Quickly gaining on Trump, and in some polls actually surpassing him, is the aforementioned Carson, who appears to have great appeal among those who are sick of the status quo but who prefer a candidate who speaks in a thoughtful and dignified way rather than with incessant bluster more suited to the Jerry Springer show. *(I'm gonna build a Great Wall and make Mexico pay for it; I build the best walls in the world; I'm the best negotiator; I can do deals around the Iranians and Chinese; if people aren't nice to me I'm gonna take my ball and go home; blah, blah, blah....')* In Trump's world, all problems have an easy bumper sticker solution. With all the oxygen sucked out of the room by him, along with an understandable loathing among the electorate for all sitting politicians, none of the other Republican candidates have thus far been able to gain much traction with the possible exception of fellow political outsider Fiorina.

Personally, I want to like Carson. His uncompromising comments about the incompatibility of Islam and a free society ware spot on. So were his observations about how gun control contributed to the rise of Nazi Germany and the subsequent Holocaust. However, I'm still uncomfortable with other comments he's made about gun rights that make me wonder just how strong a supporter he really is on the 2nd Amendment. (his remarks about resisting an active shooter notwithstanding)

This clip from 2013 is an example of the kind of fuzzy thinking I'm referring to:

https://www.youtube.com/watch?v=T1wQrVNmo80

On most issues, being thoughtful and considerate of all sides can be a good thing – but not on the 2nd Amendment. If he's unclear that the 2nd Amendment includes the right of law-abiding citizens to possess semi-automatic firearms (which means practically all of them except revolvers, pump-actions, and muzzle-loaders), regardless of whether they live in the city or a rural area, then we don't need him to be President. The last thing we need is yet another Republican willing to 'consider the fears of all sides', be 'reasonable', or to 'reach across the aisle' and 'compromise' on our most fundamental and essential right. If we want more so-called 'common-sense' laws restricting gun rights we might as well just vote in another damned Democrat into the White House.

And speaking of the Jackass Party, the Democratic presidential circus is far more absurd than the Republicans could ever hope to be, so long as you don't count Trump as a real Republican. The fact that, in spite of being one of the most loathsome, dishonest, and probably criminal Americans in public life today, Hillary Clinton still remains the odds-on favorite to win her party's nomination boggles the mind. The only shadow of competition to her upcoming coronation so far has come from an unapologetic, loose-cannon, self-proclaimed socialist hippie (the left-wing-nut version of Trump) who never bothered to morph into a yuppie like the fellow leftists in his generation did; or a less-than-statesmanlike Vice President who believes his political mission, should he run and win the Presidency, is to 'preserve and expand the Obama legacy.' Bring me a pail.

Even worse, I fear that demographic shifts to the left, politically correct brainwashing, and the Culture of Entitlement makes it mathematically impossible for a Republican, and especially a truly conservative one, to ever win the Presidency in the United States again. I hope I'm wrong. We'll know next November. If, after the utter Democratic-led disaster this country has suffered through over the past 7 years, the Republicans still lose the 2016 general election it will be absolutely clear that we Traditional Americans will never be able to restore America through the current political process. If that occurs we'd better come up with a Plan B pretty damn quick or be prepared to watch our old way of life die forever.

Enough on presidential politics. What else did I miss from the last three months? Let's see…the Trans-Pacific Partnership agreement was signed, with little to no fanfare, by the participating nations and has gone to their respective governments for approval. Facing a simple-majority up-or-down vote in the US Congress and enjoying the support of globalists in both parties, this freedom-killing monstrosity is sure to pass with no problem. Also, at the beginning of October Obama's attorney general announced that the Justice Department will be implementing the UN's new law enforcement initiative euphemistically called the 'Strong Cities Network' in major American cities. Its supposed aim is to combat 'violent extremism' around the globe. However, considering this so-called 'president's' world-view that Islam does not contribute to violent extremism and that the West is the source of all the world's ills, my guess is that this global police initiative will be aimed at whites who advocate taking a stand against the spread of Islam's murderous ideology and other Third World pathologies. Here's a link to Pamela Geller's take on this:

http://www.breitbart.com/big-government/2015/10/02/obama-administration-and-un-announce-global-police-force-to-fight-extremism-in-u-s/

This subject deserves a post all its own, but this current one has grown far longer than I intended and my hand is really starting to throb. Let's just say for now that the march to global tyranny proceeds without pause.

Finally, one administrative comment about the appearance of my website. Back in September I noticed that the traffic to my site had accelerated greatly and I was pleased with the notion that I actually had a growing readership. Alas, my ego was quickly deflated when I discovered that my site had been targeted by spam bots in Ukraine and the vast number of hits recorded to that point had come from that source. Since I have no desire to mislead what readership I do have into believing I have a larger following than I actually do, I decided to remove the visit counter from my blog page.

For those of you who do happen to read my ramblings, I apologize for my forced absence and I hope all is well with you and yours. I also hope you had a good end to the summer and are enjoying a lovely fall. God bless.

18 – Nous Sommes en Guerre

First published on November 15, 2015

On the evening of Friday the 13ᵗʰ in November 2015, nine jihadists launched multiple coordinated attacks on various sites in the heart of Paris, killing 130 and wounding 368 – with 89 of them slaughtered while attending a rock concert at the Bataclan Theater. Other targets included a soccer stadium and numerous cafes and restaurants filled with people out to enjoy a Friday night in the City of Lights.

Most of the attackers were French and Belgian citizens of Moslem descent. Two were Iraqis who most likely infiltrated into Europe amongst the wave of Moslem 'refugees' that have flooded the continent. (Angela Merkel's legacy)

It was the most sophisticated Moslem attack on an urban center since Mumbai in 2008, and the worst attack on France since World War Two. The fact that the majority of the attackers were native-born Europeans was particularly disturbing, as it portended far more of these types of atrocities to come. The ever-growing population of non-assimilated Moslems, hostile to the native culture and gathered in 'no-go zone' neighborhoods throughout the West, serve as breeding grounds for home-grown jihadis and makes an endless terror campaign against our countries inevitable – for at least as long as we tolerate it.

In the year-and-a-half since the Paris massacres we have seen the continuation of this war against us in Brussels, San Bernardino, Nice, Orlando, Berlin, Manchester, London, and countless other smaller attacks that were underreported as 'mere' local crimes where the ethnicities of the Moslem perpetrators and non-Moslem victims went unmentioned.

*In this essay I state the obvious, politically-incorrect truth that these attacks will not stop until **we** stop them, and the only way to do **that** is to remove the threat at the source —by addressing the one culture that preaches 'holy war' against us and murder as the primary tenets of its belief system.*

Far too many in the West have been conditioned by the Left to view Islam as merely another 'religion' and, either through willful ignorance or deliberate deception, choose to ignore its hostile political and ideological aspects. At the dark core of Islam is the innate, self-perpetuating drive to conquer the entire world and subdue everyone in it. It is the equivalent of a cultural virus — its fundamental purpose is to subvert every society it comes in contact with and convert or coerce the target populations into new followers.

When they first infiltrate a society, Islam's adherents pretend to be agreeable and adhere to some of the local norms. But once their percentage of the population in an area reaches a certain 'critical-mass' level they become more demanding and belligerent, and once they become a majority the mask comes off and they begin to work to implement Sharia Law and impose their creed upon all others. At their most orthodox extreme, the Islamists kill all who won't convert or pay the jizya tax and 'willfully submit'.

Then this process of cultural and demographic jihad repeats, and the new converted/conquered territory acts as a forward base to spread the doctrine further afield.

They cannot be allowed to do this in our country. Although the politically correct Left has managed to block all but the most limited measures to address the Moslem threat during the first six months of Trump's Presidency (because a large portion of the American people still refuses to acknowledge the scope of that threat), as the attacks against us continue to go on and on and increase in savagery a tipping point will eventually be reached. Then the majority will demand whatever measures are deemed necessary to remove that threat, once and for all.

If our leadership continues to be prevented by the Left from taking relatively tame measures now to secure our people and way of life from this existential threat, then far more draconian measures will become inevitable down the road.

At that point, internment camps (or worse) may be seen yet again in America, and those who will scream the loudest in protest against them will be the ones who are most responsible for their return.

***

We are at war.

The coordinated attacks in Paris Friday night that killed over 120 and wounded 300+ were not just attacks on France. They were, unfortunately, only the most recent in a long string of heinous atrocities committed against non-Moslems by adherents of orthodox Islam.

For decades they have declared time and again through their words and deeds that they are at war with 'infidels' in general and the West in particular. They have gunned down and bombed countless numbers of our innocent brothers and sisters. They have viciously beheaded and theatrically murdered many others for propaganda purposes to encourage their vile followers and put fear into the faint of heart amongst their enemies. They have committed mass murder by flying airliners into skyscrapers.

They will continue to do so.

They will not stop.

These attacks will only increase in frequency, scope, and sophistication.

And what is the typical response in the West to these types of attacks?

Candle-light vigils. Piles of flowers stacked at the murder sites. 'Solidarity' campaigns on social media #Je Suis Charlie #Pray for Paris #Love not Hate #Please-don't-make-me-have-to-actually-DO-something-and-nut-up-and-take-responsibility-for-my-own-safety-and-security. Vacuous promises of 'justice' against 'hate and extremism' by so-called leaders who lack the courage to acknowledge we are at war or even name the enemy.

Meanwhile, our enemy laughs at those effeminate, empty gestures while preparing the next slaughter.

Then there are those who acknowledge that we are in a war and that something must be done, but push for a 'cure' potentially far more dangerous to our safety and liberty than the Islamic 'disease' they propose to fight – a police state. They say that, if only the TSA, FBI, CIA, NSA and a multitude of other alphabet-soup agencies out there in the black-budget, secret-government ether were given more sweeping powers to search us, spy on us, seize us, and drop us into Guantanamo-style bottomless pits they will finally be able to protect us from future attacks.

I feel safer already. Unfortunately, ridiculous big brother measures such as making us stand in longer lines at airports and watch while grandmothers and children of obvious European descent get molested by TSA agents do nothing to prevent Moslem men from hijacking airplanes. Yet that is the kind of 'safety' a politically correct police state offers.

Those are the two options offered to the Citizenry by the political left and right in the modern West – be slaughtered by the enemies of our traditional culture or be tyrannized by the State.

But there is a third choice – emulate the courage and manliness of our Founding Fathers; take responsibility for the safety of ourselves, our families, and our communities; and take our country back.

There are things we must do immediately and longer-term. Following the jihadist attack on our military personnel in Chattanooga this summer, I advocated in an earlier post on this blog that we must all become Minutemen and be ready and willing to defend our communities against the Moslem (or any other) threat. It is more important now than ever before that we do so. If we don't defend ourselves no one else will. We must be our own first-responders.

Longer-term, we must eradicate the enemy from our midst. At least one of the Paris attackers came from Syria and entered Europe within the last month hidden among the wave of so-called 'refugees' swarming that continent. At least one other was a 'French' Moslem whose ancestors probably emigrated to France sometime within the past 50 years. We should not be shocked when, after importing millions of people into the West who profess murderous hatred for us and our way of life, some of them violently act on that hatred and attack us.

To all my brothers and sisters in the West – these are **our** countries. No one from outside has the 'right' to come here and destroy them. Nor do we have the moral obligation to commit cultural suicide for so-called 'humanitarian' reasons.

In America, our borders should be immediately closed to any further Moslem immigration. Those already here should be required to publicly renounce all passages and teachings in the Koran or hadiths that advocate violence against non-Moslems, particularly Surah 9:5

(The passage infamously known as 'The Verse of the Sword'). In addition, they should also be required to take a public loyalty oath to support and defend the Constitution of the United States against all enemies, foreign and domestic, and to renounce Sharia law, which is utterly incompatible with that Constitution.

Those who refuse to do so should have their citizenship stripped or legal residency revoked and be immediately deported. Furthermore, it should be made clear to those who choose to take the oath that any subsequent hostile actions taken by them against the people of the United States or in support of such actions will be considered treason and they will be subject to the traditional punishment for that crime.

That must be the unconditional price they must pay for the privilege to live in our country. Nothing less will suffice. The politically correct Left will scream bloody murder that this violates the religious rights of Moslems in America. But their religious freedom ends when the so-called 'religion' in question is a death cult whose most sacred text advocates the murder of the rest of us.

There are many enemies of our traditional culture that have burrowed their way into the heart of Western societies, and we will eventually have to deal with all of them in one way or another, but the most immediate and existential threat we face right now is from orthodox Islam. Islam, whether we like it or not, is locked in a holy war with the West that has been on-going since that evil cult's founding in the 600s and its subsequent spread by jihad and murder.

There will never be peace with Islam unless they decide to reform and renounce their belief that God commands them to subjugate and kill non-Moslems. Until then we have no choice but to wage total war against them, drive them from our shores, take the fight to their lands, and destroy their ability to ever effectively wage war against us again. A good start would be to carpet-bomb and utterly destroy Raqqa, the self-proclaimed capitol of the Islamic State, a la Berlin or Tokyo during the last Total War.

It's a hard choice to make but one thing is certain - if we don't have the resolve to do so we'd better get used to the sight of ever-increasing rivers of innocent blood flowing through our streets.

For that is the price *we* must pay for moral cowardice in the face of this enemy.

19 – 2016 – The Tipping Point

First published on January 11, 2016

My thoughts in this essay draw heavily upon ideas from a book titled The Fourth Turning, *by authors William Strauss and Neil Howe. It is easily one of the most interesting and compelling works on history and sociology I've come across during a lifetime of study in both areas. I highly recommend it.*

The book proposes and describes a generational cycle theory of history that, among many other things, postulates that approximately every 80 years or so America enters a period of Crisis that convulses the society, reshapes the existing civic order, and threatens the very survival of the Nation. These recurring Crisis periods tend to last approximately 20 to 25 years and reach a society-transforming climax near the end of that time.

The driving mechanism behind the 80-year cycle (called the 'saeculum' by the authors, which is a Latin word describing a length of time equal to a long human life) and each of four 20-year phases of that saeculum (which they call 'turnings') is the tendency for groups of people (generations) who share the same formative years (from birth to approximately age 25) to develop similar collective personas with their temporal peers.

Although there are, of course, an infinite number of personality differences between members of a generation, there are also many common attitudes and temperaments that result from being immersed as children in the same culture and having the same 'big-news events' of their youth imprinted on their group psyches. The events of their childhood and early adulthood will tend to shape a generation's outlook for the rest of their lives.

Each generation's shared worldview will differ greatly from other generations because the phases they grew up and came of age in also differ. The generation that grew up under the shadow of the Great Depression and World War II has a very different collective persona than the one that grew up enjoying the post-war peace and prosperity of the 1950s and early 60s. The generation that grew up immersed in the spiritual exploration and cultural upheaval of the late 1960s and early 70s has a much different outlook than the one that grew up during the ensuing pessimism and societal erosion of the 1990s.

When those generations then mature, eventually take command of their society, and come to dominate the culture, their worldviews predominate and in turn create an environment that shapes the younger generations' personas.

In other words, history shapes generations who, as they get older, themselves shape history. Then the cycle repeats, which leads to the oft-observed phenomena that history, although it doesn't exactly repeat, certainly appears to rhyme.

The authors of The Fourth Turning *go on to describe four different recurring turnings of the saeculum along with four different repeating generational archetypes – both of which share similar characteristics with their predecessors in earlier saecula. Describing those in detail is beyond the scope of this introduction to the next essay, but I would refer those readers who are interested in the subject to the aforementioned book.*

For the purpose of this essay, the important point from the book is that, although it was published in 1997, it successfully predicted that, "Sometime around the year 2005, perhaps a few years before or after, America will enter the Fourth Turning" (Crisis).

Cycles and phases of history, being organic phenomena like the people who shape them and not deterministic, vary slightly in length from saecula to saecula – thus the need for the authors to mention that leeway of a few years on the other side of the year 2005. They arrived at that year by averaging out the lengths of the previous cycles in Anglo-American history dating back to the mid-1400s.

In 1997 their prophecy was largely derided by academia and society at large as ridiculous and dismissed as something akin to tin-foil-hat pseudo-history. After all, in the late 90s America didn't seem to have a care in the world. In the geopolitical arena, the United States still basked in the glow of its Cold War triumph and relished the role of being the world's sole remaining, unchallenged superpower. We felt invincible and untouchable. In the realm of economics, a seemingly unending cornucopia of fiat money and easy credit made the good times roll in a way not seen since the Roaring 20s. Things couldn't be better. Everyone felt and acted rich, whether they were or not. Most lived way beyond their means – and enjoyed every minute of it.

Though there were ominous signs and pessimistic projections that there would be a terrible price to be paid someday for our high-levels of national indebtedness and unfunded liabilities assumed by over-promising unsustainable levels of 'entitlements' to the people, that was considered by most to be hypothetical problems that could be kicked down the road and dealt with somehow, by someone, at some later date.

Then came the stock market crash of March 2000 (when the internet bubble burst) and, of course, the horror of 9/11 – and the world changed forever.

There has been much speculation and debate among students of Strauss and Howe's generational cycle theory over exactly when America entered the current Fourth Turning/Crisis period. In the geopolitical sphere 9/11 and the ensuing War on Terror was a clear demarcation point into a Crisis phase. However, the economy seemed to rebound from the 2000 market crash and the wheels didn't really come off until the financial crisis of 2008.

Whether or not the current Fourth Turning/Crisis started in 2001 or 2008 is important to us because the date the Crisis began gives us a vital clue as to when the Crisis climax (that moment of maximum danger and opportunity that marks the end of one great cycle and the beginning of the next) will likely occur – usually a couple of years before the end of the Crisis phase itself.

The average length of the Crisis phases of the six Anglo/American saecula that date back to the English War of the Roses is 24 years. (Not counting the anomalous Civil War crisis, which burned itself out in a relatively-short, yet horrific, five bloody years after it started.) So, if the trigger event was 9/11, we can expect this current Crisis to climax sometime around 2023; while if it began in 2008 the climax should arrive around 2030, give or take a couple of years.

I lean towards the belief that the trigger event was 9/11 – it fits all the criteria of a shocking, society-transforming event. Also, it can be argued that the 2000 market crash was the real beginning of the economic Crisis that continues to fester to this day, the next crash postponed until 2008 by obscene levels of credit creation generated at the world's central banks. So, using 2001 as the starting point, I expect the Crisis climax to occur sometime between 2021 and 2025.

What will a Crisis climax entail? Fourth Turning/Crisis phases have always resulted in total wars breaking out, usually in the second half of the 20 to 25-year period, either in the form of civil conflicts, wars against foreign enemies, or some combination of both. The Crisis climax tends to coincide with turning-point battles in those wars, after which it becomes clear what combatants are going to triumph and who will be the vanquished.

And when I say total wars I don't mean the 'fight 'em to a draw' kinds of conflicts we've gotten used to during the past 60 years such as Korea, Vietnam, Gulf War I, and the current, seemingly endless War on Terror – I'm talking about an epic, absolute struggle to the death where one side is completely obliterated and pummeled by the other until their will to fight is beaten out of them a la the leveling of Germany and Japan in 1943-45 or Sherman's March to the Sea in late 1864. (Exactly 80 years apart, by the way.)

The climaxes of the three previous Crises were D-Day in 1944 during the Great Depression/World War II Crisis; 81 years before that The Battle of Gettysburg in 1863 during the Civil War Crisis; and 82 years before that The Battle of Yorktown in 1781 during the American Revolution Crisis.

The 80th anniversary of D-Day will be in 2024.

Therefore, what the cycles of history (as interpreted by Strauss and Howe's theory) tell us is this – we are currently 16 years into a Crisis phase that will last somewhere between 20 to 25 years.

If previous patterns hold, we should expect some kind of total, 'fight until the enemies' capitols are firebombed to the ground and their people completely subjugated' style of civil/foreign wars to break out in the near future, since there must be enough time for those wars to develop in order to fight the pivotal battles sometime in the 2021 – 2025 timeframe.

Even though I didn't go into this level of detail in my original essay, this is what I meant in the first paragraph when I said, "The Great Crisis of our era is upon us." In Fourth Turning *terms, what I should have said was, "The Great Decisive War of this Crisis period, that began in 2001 and is now moving into its final five to ten years, will begin very soon." I identified 2016 as the probable year when America would start down the road towards such a decisive conflict.*

That turned out to be the case. We the Deplorables, an army of Traditional Americans tens of millions strong, raised our voices in righteous indignation and rebelled against our myriad enemies among the globalists, the Cultural Marxist Left, the orthodox Moslem world, and all else who have worked tirelessly to destroy us and our culture over the past century. The unhinged, bellicose sentiments expressed by our enemies in reaction to the election of our chosen champion, President Trump, only further confirms that a Second American Civil War, at the very least, is imminent. Rising tensions overseas increase the odds of a Great Power conflict erupting as well.

This is a daunting prospect, to say the least, but if there is one silver-lining it is this — we will finally have an opportunity to take the fight to our enemies, cleanse our society of the toxin of political correctness and, God-willing, restore a Traditional America where future generations can enjoy the same blessings of life, liberty, and prosperity we were endowed with by our ancestors.

Freedom isn't free, and now is the time for those of us alive at this moment in history to do our part to pay up and preserve it. The curtain is about to go up on the next great act of the never-ending American drama and we all, in our own ways, have important roles to play.

Perform them well — posterity is counting on us.

***

The world is teetering on the brink. The Great Crisis of our era is upon us. Its severity will rival the worst faced by our forefathers — whether it be the dual crises of the Great Depression and World War II, the Civil War, or the Revolutionary War.

Great crises like these only happen every 80 years or so, but when they do, they utterly tear apart and reshape the world's political and economic order. Nations and empires rise and fall. Civilizations are either reinvigorated or collapse into savagery. Entire peoples are enslaved or win their freedom.

The next five to ten years will literally determine the fate of the West and of America. We will soon know whether the traditional values and liberties we hold dear will endure or if our culture will become a mere footnote in the long, sad human history of despotism and tyranny.

For decades globalist Cultural Marxists have tirelessly worked, using totalitarian tools such as political correctness and revisionist history, to undermine our culture, denigrate our past glories and heroes, and erode our moral character. Their efforts have borne bitter fruit as a majority of people in our societies now lack the will or moral courage to resist the on-going Cultural Marxist revolutionary coup.

Our enemies have also relentlessly worked to degrade our ability to resist. In most European countries (with the notable exception of Switzerland), as well as in Canada and Australia, the people have effectively been disarmed. Only the American people retain the ability to defend themselves, though the Cultural Marxists in the federal government continue to try and disarm them as well.

Over the decades, they have also lowered our defenses by eliminating our borders. They then actively encouraged and coordinated the mass importation of third-world aliens who, for the most part, are indifferent to our traditional culture (at best) and are unlikely to assimilate into it. This has resulted in the further degradation of that culture.

With their preparations for our downfall nearly complete, the Cultural Marxists have moved to the end game of their strategy against us – the introduction of an existential threat in the form of a mass Islamic invasion.

While a large portion of the Moslem world has long dreamed of restoring the Caliphate and resuming their millennia-long jihad against all non-Moslems, it wasn't until the arrival of the Obama administration that their dream really became possible. Of course there were orthodox Moslem jihadi terrorists prior to Obama such as Osama bin Laden, but their operations were limited to (relatively) infrequent attacks orchestrated from remote locations such as caves in the mountains of Afghanistan. Even though they were able to occasionally hurt the West, (including their greatest success, the 9/11 attacks) they never had their own state – a base of operations with the financial resources and infrastructure from which to recruit, train, equip, and send forth armies of jihadists.

Enter Barack Hussein Obama. From Day One of his administration, nearly every policy decision and action he has taken regarding the Middle East has had the effect of directly empowering and enabling the establishment of just such a Caliphate.

Members of the Muslim Brotherhood and other terrorist sponsors have been welcomed in the White House with open arms, and Obama has provided on-going financial support and repeatedly sought their counsel during his tenure – all while shamefully undermining and publicly displaying the utmost contempt towards our traditional ally Israel (the only outpost of Western Civilization in the region) and her resolute leader, Prime Minister Netanyahu.

He quickly moved to undercut the coalition-established Iraqi government by removing nearly all US forces from the theater, leaving a power vacuum in that country that was quickly filled by the Shia jihadis of Iran and the Sunni jihadis who later morphed into ISIS.

In 2011, on behalf of his Muslim Brotherhood allies, he and his fellow Cultural Marxist leaders in Europe helped foment the so-called 'Arab Spring' in Libya, Egypt, and Syria – all while telling the public they took those actions in the name of 'democracy'. Despotic but secular rulers Qaddafi and Mubarak fell in Libya and Egypt and Muslim Brotherhood jihadis immediately took over both countries. Fortunately, the Muslim Brotherhood regime in Cairo was quickly deposed in a military coup or the situation would have become even worse.

In Syria, secular dictator Assad was able to hold on in Damascus with Russian help but still lost the eastern 2/3 of the country in a civil war that rages to this day – land that has since been occupied by Sunni jihadis, those 'moderate Syrian rebels' that were armed and equipped by the Obama administration and who have since metastasized into the evil Islamic State.

Obama then refused to provide support for the only halfway-decent participant in the Syrian Civil War and the only serious opposition to ISIS on the ground other than the remnants of Assad's Syrian Army – the Kurds. Not only did Obama not provide support for them, he later gave a fellow Islamist, neo-Ottoman Turkish President (and wanna-be Sultan) Recep Erdogan, the green-light to bomb them.

After public outcry arose following some of the more egregious ISIS atrocities, Obama reluctantly authorized a pathetic joke of an air campaign against them, but ensured that it would be ineffective by limiting the military to a handful of sorties a day, targeting non-essential facilities and avoiding attacks on enemy personnel, and refusing to allow pilots permission to even drop their ordinance on the majority of those missions.

Make no mistake – the actions of Barack Hussein Obama and former Secretary of State Hillary Rodham Clinton are directly responsible for the formation and subsequent thriving of ISIS. The blood of the countless Christians brutally raped and murdered in the subsequent genocide, along with all of the innocent people Islamic State jihadis have killed so far around the world and the many, many more that will be butchered by those monsters in the future, are on their hands.

As if all that wasn't bad enough, Obama capped it off by normalizing relations with our enemies in Iran and all but handing the mullahs in Tehran the Bomb.

Obama's behavior towards the Moslem world has been what one would expect of an active Islamic jihadi agent in the White House rather than just some mere sympathizer – the ultimate 'Manchurian Candidate', if you will – while Clinton's has been that of an opportunistic traitor to her nation, her people, and her culture. May they both rot in hell.

Meanwhile, on the home front, Obama and the Cultural Marxists in Europe such as *Hausfrau* Merkel in Germany have done everything in their power to run interference for the jihadis that have attacked the West. To this day, Obama still will not utter the words 'Islamic terrorist', preferring softer terms such as 'workplace violence' or 'mentally-ill person' when speaking of Moslem jihadis who kill Americans. And his 'solution' to the increasing wave of jihadi attacks on American soil? More gun control. Can't have Americans fighting back against the jihadis, after all.

Chancellor Merkel, who has been instrumental in laying Europe bare to a Moslem invasion of a million-plus 'Syrian refugees' – the majority of whom are single young men of military age (i.e. jihadis dispatched by ISIS) and hail from Moslem countries other than Syria – has been among the many Cultural Marxist European leaders who have actively covered-up the organized mass rape and sexual assault of thousands of women by those Moslem 'asylum-seekers', in dozens of cities across a half-dozen European countries, this past New Year's Eve. Can't risk them being discriminated against because of the actions of a few tens of thousands of bad apples.

Of course, it won't be long before those misunderstood 'migrants' move up the ladder of violence and start organizing riots and mass murders of native Europeans even worse than the Paris attacks last November. To add insult to injury, any native Europeans who dare to criticize this unchecked Moslem invasion are labeled 'racist' or 'islamophobic' and face prosecution from their own governments for daring to utter 'hate-speech'.

For her on-going efforts to destroy Western Civilization in Europe, *Time* Magazine named Merkel 'Person of the Year' in 2015. May she also rot in hell – and the editors of *Time* with her.

Though the situation in the West is beyond dire, all is not yet lost. The flagrant, over-the-top lies about Islam and jihad the Cultural Marxists incessantly spew to try and conceal the true nature of that death cult may turn out to be the final straw that breaks the back of Political Correctness. Their Orwellian multicultural fairy tale about how Islam is a 'religion of peace' and how Moslems are 'no different from the rest of us' has absolutely no relationship to the reality on the ground and rings hollow in the face of events like the massacres in Paris and the New Year's Eve mass sexual assaults.

The backlash against the Moslem invasion in Europe is picking up steam. Many Europeans have finally come to their senses with the frightening realization that the utopian multiculturalist snake-oil the Cultural Marxists have sold them has left them huddling in their homes, defenseless and afraid to walk their own streets. There are reports from Europe that less-than-lethal weapons (the only ones available to most Europeans) are flying off the shelves in the wake of the increasing Moslem crime and violence sprees spreading across the continent. So-called 'right-wing nationalist' political parties are rising in the polls.

With millions of potentially hostile Moslems already embedded in their societies and many more jihadis on the way, it is doubtful the remaining native Europeans will be able to preserve themselves without eventually being forced to fight a civil war against those Moslems. Unfortunately, being disarmed, they will, at least initially, find themselves at a serious disadvantage against armed jihadis – just as they were during the Paris massacre. It remains to be seen whether they will have the necessary will and means to do what it will take to repel this existential threat. I hope I'm wrong, but I fear it may already be too late for Europe.

America is a different story. A significant minority of Americans are completely fed-up with Political Correctness and the entire Cultural Marxist attempt to destroy their way of life. Their numbers are hard to quantify but, using current national poll numbers of likely Republican primary voters as a proxy, we can make an educated guess. Nationwide, Trump is currently polling at 35% and Cruz 20%. Adding them together gives us a figure of 55% of those who identify themselves as Republican. Making a very conservative (no pun intended) estimate of the percentage of the overall US population who self-identify as Republican primary voters at 25%, we arrive at a number of 13.75% for that percentage of the US population who support either Trump or Cruz. (25% times .55) Multiply the approximate US population of 300 million (not counting illegal aliens) by 13.75% and we have at least 41 million people who support either Trump or Cruz (and there could very well be many more than that).

The questions of whether either Trump or Cruz are authentic conservatives or would make a good president are irrelevant (although those are very valid questions, to be sure). For the purpose of this discussion what matters is that they are the only two candidates in the current political field who are using consistent, unapologetic, strong language against political correctness and the Cultural Marxist agenda.

All the other Republican candidates (with the exception of Huckabee, who I believe to be an authentic conservative and a good man, but is not polling well because he doesn't come across as angry enough) fail in at least one or more key issues (Rubio on immigration, Carson on guns) or are flat-out establishment RINOs (Bush, Christie, Kasich, etc).

Thus the supporters of Trump and Cruz are likely the type of people who have had their fill of political correctness and Cultural Marxism and are ready to push back against further destruction of their country or encroachments on their liberties.

Signs of the growing backlash against Cultural Marxism in America are increasing. In spite of an all-out propaganda offensive against gun ownership during the first seven years of the Obama regime, purchases of firearms have remained at or near record levels during that entire time. It is safe to assume that a large percentage of those firearms were bought by the 41 million-plus Trump and Cruz supporters. And now that they can see what is happening to their European brothers and sisters vis-à-vis the Moslem invaders they are likely to be even more determined not to let that happen in America without a fight – and 41 million pissed-off, well-armed people can put up quite a fight.

Even if only a hard-core, rule-of-thumb 3% of that group are actually willing to take up arms that still gives us a number of one-and-a-quarter million potential riflemen – a number larger than most countries' organized militaries and one of the largest partisan forces in history. Not a force to take lightly.

Along these lines, as I write this, a group of citizen militiamen led by Cliven Bundy's sons, in an attempt to bring public attention to the federal government's repeated violations of citizen's property rights in the West, have occupied federal buildings on a wildlife refuge in Oregon and are now in their second week there. They say they refuse to leave until the federal government returns vast tracts of illegally-seized land to state and county authority, where they claim it properly belongs.

As the federal government continues to overstep their constitutional authority in this and countless other aspects of American life, there will no doubt be many more standoffs between Traditional Americans and federal agencies in the future, any one of which has the potential to spark a larger armed conflict between them. (The 2014 standoff at the Bundy Ranch in Nevada came within 5-pounds of trigger-pull away from becoming a 21st century version of the Battle of Lexington.)

And on this past Friday, Governor Greg Abbott of the Great State of Texas called for an Article V Convention of States to amend the Constitution and reassert states' rights against myriad unconstitutional federal encroachments. God bless him and God bless the people of Texas for voting a true patriot into office. Such a call, from the governor of one of the nation's largest, most populous, and economically-powerful states, would have been unthinkable a decade or two ago and should give the regime in Washington pause. (assuming they have any sense at all and their hubris hasn't completely blinded them to reality)

The bottom line is, the population of the United States is now divided into two mutually-loathing, hostile camps, and the time for dialogue is quickly passing away. There doesn't seem to be much point in talking anyway – all the arguments on both sides have been made time and again and nobody is listening anymore.

The Cultural Marxists are determined to implement their agenda, come what may, to complete their destruction of Traditional America. No amount of attempted persuasion, rhetoric, or concessions on our part will dissuade them from that ultimate goal.

Traditional Americans, on the other hand, as they increasingly come to understand there can be no compromise with this enemy, face the sobering realization that they will soon have no choice but to stand their ground or else find themselves at the mercy of Marxist masters who despise them and hostile foreign invaders who wish to kill them.

If we Traditional Americans don't resist now, while we still can, we will never get as good a chance to resist again. Nor will our children or grandchildren.

Unfortunately, this situation, with two irreconcilable, mutually-loathing enemies, is a perfect recipe for future conflict. Barring some miracle where a Trump or Cruz gets elected and follows through with meaningful reforms, and quickly, *real* counterrevolution becomes increasingly likely.

As if the possibility of civil wars in Europe and America weren't enough, the world faces other epic crises in the near future as well. The global economy has resumed its plunge into a Greater Depression, one that began in 2008 and was postponed for seven years by an unprecedented binge of central bank money and credit creation.

China's 'mother-of-all-bubbles' economy has popped and is now in freefall, dragging down the rest of the fragile world economy with it. As a result, global trade has collapsed. The Baltic Dry Goods Index, which measures the volume of shipping throughout the world, has reached its lowest level since the Index's inception in 1985 – even lower than during the depths of the Crisis of 2008.

Global economic activity has declined so much, and demand for energy has dropped so far that, in a week that saw Iran and Saudi Arabia engage in unprecedented, highly bellicose sabre-rattling as the Islamic world moved closer to an all-out Shia-Sunni religious civil war (right on top of the world's largest oil fields) the price of crude actually *dropped*.

This plunge in oil prices has also hit Russia particularly hard. As US influence and power in the world wanes, the ruling regimes of economically-strapped regional powers such as Russia and China will become increasingly tempted to divert their domestic population's attention from how difficult their daily lives have become by using the time-honored tactic of picking fights with neighbors. Watch out Japan and Taiwan. Look out Lithuania and Estonia. And with most of the United States' cold-war era alliances and treaty obligations still on the books, there's no guarantee that the US won't be dragged into a regional war and escalate it into a great-power conflict.

All these numerous crises and others – the Moslem world's Clash of Civilizations with the West, citizens rebelling against increasingly tyrannical governments, the specter of global economic collapse, the increasing risk of a World War III breaking out, the ever-present threat of race war, and no doubt still more I've neglected to mention because I've either forgotten them or they're beyond the scope of this post – all of them coming to a head simultaneously, feeding off each other, and forming some monstrous socio-economic grand-strategic 'super-storm' is the reason I declared at the beginning of this post that the Great Crisis of our era is upon us.

There is no way to predict exactly how this Crisis will play out, but the cycles of history indicate the events of the next few years will shake the world to its foundation in a great paroxysm the likes of which has not been seen by anyone under the age of 70 – and that those events will be commemorated and celebrated by our descendants (or cursed, if things go badly) and dissected by future historians for at least the next 70 years, and probably beyond.

God-willing, future generations will celebrate our ultimate victory over the enemies of civilization and decency with fireworks, parades, and statues for heroes yet to arise from our midst. If we are steadfast, future generations will be able to look back and say, though a heavy price was paid, the sacrifices made during the Great Crisis weren't in vain because we were able to preserve a good world for them.

They will be able to remember those events with pride in us for what we did, just like we do for our fathers and grandfathers who won World War II and why we still honor the heroes of the Civil War and the Revolution. If we fight the good fight, perhaps, just perhaps, around the year 2160, some future reenactor of the 2nd American Revolution will have reason to be ecstatic to find a long-forgotten pair of antique 511 Tactical boots in a dusty attic that he can add to his Patriot's 'uniform'.

Speculation about the distant future aside, the leading edge of this Great Storm has arrived, here and now, in 2016. Each of us must get right with God and ask Him for the courage and strength to do what we must to protect our families and communities from Evil in the dark years ahead. We must continue to prepare as best we can with the resources at our disposal and steel ourselves for what's to come. With the help of Providence and each other we will preserve something worthwhile to pass on to our children and grandchildren.

Keep the faith – for we will have many good, like-minded people fighting the same fight with us, each in their own way, according to their strengths and abilities. We will have allies from among people we've known all our lives and will discover new allies from surprising, unexpected quarters – if we remain open to possibilities.

Many Traditional Americans wear the uniform of the military or of federal, state, and local law enforcement agencies, yet share our disgust and dismay at what the Cultural Marxists have done to our country. Others may come from a different ethnic group but may turn out to be individuals who don't share the typical dysfunction of their co-ethnics.

There may be times in the years to come when we're forced to assume the worst in others because the risk of misplaced trust is too great. But, whenever circumstances allow, we should try to evaluate each person and the 'content of their character' one by one. Some of them will be decent people and will be on our side, even if they may not look it at first glance. It would be a shame to squander a good ally, or worse yet, make an unnecessary enemy — we'll have more than enough of them to go around.

Remember - none of us will be alone in this struggle.

Together, we will prevail.

May God bless us all and see us through.

Keep your powder dry…

20 – Insurrection Election

First Published on March 30, 2016

At the beginning of the 2016 Presidential election cycle I was a supporter of Senator Ted Cruz. I liked what he had said and done as a first-term Tea Party member of the Senate, and his credentials as an America-First conservative seemed impeccable.

But by the end of March 2016, against all odds and to the bafflement of most prognosticators, Ted Cruz was the only person standing in the way of Donald Trump and the Republican Party's nomination for President. Then Cruz found himself under scrutiny more intense than any he had yet faced in his political career – and details about him came to light that called into question his Tea Party bona fides.

This essay chronicles the thought process I used in the days leading up to the primary I voted in to decide which of the five remaining candidates to vote for. The conclusion I arrived at surprised me, to say the least.

This essay also served as an announcement to my fellow Traditional American friends that I was switching my support from Ted Cruz to Donald Trump and gave my reasons why. The primary one was that, even though voting for Trump was a risk at the time because we weren't sure what to expect from him, I believed he was the only candidate who had a chance to keep Hillary Clinton out of the White House.

Thank God that's one prognostication that actually came to pass.

***

The 2016 Presidential Election, no matter which candidate eventually 'wins', is going to be historic. It already is. The phenomenon that is Donald J. Trump, and specifically the revolutionary fervor of many Traditional Americans he has tapped into, has made it so.

I have wanted to write about this election for some time but, until now, my thoughts on it weren't clear enough to do so in a meaningful way. At the time of the first primaries and caucuses, there were up to 17 candidates on the Republican side and the specter of indictment hung over Hillary Clinton on the Democratic side. There were too many variables to even guess how the process might play out.

Now, by late March, the field has narrowed to five and the possible outcomes are more foreseeable. On the Democratic side, the long-talked-about prosecution of Hillary appears to have turned out to be just another chimera in the 30+ year history of unpunished corruption and criminality that defines the Clintons (at least so far).

That said, Hillary hasn't just coasted to coronation as the Democratic nominee as most expected she would. The rise of 74-year-old self-proclaimed socialist Bernie Sanders was surprising and showed that even the far-left in America, mostly young Millennials, are also disgusted with the political status quo that the Clintons represent on the Democratic side.

Democratic Party elders, however, through the creation of 'super-delegate' status given to sitting Democratic elected officials and party leaders, have ensured ahead of time that Sanders' populist insurgency would not seriously threaten Hillary's eventual nomination.

Though a brazen, in-your-face tactic, the creation of 'super-delegates' illustrates, yet again, that the Democratic leadership has more dictatorial control over their party than their opposition does. They went ahead and rigged the process from the start, right out in the open, confident that the vast majority of leftist voters would not jump ship even if they were unhappy with that process. Time will tell if they are correct on that, but at least they will be able to anoint their nominee with a minimum of fuss and convention drama.

Not so with the GOP. The party leadership, blinded by their hubris and over-confident that the old formula of 'throw a few hundred million bucks at pliable media organs such as Fox News and buy saturation campaign advertising for their favored candidate' would produce the milquetoast Romney-esque nominee the party leadership wanted, completely underestimated the level of anger and frustration the Traditional American, grassroots conservative base now has towards that kind of 'business-as-usual' attitude in the Republican Party.

Election cycle after election cycle, the Republican Party has taken its conservative base for granted, dismissively saying, "Who are they going to vote for, the Democrats?" So, election after election, they foist upon conservatives RINOs (Republicans in name only) like McCain or Romney and force them to hold their nose and vote for 'the lesser of two evils'.

But, regardless of how often conservatives vote Republican, nothing fundamentally changes. Republicans continue to take the country towards the same politically correct, socialist, fiscal and cultural cliff as the Democrats – just half as fast.

Republicans, despite all rhetoric to the contrary, have not eliminated a single unnecessary federal agency such as the Department of Education, Department of Energy, or the Internal Revenue Service. They have done nothing to curb governmental spending. They have done nothing to push back against the political correctness and Cultural Marxism destroying Traditional American culture.

Traditional Americans have noticed. The final straw came after the mid-term election in 2014, when frustrated conservatives handed the GOP a landslide which gave them full control of both houses of Congress. Conservatives gave the Republicans that landslide with the understanding and mandate that they would eliminate the disaster that is Obamacare and hold Obama accountable for his myriad unconstitutional abuses of power, such as using the IRS as a tool to target political opponents (one of the impeachable offenses Nixon would have been charged with had he not resigned first) and ruling by executive fiat.

And what have the Republicans done with their newfound Congressional majorities? Held some hearings, but other than that, not a damn thing. Breaking their campaign promises, they did not use the 'power of the purse' to defund Obamacare. They also continued to raise the federal debt ceiling time and again, until the total admitted debt is now approaching 20 trillion dollars (total unfunded liabilities for 'entitlement' programs are actually in the hundreds of trillions). Even after the release of videos showing Planned Parenthood officials hawking baby body parts, the Republicans caved to Democratic demands and continued to fund that evil organization in their latest budget.

The Republicans didn't have the spine to take any action on those and many other issues, lest they be accused of being 'mean-spirited', 'obstructionists', or 'agents of gridlock'. They learned all the wrong lessons from their weak attempts to shut down the government during the Clinton Administration in the mid-90s, when they allowed the Democrats and liberal media to paint them as 'heartless' and 'uncaring' with the public. Needless to say, they certainly didn't have the courage to impeach Obama for his many unconstitutional acts, though they were more than justified in doing so. The bottom line is – they appear to care more for their political careers and personal power than they do the good of the nation.

Yet even worse than all of their inaction was one of the few things the Congressional Republicans *did* do. To add insult to injury to the American people, they showed their true globalist colors when they rammed through fast-track trade authority for Obama so he could expedite passage of the secret, 800+ page, sovereignty-killing Trans-Pacific Partnership Agreement.

The Republicans later took credit for being 'bipartisan' on this issue, but what this action really demonstrated is that, for all of the Republican vs. Democrat posturing to the contrary, both parties work for the same 'one-world' international masters. Republican blither about their being in favor of 'free trade' is a flagrant lie. NAFTA, GATT, and now the TPP isn't about 'free and fair trade' at all – it's about globally-*managed* trade, managed for the benefit of the 'too-big-to-fail' multi-national banks and corporations at the expense of American economic prosperity and independence.

Traditional Americans have watched all this transpire with disgust and have grown increasingly angry at the blatantly-rigged system destroying their nation and way of life.

Which brings us back to the Election of 2016. From the get-go, the Republican Party elite completely misread the foul mood of Traditional Americans, assumed this election would be like all the others, and put forward Jeb Bush as their anointed candidate. (with Rubio as a back-up.)

The primaries completely blew up in their face. Despite spending nearly a half billion dollars on first the Bush and then the Rubio campaigns, both establishment candidates went nowhere, and approximately 80% of the Republican primary electorate voted for 'outsider' candidates Trump, Cruz, Carson, Paul, and Fiorina.

But it was Trump who most subverted the Republican primary process. In spite of his past support for liberal positions and politicians, a large percentage of the conservative base found his unapologetic, politically incorrect, Jerry Springer-style thrashing of the media and establishment politicians appealing. In addition, he said the right things about immigration, the radical Moslem threat to the West, the Second Amendment and, unlike other Republicans in the past, didn't back down in the face of politically correct, Cultural Marxist attacks on his positions. The fact that he also seemed beholden to no one only added to his appeal.

Starting at around 35% support of the Republican electorate in early primaries, Trump's numbers steadily rose as opponents dropped out of the race (in spite of continual establishment predictions of his imminent collapse) until he now stands at about 45%. His only remaining competition is former 'outsider' Cruz, who the establishment is now rallying around, and establishment-friendly Kasich, who has no mathematical chance of getting the nomination but remains in the race as a spoiler (or kingmaker) who is positioning himself as an alternative candidate (or Vice-Presidential nominee) should there be a contested or brokered convention.

So, how should Traditional Americans in states yet to hold their primaries or caucuses vote now? Let's look at the pros and cons of the five remaining candidates.

First, the Democrats. Obviously, Hillary Clinton is not an option. She is the one candidate who, if elected, is most likely to trigger war against Traditional America. She has proven over the decades that she is utterly evil and completely without scruples, and no doubt will ruthlessly wield whatever power she can get her hands on. Her election would finally and conclusively prove that the Rule of Law is dead in the United States and the current political system is beyond redemption.

Bernie Sanders, ironically, might be the most sincere of the five remaining candidates. He appears to really believe what he preaches. Although he is correct in opposing international trade deals as damaging to US workers and challenging the inordinate influence of globalist 'too-big-to-fail' mega-banks, unfortunately, most of what he preaches is pure, unadulterated socialism that often verges on communism. His philosophy is not compatible with Traditional American values, and he obviously is not a good choice for president.

Now to the Republican candidates. First, John Kasich. Kasich is a RINO who appears to hold pretty much mainstream Republican views on most issues, but his 'reasonable' persona has not served him well in this year of the angry voter and has left him far behind in the delegate count. His comments that it is 'impractical' to deport the estimated eleven million illegal aliens from the United States is problematic and made his rhetoric on illegal immigration much softer than that of Trump's. (How about we just start with deporting the illegal aliens who commit violent crimes? Can we at least do that, Governor Kasich?)

But most problematic for Kasich is that he has been a staunch supporter over the years of every sovereignty-killing 'free trade' agreement that has come down the pike, from NAFTA all the way to the TPP. That's an automatic deal-killer for me.

Which brings us to the final two candidates, Cruz and Trump – the only remaining Republicans who were considered 'outsiders' at the beginning of the race and the only ones I believe Traditional Americans should consider voting for. However, both have significant pros and cons, making the choice between them a tougher decision than it might appear at first glance.

When the race first started the candidate I felt best about was Ted Cruz. He has an excellent track record of defending Second Amendment rights and has long spoken like a cultural conservative who is a strong supporter of the Constitution and American sovereignty. On the surface, there is a lot for Traditional Americans to like about Cruz.

However, with just a little bit of research, I discovered that Cruz has *very* disturbing ties to globalist organizations and institutions, in spite of claiming he is a champion of American sovereignty. His wife, Heidi Cruz, was an investment banker who worked for Merrill Lynch and J.P. Morgan prior to becoming a member of the globalist think-tank the Council on Foreign Relations (which Ted Cruz rightly called 'a pit of vipers').

While a member, she co-wrote a CFR position paper in 2005 titled "Building a North American Community", which advocates the blurring of national borders and the creation of what amounts to a 'North American Union'. Here is the link to that document:

http://www.cfr.org/canada/building-north-american-community/p8102

Heidi Cruz's bio as listed in that document is the following:

> **HEIDI S. CRUZ** *is an energy investment banker with Merrill Lynch in Houston, Texas. She served in the Bush White House under Dr. Condoleezza Rice as the Economic Director for the Western Hemisphere at the National Security Council, as the Director of the Latin America Office at the U.S. Treasury Department, and as Special Assistant to Ambassador Robert B. Zoellick, U.S. Trade Representative. Prior to government service, Ms. Cruz was an investment banker with J.P. Morgan in New York City.*

Subsequently, Mrs. Cruz worked for Goldman Sachs, where she is a managing director, but is currently on a leave of absence during her husband's campaign. In 2012, she was able to secure a low-interest loan from her employer to finance her husband's Senate campaign, when he ran as a Tea Party champion. Ted Cruz also received a loan from Citibank. The total amount of those loans were nearly 1.5 million dollars.

This begs the question – if Ted Cruz is really such an 'outsider' and 'threat to the establishment' that 'nobody in the Senate likes', why were multinational banks Goldman Sachs and Citibank, tools of the globalist cabal that has ceaselessly sought to destroy national sovereignty around the world and has helped to rob the American people of countless trillions of dollars, so quick to finance Cruz's political ambitions? Furthermore, are we supposed to simply ignore the fact that his wife's career has been to work for the banksters on

Wall Street and those who would love nothing more than to destroy our nation and establish global government?

None of this passes the smell-test. Unfortunately, it's begun to look more and more likely that Cruz is just another establishment, globalist minion in 'conservative' clothing a la the Bush family.

In addition, Cruz has made comments these past few weeks that do not inspire confidence. I was personally very disappointed in Cruz's reaction following the leftist Soros-paid agitators' disruption of the recent Trump rally in Chicago. After a brief sentence criticizing the 'protestors' Cruz went on, at length, to condemn Trump for the hostile 'climate' of his campaign, all but blaming Trump for creating the environment for such protests to thrive.

Cruz made a serious error in saying that. Regardless of what one thinks of Donald Trump and what he says, he has the First Amendment right to say it – especially at a private venue he paid for. Just because others find Trump's rhetoric distasteful doesn't give them the right to intimidate his supporters or to infringe upon his free speech.

If Cruz was really the champion of the Constitution he says he is, he would have given an unequivocal condemnation of the 'protestors' and unqualified support to Trump's right to speak. Instead, he chose political expediency – the opportunity to score a few points at Trump's expense – over staunch defense of the First Amendment. That also doesn't inspire confidence in Cruz.

Another thing Cruz said recently (more precisely, how quickly he backpedaled from something he said) was another possible window into his character and was also concerning. In one of his stump speeches, in an attempt to appear tough on terrorism, he advocated 'carpet-bombing' ISIS. I think that is an excellent idea. Raqqa, the de facto capitol of the 'Islamic State', would be a great place to start – take the war to their people like they've been taking it to ours. Break their will to fight. Total War – just like the Axis powers were taken out in World War Two. In other words, Cruz was absolutely right. Way to go, Ted.

But not so fast. Not long after he made that statement, Cruz appeared on the Bill O'Reilly Show on Fox News and O'Reilly pressed him on his 'carpet-bomb' statement. O'Reilly pointed out to Cruz that when people use the term 'carpet-bomb' they mean total destruction such as what occurred at Dresden or Tokyo and that innocent women and children are killed in such raids. O'Reilly then 'graciously' gave Cruz a chance to 'step back' from his 'carpet-bomb' statement.

Cruz immediately did so and instantly started parsing his language, Clinton-style, saying what he *really* meant was that the tempo of the air war should be greatly increased, with far more sorties against command and control assets, oil facilities, and other targets that could be hit with precision bombing.

Cruz was right when he told O'Reilly that the number of sorties against point targets should be greatly increased – but he was also correct in his original statement that carpet-bombing should be used as well against ISIS area targets such as cities where they have high levels of civilian support. If Cruz really meant to say that we should use the weaker option he should have originally said so and not implied he would resort to a tougher one just to impress the voters. The quickness with which Cruz was willing to yield to O'Reilly's politically correct pressure makes me wonder what other of his positions he will cave on when pressed.

Since the neutering effect of political correctness on our ability to truthfully discuss issues and policy options is one of the most serious problems we face as a nation, Cruz's apparent weakness on this point is not a matter to take lightly and should be monitored closely.

I've spent a significant amount of time pointing out what I believe to be Cruz's flaws as a candidate, but what about the remaining candidate – Donald Trump?

Unfortunately, like Cruz, Trump has some strengths but many glaring flaws as well.

First, his strengths. Trump's greatest asset in this election is that he is financially independent and doesn't appear to be beholden to anyone. His campaign is self-sufficient and he doesn't have to worry about his livelihood. Trump has parleyed this independence into an ability to speak his mind without having to worry if what he says is politically correct or not. He has done so with great effectiveness, first speaking out about the need to secure America's borders, then about the need to halt the immigration of Moslems until they can be properly vetted, and other issues formerly considered 'taboo'. Even better, when the inevitable demands come for him to apologize and retreat from his comments he refuses and usually doubles down and says something even more politically incorrect.

This, in a nutshell, has been the secret of Trump's success so far. His supporters instinctively realize that political correctness is the main weapon our enemies have used to intimidate and silence any who don't go along with their Cultural Marxist agenda. By effectively taking on the self-anointed politically correct priesthood, Trump has done this nation a great service.

The same goes for his interactions with the mainstream media. Starting years prior to this election, when Trump was merely considering a run for the presidency, the media consistently and nearly universally ridiculed him. Since he announced his campaign last year this dismissive disdain from the media has increased exponentially. Some of the criticism is legitimate but much of it is misleading or outright dishonest, such as when they claim that Trump was saying all Mexicans coming to the United States are criminals or all Moslems terrorists. Trump never said either of those things but that doesn't stop the media from taking his comments out of context and crowing that he is a 'racist' or 'hater'.

But what Trump understands, and those in the media still don't, is that an ever-growing portion of the American people now know the mainstream media is just the propaganda organ of the establishment and they simply don't believe them anymore. They wouldn't believe them if they said the sky is blue or the Sun rises in the east. So, the more the media attacks Trump the more people flock to his banner. The media, more than anyone, have created the Trump phenomenon.

Now for the bad side of Trump. Even though he is uniquely able and willing to speak his mind (Damn the PC torpedoes, full-speed ahead!), he tends to say whatever is on his mind at that moment in a mostly incoherent, stream-of-consciousness, rambling manner. He is rarely able to stay on one topic even in the span of a single sentence. He is long on easy-sounding, bumper-sticker slogans – 'I'm going to make America great again', 'I'm going to build a great wall and make Mexico pay for it', 'I'm going to get our jobs back', 'I'm going to make great deals with other countries, cause I'm a deal maker', etc., etc., etc. – but short on any details on how he will actually accomplish any of it.

Nor have his positions on most issues been consistent over the years. Though he is now hitting upon all the talking points that conservative Americans want to hear – that he is against abortion, he is a strong supporter of the Second Amendment, he is strongly opposed to illegal immigration, etc. – Trump has said the exact opposite at different points in the past. Also, it is well-known that he has donated heavily to some of the most liberal politicians in America.

Some of my friends who are Trump supporters rightly point out that people's opinions can change over time and that doesn't mean he's lying about what he believes now. They also say that Trump was just being pragmatic when he donated to those liberal politicians and that he also donated to Republicans – it was just the price of doing business.

That may be true in many cases – for example his problematic comments about gun rights were mostly made in the late 1990s and early 2000s. However, there is one issue where Trump's change of heart was much more recent, and on the very issue that first catapulted him to the front of the Republican pack – illegal immigration.

Last July, I wrote a blog post where I pointed out how, in November, 2012, Trump stated that Romney lost the election to Obama because he was seen by Asians and Latinos as hostile to them, and that that the Republican Party will continue to lose elections if it comes across as "mean-spirited and unwelcoming towards people of color". He went on to say that the "Democrats didn't have a policy for dealing with illegal immigrants, but what they did have going for them is they *weren't mean-spirited about it*. They didn't know what the policy was, but what they were *is they were kind*." (emphasis added)

Don't take my word for it. Read the article yourself here:

Less than three years later, this same guy did a complete 180 and stole the spotlight right out of the gate with his now infamous comments on the need to 'build a great wall' on our southern border and to deport all the illegals.

I'm sorry, but I'm throwing the bullshit flag here. If Romney was stupid for being 'mean-spirited' towards illegals in 2012, for advocating a policy of 'self-deportation' that was far more tepid and mild than what Trump is calling for now, then Trump's an even bigger idiot now by his own definition.

I don't believe someone completely changes their mind that radically, on such a basic issue as illegal immigration, in less than three years. Either he was just talking out his ass in 2012, or he's lying now, or even worse, he doesn't care what he said then because he has since changed his mind for expediency's sake. None of these explanations reflect well on Trump.

Let's use Occam's Razor, the scientific principle that the simplest explanation is the one most likely to be true, on Donald Trump.

If he's had many conflicting opinions about issues important to Traditional Americans over the years, it may be because he doesn't have a consistent moral or philosophical compass.

If he comes across as someone full of bluster but lacking in knowledge on policy issues it may be because he doesn't have that knowledge.

If he shows a consistent pattern of lashing out and personally attacking, Jerry Springer-style, any who disagree with or oppose him, ('Little Marco', 'Lyin' Ted', etc.) maybe it's because he is unable to win arguments with logic or reasonable discourse.

I've heard Trump supporters say that he actually is much more shrewd and sharp than he appears but is 'dumbing-down' his message to appeal to a broader segment of the electorate, and that we will see the 'sharp Trump' after he's elected. That's like saying, "You have to pass the bill before you can see what's in it." We know how well that worked out.

But even if that *is* true, it makes the situation even worse. If Trump is indeed 'dumbing-down' his message to appeal to the lowest common denominator, that shows a level of condescension, cynicism, and manipulation towards the American people one would expect in a would-be demagogue, not a defender of the republican principles this country was founded on.

Most of this doesn't appear to matter to many Trump supporters. As long as he 'talks tough' and pokes the PC bastards in the eye, that's good enough.

But it *should* matter to us. Even though I agree it's a good thing that those who push political correctness be taken down a few notches, it is dangerous to get swept up in emotion when picking a president – even if that emotion *is* righteous anger. The last time the American electorate did that they chose Barack Obama, the worst president in this nation's history. Don't think frustrated Traditional Americans can't make the same mistake, or that Donald Trump can't end up being a **very** bad, even ruinous, president.

That said, with all of Trump's negatives, is there any logical reason to cast a vote for him? Surprisingly, yes. There is one issue that Trump has been consistent on for decades – economic nationalism. Going back to NAFTA, and all the way up to the present TPP, he has opposed so-called 'free trade' agreements. He has advocated tariffs on imports to off-set unfair trade practices other nations use against us, such as when China pegs their currency to our dollar or when the Chinese Communist Party gives governmental subsidies to 'privately-owned' Chinese companies, making it impossible for American companies to compete on a level playing field.

Those positions fly in the face of the-powers-that-be who are pushing globalism at the expense of America's independence and prosperity. And it is clear by their response to Trump that they see him as a clear and present danger to that globalist agenda.

One can judge a man by the company he keeps, but many times one can tell even more by who his enemies are. Trump is being continually attacked by: the mainstream media on the left *and* right; the political establishments of both the Democratic *and* Republican parties; the socialist, globalist Pope; all the socialist leaders of Europe and Japan; the government of the People's Republic of China; arch-globalist billionaire George Soros; and on and on and on.

In other words, Donald Trump is currently being attacked by nearly all those in the world who are pushing Cultural Marxism and doing their best to destroy Traditional American culture. That is no small thing, and *has* to count in Trump's favor.

So, how is the Traditional American voter supposed to decide between Cruz and Trump? Well, it comes down to what your world-view is.

If you are a person who believes that the left vs. right, Democrat vs. Republican, 'Mr. Smith Goes to Washington' paradigm we are taught in civics class is how the United States is governed, and that those who believe there is a higher international level of powerful people and institutions *really* calling the shots are just a bunch of tin-foil-hat-wearing kooks, then the choice is clear – you should vote for Ted Cruz. He clearly has the more consistent conservative record and his wife's ties to the Council on Foreign Relations and Goldman Sachs will be irrelevant to you, since you don't believe those organizations are anything more than a benign think-tank and investment bank.

But if, however, you *do* believe there is a globalist agenda to destroy American sovereignty and freedom, then you must seriously consider voting Trump, in spite of his flaws.

Donald Trump is the first person to run for president in a very long time who (at least up to this point) does not appear to be controlled by the system. In addition to his stance against globalist 'free trade', he has made other threats to the globalist power structure. He has called for an audit of the Federal Reserve, which is a private cartel owned and run by multinational, too-big-to-fail megabanks. He has said he will release the twenty-eight pages of the 911 Commission Report that was classified by the government and is said to implicate some of the *real* players who bankrolled the Al-Qaeda terrorists who flew the planes into the World Trade Center and Pentagon (hint – it wasn't just Bin Laden). He has called for the United States to withdraw from NATO, South Korea, and other entangling alliances of the type President Washington warned us about, and to stop bankrupting our nation by acting as the global police force of the New World Order.

By all indications, Ted Cruz will not do any of this – he has shown too many warning signs that he is in reality a globalist minion, and is therefore not a viable counter to this threat. The Bush presidencies showed us all-too-well that great damage can be done with globalist Republicans and neo-cons in office.

This is why, after much soul-searching, even though I began this presidential election season as a supporter of Ted Cruz, I have now decided to cast my vote for Donald Trump instead. All my research over the past 30 years has convinced me there *is* a globalist agenda to destroy our Traditional American way of life. It is an agenda that is far advanced, and the globalists are now ready to launch their final, overt attacks against us.

This election could very well be the last peaceful chance we get to resist this globalist takeover. I could not look myself in the eye if I didn't try to utilize every peaceful opportunity we have to preserve our freedom while it is still available (even if it may not make much difference in the long run).

My vote for Trump will not be a leap of faith – frankly, judging by what I've seen and heard from him so far, he hasn't inspired much faith in me. Instead, my vote for him will be an act of resigned necessity. In my opinion, our nation is in such overwhelming, imminent peril, that we have no choice but to throw the dice with Trump – if only on the off chance he can actually throw a monkey wrench into and at least delay the globalist machine arrayed against us. (Assuming they don't kill him first.)

But what of the possibility that Trump proves himself to be a 1930's-style demagogue, as he so often appears and what many fear he will become? If that indeed turns out to be the case, and he abuses presidential power in a dictatorial way, I would argue that we will be no worse off than if current trends continue. We have been on the road to creeping globalist dictatorship for a long, long time anyway (at least over a century), and the velvet glove that has thus far covered the iron fist is now being taken off.

We Traditional American patriots have watched for decades as the Presidency has been transformed into an increasingly imperial office. Then the globalists installed the real 'Manchurian Candidate', Barack Hussein Obama, into that office and we've had to watch him use that power to blatantly attack our security and way of life for the past seven years.

Now we face the specter of evil, power-lusting globalist minion Hillary Rodham Clinton being put into that office. Her long, sordid history shows she will not be shy in using that power to try and crush us.

Our only chance to prevent Hillary from being installed into that office is for a unified Republican Party to back a candidate to face her in November. The only Republican who has a realistic chance to reach the 1,237 delegates needed to win the nomination on the first ballot and prevent a contested or brokered convention that would most likely result in the dissolution of the party is Trump.

At this point, any other outcome practically guarantees another, even more evil, Clinton Administration and greatly increases the risk of a Second Civil War in America.

We simply can't risk that, and that is why I'll take my chances with Donald Trump.

21 – The Choice We Face

First published on June 17, 2016

This essay was written in the wake of a wave of leftist attacks against supporters of Donald Trump that swept across the nation in the Spring and early Summer of 2016. These unprovoked (and still on-going) attacks against peaceful Trump supporters were an unprecedented escalation in the struggle between Cultural Marxists and Traditionalists that has gripped this country over the past few decades and become known as the 'Culture War'.

This was the first time in modern American history that large numbers of people were repeatedly and systematically targeted by domestic terrorists solely because they attempted to exercise their First Amendment rights to engage in political speech and to peacefully assemble.

As soon as I saw the images of hordes of leftist 'Brownshirts' rioting and attacking Trump supporters in Chicago, Albuquerque, San Jose, and numerous other places I realized that I was witnessing a game-changer – that the once-venerable American tradition of peaceful and civil political discourse and competition was now officially dead in the United States.

In an effort to understand the ramifications of this new reality I undertook a detailed examination of the nature of the modern Left in the West – their mindset, strategy, and the tactics they've used up to this point against their Traditionalist political opponents. More importantly, I considered what they were likely to do with the unchecked power they would have gained had they won the White House for four more years and (after securing a decades-long leftist majority on the Supreme Court) seized control of the federal government for at least another couple of generations.

This essay is the result of that examination. It recaps how the Left initially attacked Traditionalists decades ago with the implementation of political correctness and how they used first social, then civil and legal sanctions against those who refused to adhere to the leftist demand that they self-censor their opinions. I then discussed how influential legal scholars on the Left are now advocating for the courts to eradicate the remnants of Traditional Western culture from our society, while in Europe the force of Law is already being used to criminalize what they deem to be politically-incorrect speech. Finally, I examined the aforementioned wave of organized leftist political violence against Traditional Americans and asked the following question – if the 'social justice warriors' of today are feeling emboldened enough to openly assault en masse those who disagree with them, what will they try to do once they believe they have total power over us?

I reached the conclusion that they will do what the Left has always historically done in country after country whenever they have gained power – they will disarm their opponents, force them to comply with their totalitarian edicts, round up those who refuse and throw them into gulags for 'reeducation' and, ultimately, if that doesn't beat them into compliance, 'liquidate' them.

The utopian ideology of communism/socialism/modern liberalism/progressivism is a secular religion that views all other political philosophies and ideas as heresy and those who advocate for them as evil. In their minds, the glorious, egalitarian end they seek justifies any and all means they deem necessary to bring it about, including (but not limited to) deceiving, lying, smearing, cheating, stealing from, intimidating, assaulting and yes, murdering those unenlightened enough to stand in the way of 'Progress'.

Functionally, there is no difference between the virulent secular creed of Leftism and the abominable, murderous pseudo-religion known as Islam – which explains why proponents of the two, despite superficial differences, are natural allies against Traditionalists in the West who are the defenders of Judeo-Christian values and individual liberty.

When I first wrote this essay in June 2016, the idea that the election of another Democratic President could spark a chain of events that would ultimately lead to the attempted leftist genocide of Traditional Americans and/or civil war sounded ridiculous and over the top. After all, 'normal' progressives are peaceful people, care about others, and would never advocate violence – if you don't believe me just ask them.

However, the unprecedented irrational and unhinged behavior of even 'mainstream progressives' in the months leading up to Trump's election and during the first half-year of his Administration put the lie to that belief and undeniably illustrated the Left's true colors. Their unbridled rage indicated that the worst case scenario laid-out in this essay was, in retrospect, not only possible but likely. Even if it turns out that most 'progressives' would not personally engage in violence against Traditionalists, it is clear they will do little to stop the more aggressive, blatant communists in their camp from doing so – just as allegedly 'moderate' Moslems do little to stand up to the murderous jihadis in their midst.

172

Since Trump's election, countless leftist members of the mainstream media, academia, Hollywood, and politicians have publicly called for the President's assassination and the killing of other Republicans. One leftist acted on those calls and attempted a mass shooting of a group of Republican congressmen at a public park while they practiced for a charity baseball game against their Democratic colleagues. Meanwhile, other Democratic congresscritters accused Trump, and by extension all who voted for him, of being 'traitorous' and 'less patriotic' than themselves.

Not exactly a recipe for future peace in this country.

I am now convinced that, if the Left in America ever got their way and acquired unchecked political power, their Marxist leaders (such as those in charge of the modern Democratic Party) would not hesitate to disarm us, imprison us, and yes, ultimately kill us.

Fortunately, what the momentous events of 2016 showed the world is that the Left will not gain unchecked power over Traditional America without a fight – the scale of which they clearly don't comprehend yet and one they will not win.

***

For the past thirty years, we have all lived under the specter of political correctness – the main weapon Cultural Marxists have used to silence any who opposed their radical leftist agenda to destroy the traditional culture of the West.

Political correctness originally began as an attack on language in order to allow the Left to set the parameters of the linguistic battlefield in the on-going philosophical and legal war against the defenders of Traditional Western culture. By forcing their enemies to have to continually navigate through semantic minefields and jump through verbal hoops, the Left has successfully held the initiative throughout the so-called 'culture wars' and kept Traditionalists off-balance and unable to effectively respond.

From the beginning, those 'compassion fascists' who wielded the PC club claimed to do so for the noblest of reasons – to empower and enable those groups they claim were marginalized and victimized by the old culture. Thus the earliest manifestations of political correctness revolved around which terms used to describe groups of people were acceptable or not.

'Negros' became 'Blacks', which became 'African-Americans', and then morphed again into 'People of Color'. 'Mexicans', 'Hondurans', and 'Salvadorans' became 'Latinos', then 'Hispanics'. 'Orientals' became 'Asian-Americans'. 'Indians' became 'Native-Americans'. 'Crippled' people became 'handicapped', then 'differently-abled'.

'Homosexuals' became 'gay'; then 'lesbian, bi-sexual, and gay'; then 'LBGTQ' as 'trannies' and 'queers' were added to the mix – though how 'queers' are different from 'gays' I don't know and really don't care. (Eventually the 'acceptable' acronym will be 'LBGTQPPNF' as polygamists, pedophiles, necrophiliacs, and fetishists are added to the ever-expanding rainbow-colored kaleidoscope of sexually-deviant 'protected classes'.)

'Women' became 'wymyn'.

'White men' became 'racists'.

In the beginning, this whole debate over what labels to tag people with seemed silly and ridiculous – a 20ᵗʰ Century version of arguing over how many angels could dance on the head of a pin. But it wasn't – even though it was clearly absurd it successfully conditioned society to respond to the demands of the larval PC culture police.

Then the Cultural Marxists began to inflict their 'progressive' agenda on the American people through the imposition of new laws, regulations, and court rulings. Politically correct euphemisms provided linguistic cover for these divisive and destructive policies – racial quotas became 'affirmative action' for 'equal opportunity'. Forced bussing was called 'integration'. Subsidizing the migration of inner city populations to the suburbs (and now to rural areas) was done to promote 'diversity'. The elimination of border controls in Western nations was done to encourage 'multiculturalism'. 'Illegal aliens' became known as 'undocumented immigrants', and then simply 'migrants'. Ever-increasing Marxist redistribution of wealth through 'progressive' taxation (i.e. state-sponsored theft) became 'economic justice'. Minorities ambushing cops and rioting in the streets is now 'social justice'. Infanticide is a 'choice'. Harvesting organs from murdered infants is noble, but exposing such criminal activity is 'an assault on women's reproductive rights'.

'Tolerance' became the requirement that members of non-protected classes (white men, Christians, heterosexuals, political conservatives, traditionalists, etc.) accept all this leftist bullshit without protest. However, the PC definition of 'tolerance' is not a two-way street – there is no reciprocal requirement that people from non-protected classes be shown any of the respect or consideration that is demanded for the 'victim' classes.

Nor does the Left's definition of 'diversity' include diversity of opinion. Just as the Economic Marxist doesn't believe in the free market exchange of goods and services, the Cultural Marxist doesn't believe in freedom of speech or real debate in the 'marketplace of ideas'. Any dissenting opinion must be crushed. Any who dare disagree with the leftist agenda are branded 'racists', 'homophobes', 'insensitive', or some other pejorative.

In the beginning of the era of political correctness, such heretics were punished through non-judicial means. If they worked for a corporation headed up by weak-minded fools who bought into the notion of 'white guilt' and lacked the moral courage to stand against the PC onslaught (as most large companies were) they would find their career scuttled. If they worked for a government agency or served in the military their career would end even faster. If they were a business owner, they would find their company boycotted or subjected to frivolous lawsuits. If a public figure or celebrity, they were ostracized and blacklisted. If they had a TV show they were pulled off the air. If a sports caster, from Jimmy 'The Greek' Snyder in 1988 to Curt Schilling in 2016, they were vilified and flushed down the memory hole.

As part of the punishment for the sin of political incorrectness, the heretic was expected to publicly recant, debase themselves, and beg forgiveness from those in the protected classes they had supposedly 'victimized' with their 'insensitivity'. Many humiliated themselves in an effort to repair the damage to their careers, but it rarely worked. The leftist arbiters of the new 'virtue' were not known for mercy.

This had a chilling effect on free speech in the public sphere, as members of non-protected groups learned to self-censor their opinions for fear of reprisal, no matter how outrageous, insulting, or over-the-top political correctness became. For any person in a non-protected class under the age of 50, they have been denigrated and discriminated against in the workplace their entire adult life, yet dared not speak a word against it. Traditional Americans have had to watch while their culture was poisoned by the Cultural Marxists yet felt they could not speak out fully against it, which only served to further the decay and embolden our leftist enemies.

That is where we find ourselves as a society today in 2016. It is a terrible state of affairs – the country we once knew has transmogrified into something that is evil and would be unrecognizable to our ancestors as recently as 50 years ago.

Unfortunately, as bad as things are now, it's about to get much, much worse.

The Cultural Marxists managed to cause all the damage I've just described while there still remained a vestigial trace of 'checks and balances' in the system and conservative traditionalists still held some positions of authority to act as a brake on the Left's worst impulses.

Those safeguards are now disappearing. As electoral demographics have shifted left as a result of unfettered immigration from the Third World the balance of power has shifted left as well. Having an unapologetic communist and racist occupy the White House the past seven years hasn't helped. Neither has the passing of Justice Scalia, which has thrown the balance of the Supreme Court into doubt. And even though Traditionalists elected enough Republicans to Congress in 2014 to hand both the House and Senate over to the GOP, the cowardly party leadership have proven themselves impotent to take on either an out of control Obama or a Supreme Court that went off the rails even before Scalia's death with its disastrous 2015 ruling on Obamacare and unfounded ruling on homosexual marriage.

The Cultural Marxists have recognized this shift in power in their favor and are aggressively moving to exploit it. Just months after the high court ruling on homosexual marriage, the Left has belligerently pushed its campaign to normalize transsexuality in the media with breathtaking speed in a blatant, all-out assault on the remnants of the traditional culture. (The nauseating saga of Bruce Jenner being the most unavoidable example.) They have since upped the ante by demanding that men who 'self-identify' as women be allowed into female bathrooms and locker rooms in spite of the risks to the safety of women and young girls. (Or the fact that it is completely unnecessary.) It is obvious that sexual criminals who prefer victimizing females will gladly identify themselves as 'tranny' to gain access to such a fertile hunting ground.

This latest affront was too much for Governor Pat McCrory and legislature of the Great State of North Carolina, who courageously passed a common-sense law in response requiring that people use the public restroom matching the sex that is officially listed on their birth certificate (i.e. an objective, biological standard) rather than a purely subjective 'gender identity' chosen by each individual.

The Left immediately went completely apoplectic, attacking North Carolina with language usually reserved for people who disembowel puppies and kittens for fun. They also rolled out their usual tactic of calling for an economic boycott against the state.

What sets this latest politically correct affront to Traditional America apart from previous ones is that 'President' Obama, already drunk on wielding unchecked executive power to further the Cultural Marxist agenda on immigration and gun control, has decided to unleash the power of the Department of Justice and the rest of the executive branch against North Carolina – threatening to sue the state and withhold millions of federal funds if they don't comply with his edict to rescind their law.

An article in Time magazine in early May spells out the crux of the Obama Administration's specious 'argument' against the North Carolina law:

> In the letter, the Justice Department alleges that this law violates federal civil rights protections because discriminating against transgender people is a form of sex discrimination. The bulk of the letter concentrates on the treatment of state employees. And the argument is this: If the state allows "non-transgender" employees to use the sex-segregated bathrooms that align with their gender identity but denies that right to transgender employees, then the latter are not receiving full and equal access to bathrooms—and that's sex discrimination. The letter demands that the

state cease implementation of the law.

Here's a link to the Time article:

http://time.com/4318812/bathroom-law-transgender-north-carolina/

So, in essence, what the Cultural Marxists are arguing in this case is what they argue in so many others – that their subjective opinion trumps objective fact. Their 'gender identity' is more valid than biology and countless generations of tradition. Their feelings rule over all. A is *not* A. Reality is 'homophobic', or 'racist', or 'hateful'.

What we must always keep in mind is this - their will is, and will always be, impervious to logic from us or anyone else who disagrees with them. When this fanatical mind-set becomes coupled with the force of law, they become exceedingly dangerous.

A chilling example of this threat comes from a leading Cultural Marxist law professor at Harvard University named Mark Tushnet. On May 6, 2016, he published a blog entry with the seemingly innocuous title, "Abandoning Defensive Crouch Liberal Constitutionalism." In it, Professor Tushnet gives us a glimpse into our enemy's strategic plan going forward against Traditional Americans. It is not a pretty picture.

First, he incorrectly laments that,

> *"Several (liberal) generations of law students and their teachers grew up with federal courts dominated by conservatives. Not surprisingly, they found themselves wandering in the wilderness, looking for any sign of hope. The result: Defensive-crouch constitutionalism, with every liberal position asserted nervously, its proponents looking over their shoulders for retaliation by conservatives…"*

What utter bullshit. If the federal courts were indeed 'dominated by conservatives' *Roe v. Wade* would not have been the 'law of the land' for 43 years. Obamacare would have been overturned. Homosexual marriage would not be considered a 'constitutional right'. As for 'every liberal position (being) asserted nervously', when was the last time any of us saw a leftist being timid when flapping their gums – especially a leftist lawyer, jurist, or lawmaker?

The Professor goes on to obliquely celebrate the death of Justice Scalia and expound on the opportunities this presents the Cultural Marxists:

> *It's time to stop. Right now more than half of the judges sitting on the courts of appeals were appointed by Democratic presidents, and – though I wasn't able to locate up-to-date numbers – the same appears to be true of the district courts. And, those judges no longer have to be worried about reversal by the Supreme Court if they take aggressively liberal positions. (They might be reversed, but now there's no guarantee.) And, we shouldn't focus on the Court's docket this year, which was shaped by conservative justices thinking that they could count to five on a bunch of cases. The docket will look quite different if they can't see that path to five votes when they decide which cases to review.*

He then rhetorically asks, "What would abandoning defensive-crouch liberalism mean?" He gives several points, but the most striking are:

> ### A jurisprudence of "wrong the day it was decided."
> *Liberals should be compiling lists of cases to be overruled at the first opportunity on the ground that they were wrong the day they were decided… What matters is that overruling key cases also means that a rather large body of doctrine will have to be built from the ground up. Thinking about what that doctrine should look like is important – more important than trying to maneuver liberal goals through the narrow paths the bad precedents seem to leave open.*

You can bet the list of cases the Cultural Marxists will seek to 'overrule' and 'build from the ground up' a 'rather large body of doctrine' include *McDonald v. Chicago* (Which held that the Second Amendment applies to the states.) and *District of Columbia Et al. v. Heller* (Which held in part that the Second Amendment protects the right to possess a firearm unconnected with service in an organized militia such as the National Guard, and to use that arm for traditionally lawful purposes such as self-defense within the home.)

It took only a little over a month after Professor Tushnet's call to Cultural Marxist jurists to attack established precedents standing in the way of their agenda for the liberal-dominated 9th Circuit Court of Appeals to issue a ruling that would directly overturn *Heller*.

http://www.nbcnews.com/news/us-news/9th-circuit-court-appeals-says-no-right-concealed-gun-carry-n589041

Other cases to come will no doubt include those governing free speech that offends leftist sensibilities such as the so-called 'fairness doctrine', which would effectively eliminate conservative talk radio and freedom of expression on the internet. We can also expect so-called 'hate speech' from Traditionalists to be criminalized, as it already is in Europe. (More on that in a moment.)

Professor Tushnet continues:

> **The culture wars are over; they lost, we won.** *Remember, they were the ones who characterized constitutional disputes as culture wars (see Justice Scalia in Romer v. Evans, and the Wikipedia entry for culture wars, which describes conservative activists, not liberals, using the term.) And they had opportunities to reach a cease fire, but rejected them in favor of a scorched earth policy. The earth that was scorched, though, was their own. (No conservatives demonstrated any interest in trading off recognition of LGBT rights for "religious liberty" protections. Only now that they've lost the battle over LGBT rights, have they made those protections central – seeing them, I suppose, as a new front in the culture wars. But, again, they've already lost the war.)*

This asshole really is a sophist, isn't he? He seems to have no shortage of flawed premises he uses to try and support his arguments. First, I'm not willing to grant him that 'conservative activists' coined the phrase 'culture wars' based solely on a Wikipedia entry, but even if they did, so what? Labelling something that already exists does not make one responsible for the creation of it. There is no doubt that the Cultural Marxists were aggressively assaulting Traditional Western culture long before the term 'culture wars' ever entered the popular lexicon. Then, he tries to minimize the attempted Cultural Marxist destruction of our most basic rights as mere 'constitutional disputes'. Wrong answer, pal.

He goes on to repeatedly assert that Traditional Americans have lost and the Cultural Marxists have won the 'culture wars'. While I will agree that most of the battles have been won by his side thus far and that momentum until recently has definitely been theirs, I believe the good professor is crowing a bit too soon. Until now this has pretty much been a one-sided fight. But now the Cultural Marxists have grown cocky and overreached – and the long-sleeping giant that is Traditional America has finally started to awaken, is rubbing its eyes and looking around, and is righteously pissed off by what it sees. This war has just begun.

Then he faults us Traditional Americans for opposing 'LBGT rights' while simultaneously rigorously defending what he derides as 'religious liberty protections'. He implies that, since we didn't agree to compromise with the homosexual agenda our religious freedoms should have no future validity in liberal-dominated courts.

What a typical Cultural Marxist. Their definition of 'compromise' always is – we give them what they want now and they'll generously let us keep some of what we've always traditionally had. At least until tomorrow – when they'll be back with fresh demands.

There can be no compromise with them, because they don't believe in 'live and let live' and will not rest until all who disagree with them are utterly suppressed and subjected to their will.

Then Professor Tushnet comes to the most illuminating part of his blog entry – he continues his second point by describing how the Cultural Marxists *really* view us Traditional Americans and, more importantly, what should be done to us:

> *For liberals, the question now is how to deal with the losers in the culture wars. That's mostly a question of tactics. My own judgment is that taking a hard line ("You lost, live with it") is better than trying to accommodate the losers, who – remember – defended, and are defending, positions that liberals regard as having no normative pull at all. Trying to be nice to the losers didn't work well after the Civil War, nor after Brown. (And taking a hard line seemed to work reasonably well in Germany and Japan after 1945.) I should note that LGBT activists in particular seem to have settled on the hard-line approach, while some liberal academics defend more accommodating approaches. When specific battles in the culture wars were being fought, it might have made sense to try to be accommodating after a local victory, because other related fights*

were going on, and a hard line might have stiffened the opposition in those fights. But the war's over, and we won.

Here Professor Tushnet, the unabashed Cultural Marxist, equates us Traditional Americans (Judeo-Christians, Constitutionalists, liberty-lovers, those who believe that God's Natural Law is superior to state power) to Klansmen, Nazis, and the barbarous Imperial Japanese. He argues that we should be treated like the Nazis and Imperial Japanese were after World War II.

For those who don't remember, Nazism was totally purged from Germany and anything to do with it was subsequently made (and still is) illegal in that country. The same with the militaristic Bushido cult in post-war Japan, though the Emperor was left in place as a figurehead.

So, when Harvard Law Professor Tushnet says we Traditional Americans should be treated like the defeated Nazis, he is arguing that the power of law should be used to completely purge our beliefs and traditions from American culture.

There is no other way to interpret his statement.

Tushnet's blog post goes on to discuss legal tactical considerations to accomplish this grand strategic goal, but they are secondary in importance and I won't discuss them any further here. For those of you interested in his entire post, here is the link:

http://balkin.blogspot.it/2016/05/abandoning-defensive-crouch-liberal.html?m=1

I have taken significant time here to analyze Professor Tushnet's post because Mark Tushnet is not just some minor academic functionary shooting his mouth off. He is the 'William Nelson Cromwell Professor of Law' at Harvard University. That means that he is not merely a tenured professor – he occupies an endowed chair and has his salary paid for by the investment proceeds of an endowment set up for that purpose.

That means Tushnet is high on the food chain among the faculty at Harvard Law, one of the nation's leading institutions whose graduates are on the fast track to becoming America's future jurists – people who have tremendous power over all of our lives. In his youth he was a clerk to Justice Thurgood Marshall and was instrumental in helping to get *Roe v. Wade* passed.

These unusually candid comments from one who is so highly placed in the Cultural Marxists' philosophical camp provide a window into the soul of our enemy – a glimpse directly at their battle plan against us.

It is a clear warning as to what they intend to do to us as soon as they possibly can – totally eradicate us and our way of life.

Now there are those who will argue that I am being an alarmist. Some will say that Tushnet is not talking about *literally* killing us – he's only using martial language to illustrate his points in the context of 'the culture wars'. He doesn't *really* mean to harm us physically – he's only advocating for the peaceful establishment of legal precedents favorable to his 'liberal' opinions. What can possibly be wrong with that?

The problem is, those 'liberal' (i.e. Cultural Marxist) opinions he champions, once they prevail in the courts, become Law.

Law that is then enforced by agents of the State at the business end of guns. And flash-bang grenades. And tanks. And drones with Hellfire missiles.

As George Washington so famously observed, *"Government is not reason; it is not eloquence; it is force. Like fire, it is a dangerous servant and a fearful master."*

You cannot talk your way out of a government edict. Try telling the IRS you aren't going to pay taxes because you are morally opposed to financing foreign aid that goes to support brutal dictators overseas or that you are religiously opposed to having your money used to fund the evil baby-part peddlers at Planned Parenthood.

Good luck with that. Your mileage may vary.

When Tushnet speaks of using court rulings to impose the Cultural

Marxists' will on Traditional Americans, *that is a very real and physical threat.*

One such ruling alone, *Roe v. Wade*, has resulted in the legalized murder of nearly 50 million children in America since 1973 – a genocide four times as great as the Nazi-directed holocaust and comparable to the slaughters in the Soviet Union under the Bolsheviks and in Communist China under Mao.

Ask yourself, what do you think they'll do to *us* if they manage to successfully 'redefine' the Second Amendment out of existence in the courts and render us completely defenseless to their will? What will living in this country be like when there are no more checks and limits to their power?

Will it be possible for freedom-loving people to live at all?

All the signs we need to understand what's coming are already out there – ominous signs right here in the United States; even worse ones facing our Western brothers and sisters in socialist-dominated Europe; and the lessons to be gleaned from the historical behavior of previous socialist/communist regimes towards dissidents.

Here in the United States and in Europe, the Cultural Marxists have further escalated their politically correct war on free speech by redefining commentary critical of their totalitarian agenda as 'against the public interest' or as 'hate speech' and criminalizing it.

In April 2016, 16 Democratic state attorneys general decided to prosecute any companies that disagreed with the environmentalist dogma of 'global climate change'. Any 'climate-change denier' who dares to be a heretic against the faked 'established science' on the subject will now be punished as a thought criminal 'to the fullest extent of the law' in those states.

Here's a link to an article about this story:

https://www.independentsentinel.com/16-ags-plan-to-criminalize-climate-change-denial/

In Europe they're already arresting people for expressing politically incorrect opinions.

In February 2016, a man living on the small Scottish Isle of Bute, which had a population of 6,498 in 2011, posted a Facebook comment critical of the government's decision to relocate 1,000 Syrian 'refugees' to his island. Police subsequently arrested him for the crime of making an 'offensive' comment regarding the 'migrants'. A police spokesman stated,

> *"I hope that the arrest of this individual sends a clear message that Police Scotland will not tolerate any form of activity which could incite hatred and provoke offensive comments on social media".*

http://www.breitbart.com/london/2016/02/16/british-police-arrest-man-for-syrian-migrants-facebook-post-promise-zero-tolerance-on-offence-online/

In January 2016, Dutch police started paying visits to people who had the temerity to tweet messages critical of the government's pro-migrant policies and threatened them with charges of 'sedition' if they continued. One man had tweeted the following:

> *"The college of Sliedrecht has a proposal to receive 250 refugees in the coming 2 years. What a bad plan! #letusresist"*

'What a bad plan!' – not exactly the most incendiary rhetoric I've ever heard. No matter – it was enough to bring the man a house call by the cops.

Another Dutch man was visited by police when he said this on Facebook:

> *"There was a meeting in the council hall, an information evening, just for the people of our city."* He added: *"we had to get together at the market square to have a protest, because, I will be very honest, we're not happy with the asylum seekers in our country."*

What?! This insensitive reactionary is unhappy with jihadists and mass rapists invading his country and turning the place into a

Moslem hellhole? He was also obviously in need of some instant 'reeducation' from the police.

http://www.breitbart.com/london/2016/01/27/you-tweet-a-lot-watch-your-tone-cops-threaten-dutch-man-for-opposing-govt-mass-migration-plans/

According to an article from New Europe:

> *In recent months, police have visited the homes of many more people that criticised the plans for asylum centres. In October 2015, in Leeuwarden about twenty opponents of the programs received police visits at home. It happened in Enschede, and in some places in the Brabant, where, according to the Dutch media, people who had been critical of the arrival of refugees and ran a page on social media on the topic were told to stop.*

> *A spokesman for the national police acknowledged to Handelsblad that there are ten intelligence units of "digital detectives" monitoring in real time Facebook pages and Twitter accounts and looking for posts that go "too far".*

https://www.neweurope.eu/article/you-tweet-too-much-about-refugee-the-dutch-are-told-by-police/

People have also been arrested in Germany, Sweden, and other European countries for social media posts critical of the European Union and their home countries' governments for allowing the invasion of millions of Moslems, most of whom are men of military age, into their nations.

But the arrests haven't been limited to ordinary, run-of-the-mill European citizens. Leading opposition politicians have been arrested for speaking up against the Moslem invasion as well.

Dutch politician Geert Wilders was prosecuted for 'hate speech' crimes as far back as 2009. He was charged because he was outspoken in his belief that militant Islam poses a threat to Holland's traditionally tolerant culture. (A position self-evident to anyone who's studied the so-called 'religion of peace'.)

Though Wilders was eventually acquitted in 2011, the case set a dangerous precedent for the criminalization of political speech.

http://www.legal-project.org/issues/geert-wilders

And in France in October 2015, Marine Le Pen, leader of the opposition National Front party, was ordered to stand trial for the crime of 'inciting racial hatred'. How did she do this? She talked, during a campaign speech, about how Moslems take over streets in certain areas of the country during prayer time and, essentially, occupy French territory. She stated it was similar to the occupation in World War II. Here are her comments:

> *"I'm sorry, but for those who like talking a lot about World War II, if it comes to talking about the occupation, we can talk about it, because that (Muslims praying on the street) is the occupation of territory," she told a crowd in the southeastern city of Lyon.*

> *"It is an occupation of part of the territory, suburbs where religious law is applied. Sure, there are no armoured vehicles, no soldiers, but it is an occupation nonetheless and it weighs on residents."*

According to the Yahoo article I found this quote in, these fairly tepid comments 'provoked outrage in France'.

https://www.yahoo.com/news/marine-le-pen-face-trial-inciting-racial-hatred-143014002.html?ref=gs

Ms. Le Pen told the truth. In many areas of France, streets are packed curb to curb and are impassible during Moslem prayer time, the right of free movement of French citizens is denied to them, and the 'territory' is effectively 'occupied'. To the Cultural Marxists, however, being truthful is not an acceptable defense if that truth is politically incorrect or 'offends' the sensibilities of a protected class – in this case, Moslems.

At the time Marine Le Pen was ordered to stand trial, she was one of the leading opponents to sitting Socialist President Francois Hollande. She is, in essence, France's Donald Trump. Since Europe is farther along on its path to socialist totalitarianism than America thus far, Trump has not been criminally charged for comments he's made during his political speeches...at least not yet.

Governmental use of criminal law to silence political opposition is a major milestone on the road to tyranny, and there is absolutely no place for it in a free society.

As chilling as this is, the next trick in the would-be totalitarian's playbook is even worse – organizing and encouraging violent mobs to disrupt, assault, and terrorize opposition political rallies and events.

The Nazis infamously used their SA 'Brownshirts' to do just that during their campaign to democratically come to power in the Weimar Republic in Germany in the late 1920s and early 1930s. In addition to harassing and assaulting Jews and other people they considered *'untermenschen'*, these bands of thugs specialized in beating up (and many times killing) supporters of parties opposed to the Nazis in an effort to create a climate of fear that would keep other Germans from standing up and voting against them.

Every other dictatorship in history has done the same thing to its opposition.

Now the same thing is happening again, this time right here in the United States.

Globalist-financed and organized leftist agitators and rioters, displeased by Donald Trump's call to secure America's borders and enforce federal immigration law, violently disrupted a Trump rally and speech in Chicago in March 2016 and forced its cancellation. Emboldened by what they viewed as a successful 'protest', leftist mobs attacked subsequent rallies and Trump supporters with increasing levels of viciousness.

The anti-Trump riots reached new levels of vitriol and violence as the Trump campaign swung through the southwestern states of New Mexico and California, and began to take on overtones of low-intensity conflict and 4th generation warfare.

During a particularly violent anti-Trump riot in San Jose, the city's police did absolutely *nothing* to help Trump supporters who were openly assaulted in front of them, including women and children. They were ordered by the Cultural Marxist mayor to stand-down and let the 'protestors' do what they wanted so as 'not to incite the crowd and produce more violent behavior'.

Apparently none of the sworn officers present felt it was worth losing their jobs to uphold their oath to 'preserve and protect the Constitution of the United States against all enemies, foreign and domestic' by disobeying that unlawful order and coming to the assistance of innocent citizens being terrorized by criminal mobs intent on denying them their First Amendment rights to free speech and assembly.

This violence has been perpetrated for the express purpose of influencing the outcome of an election by intimidating citizens engaged in the political process.

According to federal statute, this fits the definition of 'terrorism'. And that makes these anti-Trump rioters, by definition, 'domestic terrorists'.

But don't hold your breath waiting for the Obama Department of Justice to launch a criminal investigation into these civil rights violations of Trump supporters. In the Cultural Marxist worldview, they had it coming for supporting the 'philosophy of hate' the leftists say Trump represents.

The inaction of the San Jose mayor and the Obama Administration on this illustrates a vital point about the new reality in America that Traditional Americans absolutely *must* understand – *wherever Marxists are in power, any who oppose them will not have the protection of the Rule of Law.*

The rules of the game have changed, and the other side is playing for keeps. American elections are no longer merely civic rituals to aid in the traditionally peaceful transfer of power.

Prussian military theorist Carl von Clausewitz once famously said, "War is the extension of politics by other means." In America today its corollary is also true – politics is the precursor to war.

For there can be no doubt that the Cultural Marxist attacks on Traditionalist Trump supporters during this election cycle have escalated to the level of 'low-intensity conflict' or '4th generation warfare'.

I discussed the nature of these two concepts in a blog post I wrote last July entitled "War On Our Doorstep – Why We Must All Become Minutemen Now", following the jihadi attack on Chattanooga that left 5 American servicemen dead. For those who haven't read it yet, it can be found here:

http://www.counterrevolutionarycorner.com/2015/07/war-on-our-doorstep-why-we-must-all.html

To summarize, 'low-intensity conflict' is a term defined by the US Army as:

> ...*a political-military confrontation between contending states or groups below conventional war and above the routine, peaceful competition among states. It **frequently involves protracted struggles of competing principles and ideologies**. Low-intensity conflict ranges from subversion to the use of the armed forces. **It is waged by**

a combination of means, employing political, economic, informational, and military instruments. (emphasis added)

Wikipedia describes '4th generation warfare' as:

> *...conflict characterized by* **a blurring of the lines between war and politics, combatants and civilians.** *It is a term coined in 1989 by...American military analysts to describe modern warfare's return to a decentralized form. (It) signifies the nation state's loss of its near-monopoly on combat forces, returning to modes of conflict in pre-modern times.* (emphasis added)

By these definitions it is clear the United States has already entered the early stages of 'low-intensity conflict' and '4th generation war'.

The important point for our discussion is to understand the importance of the changes in warfare during the past 50 years or so and how that will affect our future. As a result of those changes, the definition of 'war' has increasingly moved away from large-scale fights between industrial armies a la World Wars I and II to conflicts where smaller groups of people, sometimes even individuals, are able to wield effective force against larger entities up to and including nation-states. These changes are what have made the evolution of 4th generation warfare possible.

One of the key changes was the Information Revolution, which introduced potent, miniaturized, man-portable weapons such as Stinger 'fire-and-forget' anti-aircraft missiles and hand-held guided anti-tank weapons to would-be insurgents. Unlike earlier wars in the modern era, this allowed them to field effective combat units without having to possess a large industrial base – in other words, guerrillas and small bands became much more militarily effective.

Even more important, information technology enables grassroots movements to self-organize in a relatively leaderless way through social media, greatly increasing their security and efficiency, and also allows small groups and individuals to attack larger enemies' information-based control systems by hacking into them.

As this evolution occurred, war began to look more like the ethnic and religious civil wars we saw in Lebanon in the 1980s, in Bosnia-Herzegovina in the former Yugoslavia in the 1990s, and in Iraq and Syria today rather than the World Wars of the first half of the 20th century. 'Low-intensity conflict' and '4th generation warfare' can also be used to describe the situation in more mono-ethnic failed states such as Mexico, where the struggle has been between a relatively weak central government against militarily potent narco-terrorist drug cartels, or in Somalia, where central authority broke down completely and the resulting power vacuum was filled by tribal gangs led by rival warlords.

Most people are able to identify countries that have fallen into 'low-intensity conflict' and '4th generation warfare' after the fact, but few are able to accurately predict such calamities beforehand, especially in countries that have enjoyed relative peace and prosperity for a long period of time. This prior period of peace and prosperity would have accurately described all of the nations listed above – for all of them had been stable for decades before their eventual slides into chaos.

This failure of most people to be able to predict future changes to the status quo is largely due to a psychological phenomenon known as 'recency bias'. In layman's terms, this is the tendency of people to assume that situations are going to continue into the future the same way they've been in the recent past. And for many, many years they can be right. Long-term systems and trends tend to remain in place for a long time – and societal and cultural structures are some of most resistant to such change.

However, once the underlying conditions supporting a particular status quo erode sufficiently, a tipping point is reached, and rapid, radical change can occur seemingly overnight – catching the vast majority of people off-guard. Few citizens of the former Yugoslavia or of Syria would have expected civil war to break out even a mere couple of years before they started.

The key to recognizing when a country may be nearing such a tipping point beforehand is to study conditions in those nations that have succumbed to civil war and chaos in the past and see if any common traits were present prior to their collapses. (However, this requires an interest in the cycles of history that most modern people seem to lack, which also contributes to their being blindsided when the inevitable turnings of those cycles occur.)

When we make such an examination, it becomes apparent that certain factors make a country more susceptible to the risk of descending into civil war. The primary ones can be categorized as demographic, religious, and ideological differences.

For a more detailed discussion of some of the factors that can contribute to civil war, read my earlier blog post entitled "Multiculturalism and Diversity – What I Do Not Believe, Part 2". For those who haven't read it yet, it can be found here:

http://www.counterrevolutionarycorner.com/2015/06/multicultural ism-and-diversity-what-i.html

To summarize, here are key warning signs to look for (Some from the original post and a few added here.):

- There is a direct correlation between high levels of ethnic diversity in a country and correspondingly high levels of societal unrest in the form of ethnic tensions, race riots, secessionist movements, or even civil war.

- The root cause of this is that it is natural for human beings to identify themselves most with their tribe – that group of people with whom they share a common bond of blood, religion, language, and history. They also tend to chafe under rule by members of a different tribe. There is nothing inherently wrong with this – it is simply human nature.

- Conflicts arise when the borders of a political unit don't match the ethnic makeup of the people within those borders – whether because those borders were drawn 'incorrectly' at that country's founding or as a result of subsequent demographic changes.

- Another source of instability to a nation is having a significant minority population with co-ethnics in a neighboring country, particularly when that minority doesn't fully assimilate into the native population.

- When civil wars *do* occur in mono-ethnic nations, they tend to be religious in nature (such as the Catholic-Protestant wars in Europe in the 1600s or in Syria today) or have co-ethnics with radically different ideologies and economic interests (as occurred in the American Revolution and then later in the Civil War).

- The only way nations with populations split along ethnic, religious, or ideological lines have been able to peacefully co-exist for long as a single political unit is by adopting true federalism such as exists in Switzerland – allowing great amounts of local autonomy to the various groups, with a relatively weak central government only coordinating common issues such as national defense. (The United States had this form of government at its founding.)

- The only other way for a country with a diverse population to hold together is for one of the ethnic, religious, or ideological groups to dominate the others by force – which transforms that country into more of a multiethnic empire rather than a single, unified nation.

- Those are the only choices the people have in a multicultural, multiethnic country – to establish a republic and adopt a predominantly 'live and let live' attitude towards the other groups; or to fight a civil war in an attempt to establish the dominance of one group over the rest. If that attempt fails, the country usually then shatters into smaller, independent fragments.

- *There is no example in history of a multicultural, multiethnic country, which chose to accentuate its group differences and historical grievances rather than common values, that has successfully held together.*

After examining conditions in the United States in light of these risk factors, it becomes increasingly clear that our country is in grave danger, for many of the items on this list now apply here.

After decades of Cultural Marxist assault on our formerly unified culture, America is more 'diverse' and Balkanized than ever.

Many of our cities are on the verge of race war. (Baltimore, Ferguson, etc.)

Uncontrolled illegal immigration from Mexico has left large parts of the southwestern United States with a population that displays more allegiance to our southern neighbor than our own country.

The nation's largest ethnic group, those of European descent, are ideologically-split into two irreconcilable, mutually-loathing camps – Traditional Nationalists who believe in God-given individual liberty as enshrined in our founding documents vs. fanatical Cultural Marxist internationalists who push state-mandated, totalitarian egalitarianism upon everyone else.

Nor do the Cultural Marxists believe in true federalism or the social 'safety valve' that small-'r' republicanism provides a society by resolving differences of opinion on cultural issues with the mechanism of strong local autonomy – their doctrine demands that their dogma dominate all other philosophies with a top-down, centralized command authority. Despite all their bogus claims to be champions of 'diversity', there can be no 'live and let live' in their world view – for them 'one-size fits all'. Totalitarianism is their creed.

To add a final combustible element to this toxic brew, the globalist Cultural Marxists now in power are deliberately and 'with malice of forethought' importing into our new 'multicultural paradise' a group whose culture chiefly consists of wanting to kill all others – orthodox Moslems. They are using the jihadists embedded within the Moslem population as a weapon against us to keep us further off-balance while they implement the rest of their totalitarian agenda.

Not a recipe for peaceful coexistence.

The United States is now closer to all-out civil war than at any time since 1859 – only this time it promises to be more chaotic and brutal than the last one.

The last civil war was largely fought between two organized, de-facto nation states – this one could very well devolve into a Mad Max war of all-against-all. (What the Germans refer to as *bandenkrieg*.)

By inflaming every imaginable grievance possible, from any and all conceivable hyphenated ethnic and ideological minority groups (no matter how small or bizarre) against the majority culture, and offering only a tepid 'tolerance' as common ground, the Cultural Marxists have turned the United States into a colossal powder keg just waiting for a spark.

And 2016 has thus far produced a multitude of sparks – some of the hottest political sparks seen in our lifetime.

With the death of Justice Scalia throwing the balance of the Supreme Court in doubt, the stakes in this presidential election are higher than they've been since 1860. The Cultural Marxists know that, if they can keep the imperial presidency in their hands and add the support of the high court to rubber stamp edicts coming out of the White House, they will be able to complete their takeover of America and ensure a stranglehold on Federal power indefinitely. The Congress, even if it remains in Republican hands, will be irrelevant – the steady abdication of that body's constitutional authority to the executive and judicial branches since World War II has rendered it largely impotent.

If the Cultural Marxists retain the White House for another four years, they will be able to irrevocably change the balance of the electorate by bringing in ever greater numbers of illegal aliens and then granting them citizenship and/or the franchise, thus creating millions upon millions of new voters for the Democratic Party. They will also be able to stack the Supreme Court with socialist justices who will interpret what they see as the 'living document' of the Constitution in whatever manner necessary to justify this.

The bottom line is this – if Hillary Rodham Clinton wins the presidential election in November, there will never be a contested presidential election in the United States again.

And what will the Cultural Marxists do once they've achieved total political power? The same thing all totalitarian socialist and communist governments do – they will *use* governmental power, in the name of 'progress' towards their utopian goal of total 'equality' for all, to eliminate any possible challenge *to* that power.

In an extension of current politically correct trends, Traditional Americans will be branded as bigoted 'reactionaries' and 'extremists', who will then have the full power of the criminal justice system wielded against them.

Top priority on the Cultural Marxist agenda is the disarmament of Traditional America. In their Machiavellian calculations, we armed Americans are the only force standing in their path to total power and, as such, simply cannot be allowed to exist.

Their current hysterical push for more gun control in the wake of ever increasing Moslem attacks on us, along with their renewed efforts in the federal court system to erode the 2nd Amendment, make their ultimate intentions quite clear.

Picture how America will look after the Cultural Marxists disarm us. If they are willing and brazen enough to send mobs of leftist rioters to attack us while we still have the means to defend ourselves, just what will they be capable of when we are completely at their mercy?

The histories of countries that have fallen under the sway of totalitarian socialism in the past (and resulted in over 200 million people killed as a result) show us some likely possibilities. Traditional Americans, no longer having the means to resist, will be reduced to the wretched status of 'dissident', and will suffer the same fate all such dissidents have in past dictatorships – they will be rounded up, relocated to internment camps for 'reeducation' to ensure 'public safety' and, if they still refuse to adhere to the Party line, will finally be 'liquidated'.

In an America dominated by Cultural Marxists, the 'social justice warriors' of today will be given uniforms, badges, and guns and will be appointed the political commissars of tomorrow. They will be the ones who will make the arrests of Traditional Americans, will move them to the American gulags, and yes – will eventually murder them.

Harvard Professor Tushnet's vision of an America purged of traditional conservative cultural influences will finally be achieved.

There will be many who will scoff at these conclusions and dismiss me as a paranoid alarmist. To them I say – show me any trend in the news today that doesn't point to this ultimate totalitarian dystopia. More important – show me any sign that the Left is capable of self-regulating their most extreme impulses. For if they get their way, no one else will be around to check them.

You can't. There are absolutely no signs of the existence of a 'moderate' Cultural Marxist. You're more likely to see Sasquatch.

Absolute power will corrupt absolutely. It always does.

This is literally a matter of life and death. **Our** life and death. In the name of self-preservation, for ourselves and our posterity, we Traditional Americans **cannot** allow this to happen.

Our last chance to politically stop this Cultural Marxist juggernaut is this presidential election. Like him or not, respect him or not, Trump **must** win. And yes, even if he *does* win, the political war will far from over – but at least we will have a fighting chance to hold the line a little longer.

If Clinton wins, we will have to prepare as quickly as possible for conflict, as America will most likely fight another civil war.

Once elected, she will no doubt move to unconstitutionally criminalize firearms ownership, which Traditional Americans cannot comply with and will simply disobey.

When she orders the inevitable move to put us 'criminals' 'in our place' and seize those firearms by force, Traditional Americans will look to the example of their Forefathers and defend themselves 'with manly firmness'.

Another shot will be 'heard around the world'.

The last civil war was initiated by a contentious presidential election in a bitterly divided America. The first American Revolution was sparked by a government gun-control raid to seize the colonist's firearms. The next American civil war/revolution will likely be triggered by both.

America is out of time. We are at a momentous fork in the road. One path leads to tyranny, destruction and death; the other to a new regeneration of liberty, creation, and life.

The Great Crisis of our Age has begun, right here, right now, in 2016.

The stakes could not be higher.

The Cultural Marxists will not rest until Traditional America is completely destroyed. There can be no compromise with this enemy. There can be no reasoning with this enemy. The only choice we have now is to resist – or to surrender and beg for mercy that will not come.

Each of us must now choose a side. We must have courage. We must stand up, speak out, and be counted.

Choose well – for our nation's future depends on it.

To my brothers and sisters who are fellow veterans and former law enforcement officers, remember – your oath to 'support, protect, and defend the Constitution of the United States against all enemies, foreign and domestic' does not expire. Neither does your martial experience and expertise.

To my brothers and sisters who currently serve in the military and in law enforcement, I call on you to uphold your oath and to keep in mind that you did not swear to defend an old, anachronistic, shriveled-up piece of parchment in the National Archives – you swore an oath to uphold the eternal ideals that document represents. You swore to defend the God-given rights of the American people. No government, no power on Earth, can take those away.

If you are given unconstitutional orders by your superiors to violate those rights, you are morally and legally **obligated** to disobey. The Nuremberg Trials firmly established the precedent that 'I was only following orders' is no excuse. If you choose to enforce such unlawful orders anyway, you *will* be held accountable. If it comes to war, freedom-loving Americans will win it. The American people will find out what you've done, they will not forget, and justice will be done.

If, however, you summon the moral and physical courage to do the right thing, and stand by your countrymen at this critical hour to defend those rights, you will find yourselves honored among the pantheon of the greatest American patriots for all posterity.

And to all Americans, we must immediately make our peace with God and call upon Providence to guide us and help us stand upright in the dark and trying years to come.

With His assistance, we shall prevail.

22 – A Glimmer of Hope – But Danger Looms

First Published on June 28, 2016

The Brexit vote of June 2016 was a momentous event that marked the first defeat of the globalists in a century and was a harbinger of Trump's later election that November.

Just as in the 2016 Presidential election, the globalists pulled all their usual tried-and-true tricks during the campaign leading up to the vote to get the outcome they wanted – they had their minions in the mainstream media, academia, and government incessantly warn of dire consequences if the 'Leave' side won; they published fake polls that showed the 'Remain' camp firmly in the lead in the days leading up to the referendum in an attempt to discourage 'Leave' voters and depress their turnout; and they tried to shame people into not voting for Brexit by smearing 'Leave' supporters as ignorant, uneducated, racist rubes.

*In this essay I warned that the globalists would not take this defeat lightly and would strike back with vengeance. I explored various options open to them, including trying to undermine the vote over time by dragging out the process and possibly even forcing a second vote 'just to be sure' the people **really** want to leave the European Union. So far the delaying portion has come to pass, with the task of actually managing the Brexit process falling to Prime Minister Theresa May, a tepid conservative at best who publicly supported the 'Remain' camp during the referendum campaign. Whether Brexit ever actually takes place remains an open question as of this writing in mid-2017.*

With regard to the United States, the most important question is what the globalists are going to do about the existential threat that Donald Trump poses to their agenda. Assassination has always been an option that they haven't been shy about publicly encouraging, and it still may happen if they come to the conclusion that they can get away with it. I have little doubt they would find Vice President Pence far more manageable. Fortunately, at least so far, the powers-that-be have contented themselves with attempts to sabotage Trump's administration with ceaseless obstructionism, false narratives about mythical Russian collusion, and deep-state operatives doing everything in their power to undermine his initiatives.

Finally, I conclude this essay by warning about other, more horrifying options the globalists have available to them in their toolbox should they come to believe they're completely losing control of events. These include such apocalyptic scenarios as triggering a global economic collapse, a global pandemic, another world war, destroying the power grid, or some combination of the above calamities. All those options remain on the table for them, and the fact that we are approaching the Crisis Climax of this cycle only makes such a disaster more likely.

We can be sure of one thing, however – the Brexit vote and the subsequent election of Donald Trump were merely the beginning of a long, bitter, fight-to-the-death struggle with the evil globalist cabal that has tirelessly endeavored to enslave humanity. But that doesn't negate the fact those votes confirmed, to ourselves and our enemies alike, just how powerful we Traditionalists remain and that we have roused at long last.

We will be ignored no longer.

***

Last week's vote by the people of the United Kingdom to exit the European Union was an amazing, historic event. It was the most significant setback to the global elites' long-term plans in a very, very long time.

This occurred in spite of the fact that 'Stopping Brexit' was at the top of the globalists' 'to-do' list that came out of the recent Bilderberg meeting in Dresden. ('Keeping Donald Trump from becoming President of the United States' was also up there.)

The elite pulled out all the stops to push a fear campaign predicting all kinds of apocalyptic consequences if the 'Leave' vote won. They warned of economic collapse. Obama threatened that Britain would be forced 'to the back of the queue' in trade talks with the United States. Even more over-the-top, British Prime Minister Cameron darkly warned that a Brexit could lead to World War III.

They even stooped so low as to capitalize on the murder of a leading 'pro-Remain' Member of Parliament in the week prior to the referendum. It was initially reported that the murderer yelled "Britain First!" before pulling the trigger, thus smearing all that favored Brexit as right-wing potential murderers. (It was later revealed that the gunman was apolitical, had no particular opinion about the European Union one way or another, and was on psychotropic drugs for mental illness – but by that time the PR damage to the 'Leave' campaign had already been done.)

The people of the United Kingdom were constantly bombarded with the message that a vote to 'Leave' the European Union was hateful, racist, and xenophobic. (Sound familiar, Trump supporters?)

They voted to leave anyway.

One has to go back nearly a full century, to 1919, to find the last direct repudiation of the global elites' agenda.

That was when Senate Republicans blocked globalist President Woodrow Wilson's plan to have the United States join the League of Nations.

There can be no doubt that June 23, 2016 was a great day, for it showed that Traditionalists in the West have finally awakened and are beginning to fight back against those who would destroy them and their civilization.

Thanks to the internet and social media (The 21st Century versions of the Colonial pre-Revolutionary 'Committees of Correspondence' and the Soviet-era 'samizdat' dissident publications – but on steroids.), Traditionalist resistance to the global socialist agenda has gone viral and international, with victories in other nations providing inspiration and encouragement to like-minded individuals throughout the West.

In America, Traditionalists who have rallied around Trump have come to realize that they have far more in common with fellow overseas defenders of Western Civilization such as Nigel Farage in the UK, Marine Le Pen in France, or Geert Wilders in the Netherlands than they do with traitorous globalist minions Barack Obama or Hillary Clinton.

This viral backlash against globalism threatens to destroy the elites' entire agenda, which has as its ultimate goal the creation of a One-World government, religion, and culture.

Even the mainstream media admits that another half-dozen nations could follow the UK's example and also leave the European Union. In the United States, Trump's ascendancy shows no sign of abating, in spite of all the globalists' attempts to derail his campaign thus far.

This is cause for great optimism, and it is right that we celebrate the first great political victory that our courageous brothers and sisters in Great Britain have scored for all of us against the hated globalist tyrants.

But we must not celebrate too long nor rest on our laurels, for 'The Empire' will most certainly 'Strike Back'.

This seemingly invulnerable enemy has tasted defeat for the first time in nearly a century and, like all wounded beasts, will likely lash out in fear and rage.

It has always been the *modus operandi* of the global elite to use the least amount of obvious manipulation and intervention to achieve their aims, so as to leave their would-be victims blissfully unaware of the impending threat.

That is why they have, so far, mostly used subversive tools to achieve their nearly completed takeover of the West – Cultural Marxism and political correctness to destroy our culture; multi-national treaties and supra-national organizations to erode our sovereignty; and the use of fraudulent Keynesian central banking to enslave us economically.

However, if the global elite start to lose control over us – if we reject political correctness and reclaim our culture; repudiate globalism and re-embrace nationalism; and begin to threaten their financial stranglehold on us – they are fully capable of escalating their war against us with more overt means.

They have worked too hard and come too far in implementing their master plan, literally for generations, to simply give up when their ultimate goal is in sight and nearly in their grasp.

Politically, look for them to try and minimize the damage from the Brexit vote any way they can. It will take years for Britain to finalize their separation from the EU, and you can count on Brussels to be as punitive as possible towards them in an effort to dissuade other European nations from following suit.

Also, look for the globalists to infiltrate their minions into the 'Leave' camp, sabotaging efforts to implement the Brexit and possibly even forcing another referendum on the question 'just to be sure of the will of the people' – a tactic they've used successfully in other European nations that have voted against aspects of the EU project.

In the United States, political resistance to the globalist agenda has rallied around the presidential campaign of Donald Trump. If the global elite can somehow remove Trump from the political equation, there likely wouldn't be enough time left in this election cycle for another Traditionalist candidate to rise and take his place to deny globalist Hillary Clinton the White House.

The elites are fully aware of this and will do anything in their power to prevent the election of Trump. There is still the possibility that the globalists will try to steal the nomination from him at the Republican convention. If that fails, they always have the option of assassinating him – a prospect they have continually and actively encouraged in the popular culture.

If they *do* assassinate Trump, they will guarantee that their Cultural Marxist minion Clinton will succeed Obama in the White House and complete their socialist coup of the Federal government.

If that happens, it will close the political option for Traditional Americans to regain their country and culture back through peaceful means. Civil war will likely follow, as Traditionalists are forced to defend themselves against newly-unfettered totalitarian Marxists, finally in complete control, wielding state power against them. Such a civil war could start even sooner if the elites blatantly kill Trump and sufficiently enrage Traditionalists into action.

The globalists are also fully aware of this so, if anything bad should happen to Trump, that will be a clear sign they have decided to initiate all-out war against us.

Economically, the globalists can attack resurgent Traditionalists in the West by triggering a 'Greater Depression' to impoverish them and make them more subservient. It's harder to fight back if your family is starving.

The global financial elites have been setting the stage for such an economic collapse for some time, and they could easily kick it off now and blame Brexit for the ensuing chaos. The financial market turmoil in the days following the vote have already been blamed on the 'Leave' camp.

To impede the free flow of information and degrade the communication of the Resistance, look for the global elite to increasingly censor, or even completely cut off, the internet in certain 'problem' areas and/or with specific 'problematic' groups of people or individuals.

If the day should come when you and your friends find yourselves cut off from the outside world, grab your rifles and prepare to defend yourselves and your loved ones, for that will be a clear sign that The Purge of Traditionalists may have begun and our enemies could very well be trying to bag as many of us as possible before word spreads.

Finally, should political events continue to spiral out of the global elites' control, they can always resort to something they've turned to many times over the centuries – war.

They have repeatedly used war to profit and consolidate their power, especially in the last century – humanity's bloodiest by far. They have many options at their disposal, with varying degrees of destructiveness, to accomplish the same thing now.

In addition to triggering a nearly-instantaneous civil war in the United States via the aforementioned Trump assassination, the elites could inflict society-wide chaos throughout the West by launching an Islamist 'Tet-style' offensive, at a pace dwarfing any previous attacks, that would quickly overwhelm normal emergency response capability – a scenario extensively discussed by military analyst Matt Bracken.

You can find his essay here – whether it actually happens in 2016, or sometime later, it is well worth the read:

https://westernrifleshooters.wordpress.com/2015/11/29/bracken-tet-take-two-islams-2016-european-offensive/

The real reason the globalists have expedited the importation into the West of armies of jihadists hidden among the tsunami of Moslem 'refugee migrants' is to have just such a military option available to them.

The global elite could also use the Moslem horde as a cover to launch more false-flag attacks on the West, possibly using weapons of mass-destruction, resulting in a level of carnage that would make the 9/11 attacks seem minor in comparison.

These large-scale Moslem attacks could then be used to implement martial law, though it will no doubt be labeled some politically correct euphemism such as a 'state of emergency' or 'temporary measures to restore public safety'.

In the United States, should the global elite decide Hillary has become too much of a liability to them, they could even trigger such attacks prior to the presidential election and leave Obama in office 'for the duration of the emergency' until 'free and fair elections could be safely held'.

Last, but certainly not least, the global elites could trigger a great power war with Russia and/or China in an attempt to divert attention from themselves and rally the people behind the Flag. It's a ploy that's worked for them many times in the past.

NATO has escalated its sabre-rattling against Russia, and have aggressively forward-deployed increasing numbers of troops on her borders. NATO has even gone so far as to recently threaten that any cyber-attack against a member nation that they believe was launched from Russia could result in a military retaliation against that country.

http://www.reuters.com/article/us-cyber-nato-idUSKCN0Z12NE

http://www.zerohedge.com/news/2016-06-15/nato-says-it-might-now-have-grounds-attack-russia

It wouldn't be hard for anyone to launch such a cyber-attack and deliberately leave indicators that the Russians did it.

Tensions with China over territorial disputes in the South China Sea have also ratcheted up and provides a convenient flash-point should the globalists desire a war between that nation and the West. All it would take would be some kind of 'Gulf of Tonkin' false-flag incident to kick something off.

Such a great power conflict could easily go nuclear or, at the very least, result in the developed world's power grids being taken down by EMP or cyber-attacks. In addition, the deployment of biological weapons could result in a devastating global pandemic.

If any of these worst-case scenarios should happen, 90+% of the human race could be dead within a year or two. This fits in perfectly with the global elites' long-term plan to reduce the human race by nearly that amount to 'cleanse the Earth' and bring the population down to what they claim is the planet's 'true carrying capacity'. Once the 'pestilence' of 'excess useless-eaters' (meaning us) is culled back enough, this will result in Mother Nature restoring Gaia to a 'New Eden'.

The global elite, of course, will survive to rule over and enjoy this paradise.

We're not invited.

Unfortunately, this plan is not simply 'tin-foil hat' paranoia – their own think tanks have been openly discussing such topics in 'white papers' for decades. The general public just hasn't been paying close-enough attention to them.

The elite also seem to get off on rubbing our noses in their more apocalyptic plans for us and laughing at our ignorance. Two possible examples of where they may have publicly displayed such hubris is some very questionable 'artwork' at the Denver International Airport and mysterious monuments called 'Georgia Guidestones'.

Here is an interesting site covering the 'artwork' and other strange features of the Denver Airport:

http://vigilantcitizen.com/sinistersites/sinister-sites-the-denver-international-airport/

And here's a site about the Georgia Guidestones:

http://vigilantcitizen.com/sinistersites/sinister-sites-the-georgia-guidestones/

Check out these sites – you need to know about them.

Again, I know this sounds like real paranoid 'tin-foil hat' stuff, and we can only speculate on the true meaning of these monuments and artworks, but one thing's for certain – someone put a *hell* of a lot of money and thought into them.

At the very least they're creepy as hell, at worst downright sinister, but they're definitely worth looking at with an open mind.

If the concerns over these alleged globalist plans for human population reduction are even partially true, the people trying to rule over our lives are some *very* evil individuals who will stop at nothing to achieve their objectives.

That said, I'm not sure the global elite are quite ready to 'pull the trigger' on the quick-kill of humanity yet – I think they would ideally like to be off-planet before they do so to the rest of us. However, if they ever get desperate enough you never know.

Also, more and more members of the elite have been building bunkers off the beaten path in places like New Zealand, so perhaps they see the writing on the wall and know something we don't. Just search for 'wealthy building bunkers' and see what pops up.

To sum up, these are some of the many perils, ranging from relatively mundane to catastrophic, that we could face in our ongoing war with the globalist tyrants. They have many weapons at their disposal to choose from to use against us.

The recent Brexit vote was a great win for us Traditionalists, a much-needed first triumph to announce to the world that we've finally shown up for this fight, but paradoxically it puts us all in more immediate physical danger.

Our brave British brothers and sisters have won our first victory, but this is just the beginning of what promises to be a long and desperate struggle.

Keep your powder dry and may God protect the right!

23 – When in the Course of Human Events…

First Published July 1, 2016

This essay is another commemoration of Independence Day that reimagines the Declaration of Independence as it might be adapted for the needs of Traditionalists in America today.

It is the second essay I wrote that does so. While the one I wrote in July 2015 focused on past abuses inflicted by the Federal Government on the citizenry as justification for secession, this essay published a year later envisions a Democratic win in the November election and a worst-case scenario that could have arisen had Hillary Rodham Clinton become the 45th President of the United States.

Fortunately, thanks to the efforts of We the Deplorables, that eventuality did not come to pass in 2016. However, should the Democratic Party Marxists somehow regain control of the White House in 2020 or 2024 the idea of secession would have to be put back on the table if Traditional America hopes to preserve what's left of their culture and way of life.

Should that occur, an adaptation of the original Declaration of Independence, like the one in this essay, would be a good place to start the discussion.

***

This time last year I wrote an essay to commemorate the Fourth of July entitled 'We Hold These Truths to be Self-Evident'. Here is a link to that essay:

http://www.counterrevolutionarycorner.com/2015/07/we-hold-these-truths-to-be-self-evident.html

In it, I examined the economic, religious, and cultural state of our nation in mid-2015 and pointed out the obvious fact that, as a society, we are an extremely divided country.

I then made the observation that, *"As disgust and distrust between the Marxist Left and Traditional Americans hardens into hatred, physical separation may very well be our only long-term hope for peace."*

One year later, I stand by that statement. Nothing that has occurred since then has given any reason for optimism that we are not ultimately heading towards such a separation. If anything, the previous year has shown that events may accelerate such an eventuality far sooner than most of us now imagine possible.

In my previous essay, I then engaged in a thought exercise of how the original Declaration of Independence might be adapted to the future needs of 21st Century Traditional Americans. As for the reasons given in that hypothetical declaration justifying the need for future separation, I focused on abuses the Federal government has already inflicted on the American people in the past, especially against Traditionalists. I did not, however, speculate on possible future violations of our liberties, nor how they might impact an eventual justification for secession.

Since the middle of 2015 things have gotten much worse. The Cultural Marxists have escalated their war on Traditionalists in the West. They have imported millions of hostile aliens into our countries, then issued hysterical calls for our disarmament when the inevitable subsequent jihadist attacks against our people occurred in Chattanooga, Paris, San Bernardino, Brussels, and Orlando.

In America, when Traditionalists rallied around Donald Trump and exercised their political rights in an attempt to defend the remnants of their nation and culture, they have been repeatedly attacked by leftist-organized and funded mobs of thugs.

The level of leftist vitriol towards us Traditionalists has escalated as well, with open calls to turn the power of the state against us growing more frequent and shrill by the day.

In such an environment, it is not hard to envision scenarios that could force Traditional Americans to secede from a Cultural Marxist-dominated central government in Washington. The most immediate revolve around the possibility of another Clinton being installed in the White House.

Here's one possible scenario: By hook, assassination, or by crook, Hillary Rodham-Clinton takes the (now meaningless, at least to her) oath of office in January 2017 and becomes the 45th President of the United States of America.

It doesn't take long for her pathological personality to wield the inherently imperial power of the Presidency to aggressively implement the Cultural Marxist agenda in its entirety. A key component of that agenda, and a necessary precursor to the rest, is to disarm the American people.

In the name of 'public safety', she quickly issues executive orders implementing the 'common sense' gun-control measures of the so-called 'Australia Plan' – a de facto ban on nearly all privately-owned firearms and a legal requirement for all citizens to immediately turn them in to the authorities or face criminal prosecution.

While some Americans comply with the orders, most Traditionalists engage in mass civil disobedience and do not turn their arms in.

After increasingly ominous threats from federal law enforcement agencies fail to gain meaningful compliance, some high-profile examples are made to cow the rest of us into submission. Some of those raids are actively resisted, 'turn Waco', and become violent.

Despite the best efforts of the authorities to sanitize and manage the mainstream media coverage of the violent raids, raw footage of the operations are leaked by constitutionalists within various federal agencies to the alternative media. This footage shows federal agents engaging in cold-blooded murder of Traditional Americans. Regime efforts to censor the internet prove woefully inadequate and the footage quickly goes viral.

Grassroots groups of outraged Traditionalists organize into ad hoc 'armed neighborhood watches' and impede law enforcement agents taking part in subsequent gun-control raids with guerrilla-style hit-and-run attacks.

President Rodham-Clinton declares the individuals participating in those attacks 'terrorists' and 'enemy combatants' and orders the U.S. Military to conduct house-to-house sweeps in areas where attacks on federal agents have taken place. Any occupants of residences where illegal weapons are found are to be rounded up and sent to detention camps for further 'processing'.

Some of these sweeps are conducted, but others fail when U.S. Military personnel refuse to obey what they see as unconstitutional orders. Fratricidal clashes break out in some units when officers loyal to the regime order the non-compliant troops arrested by their comrades.

In Texas, the Governor pronounces that Rodham-Clinton's executive orders are a violation of the 2nd Amendment of the United States Constitution and of the Texas Constitution and declares them 'null and void'. He rescinds the authority of federal officials in the state to enforce gun control laws and orders the Department of Public Safety and the Texas National Guard to evict all federal law enforcement agents who attempt to do so.

President Rodham-Clinton, enraged by this defiance of her decrees, declares the Texas Governor to be in 'open rebellion' against the United States. Citing the precedent of Abraham Lincoln's arrest of the entire legislature of Maryland in order to prevent that state's secession during the Civil War, she secretly orders a mercenary unit comprised of international former special operators to launch a commando raid to kidnap and arrest the Governor.

The raid meets stiff resistance from the Texas Rangers and National Guard troops protecting the Governor and a sharp firefight breaks out. The attack is repulsed with heavy casualties on both sides. The Governor is wounded but survives. Several mercenaries are captured and, following their interrogation, Texas officials quickly deduce who is likely responsible for the attack.

The Governor, from his hospital bed, declares that the Federal government has lost its legitimacy to govern and calls the State Legislature into emergency session to consider Articles of Secession. After several days of rancorous debate with leftists in Austin, the measure is passed and The Republic of Texas declares its independence from the United States.

President Rodham-Clinton decrees that a state of emergency exists throughout the United States and declares martial law 'for the duration of the crisis'.

In response, the governors of several states in the heartland join with the Governor of Texas in calling for a Convention to form a new constitutional government.

Delegates from the various states meet near Topeka, Kansas, and begin their work. Their first order of business is to write and issue a new Declaration of Independence.

For inspiration, they look to America's first Declaration and what the Founding Fathers wrote over two centuries ago...

IN ASSEMBLY, July 4, 2019

The unanimous Declaration of the Constitutional States of America,

When in the course of human events, it becomes necessary for one people to dissolve the political bands which have connected them with another, and to assume among the powers of the earth, the separate and equal station to which the **Laws of Nature and of Nature's God entitle them***, a decent respect to the opinions of mankind requires that they should declare the causes which impel them to the separation.*

We hold these truths to be self-evident, that all men are created equal, that they are endowed **by their Creator** *with certain unalienable rights, that among these are life, liberty and the pursuit of happiness.*

That to secure these rights, governments are instituted among men, **deriving their just powers from the consent of the governed.**

That whenever any form of government becomes destructive of these ends, it is the right of the people to alter or to abolish it, *and to institute new government, laying its foundation on such principles and* *organizing its powers in such form, as to them shall seem most likely to effect their safety and happiness.*

Prudence, indeed, will dictate that governments long established should not be changed for light and transient causes; and accordingly all experience has shown, that mankind are more disposed to suffer, while evils are sufferable, then to right themselves by abolishing the forms to which they are accustomed.

But when a long train of abuses and usurpations, pushing invariably the same object evinces a design to reduce them under absolute despotism, **it is their right, it is their duty, to throw off such government,** *and to provide new guards for their future security.*

Such has been the patient sufferance of these states; and such is now the necessity which constrains them to alter their former systems of government.

The history of the present Federal Government of the political entity known as the 'United States of America' is a history of repeated injuries and usurpations, all having in direct object the establishment of an absolute tyranny over these Constitutional States. To prove this, let facts be submitted to a candid world.

- *They have betrayed the People by imposing a hostile, alien, Marxist political philosophy upon them, and have implemented all ten planks of the Communist Manifesto; including a graduated income tax, seizure of inheritances, and indoctrination of our children in government schools.*
- *They have combined with other states and entities, through their abuse of the power to make treaties, to subject us to jurisdictions foreign to our Constitution, and unacknowledged by our laws; giving their assent to their acts of pretended legislation. (NAFTA, GATT, the Trans-Pacific Partnership, etc.)*
- *Through specious use of 'The Interstate Commerce Clause', they have inserted themselves into and regulated every aspect of the lives of the People, no matter how minute, unconstitutionally usurping powers reserved to the States or the People.*
- *They have erected a multitude of new agencies, and sent hither swarms of agents to harass our people, and destroy their prosperity.*
- *They have created a secret, parallel government and military-industrial complex unaccountable to the People and destructive of their liberties.*
- *They have entangled the nation in a series of unceasing, unconstitutional wars and alliances contrary to the People's interests.*

- *On the pretext of securing the People, they have established standing armies of armed agents in our midst, and have protected them, by mock trials, from punishment for murders they have committed, including the immolation of a church along with all of its parishioners. (For example, the Ruby Ridge and Waco Massacres.)*
- *Meanwhile, they have rendered our borders defenseless, encouraging vast hordes of aliens hostile to our Traditions to freely invade our nation and murder our citizens.*
- *Even worse, they have endeavored to disarm the People and render them defenseless in the face of their enemies, including Islamic terrorists, criminal predators, and agents of despotism.*
- *To achieve this end of disarming the People, the current occupant of the Office of the Presidency of the United States has waged open war against them.*
- *They have claimed the power to assassinate citizens, without due process, or to seize and detain them in military prisons indefinitely, without trial, at the sole discretion of the occupant of the Office of the Presidency of the United States.*
- *They have embraced torture as an implement of official policy, a practice repugnant to all civilized people.*
- *They have unconstitutionally ceded authority over the nation's economy to an unelected cabal of private banks known as 'The Federal Reserve', and have allowed them to abolish real, constitutional money in favor of the false weights and measures of a fiat currency, thus enslaving the People in perpetual debt bondage.*
- *They have mortgaged the future of the People by draining the Treasury and assuming unsustainable obligations.*
- *They have enticed vast numbers of the People into dependency by redistributing to them largess stolen from their fellow citizens.*
- *They have systematically stolen from citizens, who were innocent of any crimes, through the criminal misapplication of 'asset forfeiture laws'.*
- *They have repeatedly infringed upon the People's right to the free use of their own lands and property through the imposition of onerous and unnecessary regulations.*
- *They have routinely violated the right of the People to be secure in their persons, data, and effects by subjecting them to extensive surveillance of every aspect of their lives, unconstitutionally maintaining dossiers on them, and destroying any vestige of their privacy or liberty.*

- *They have violated the rights of the People to free religious association by wielding the power of law to compel citizens to participate in practices they find morally repugnant.*
- *They have unconstitutionally abridged the rights of the People to free speech and assembly, and to seek redress of grievances, by restricting the exercise of those rights to limited, out-of-the-way areas the government has dubbed 'First Amendment Zones'.*

In every stage of these oppressions we have petitioned for redress in the most humble terms: Our repeated petitions have been answered only by repeated injury. A Government whose character is thus marked by every act which may define a Tyrant, is unfit to rule a free people.

Nor have we been wanting in attentions to our supposed representatives in the Federal Government. We have warned them repeatedly when their actions exceeded the limits on their power as set forth in the Constitution. We have appealed to their native justice and magnanimity, and we have conjured them by the ties of our common history to disavow these usurpations, which would inevitably interrupt our connections and Union.

They have denied our common history, choosing instead to sow discord among the People and to be deaf to the voice of Justice and Tradition.

We must, therefore, acquiesce in the necessity of our separation, and hold them, as we hold the rest of mankind, Enemies in War, in Peace Friends.

We, therefore, the Representatives of the Constitutional States of America, in General Assembly, **appealing to the Supreme Judge of the world for the rectitude of our intentions**, *do, in the name, and by authority of the good People of these States,* **solemnly publish and declare, that these Constitutional States are, and of right ought to be, free and independent; that they are absolved from all allegiance to the Federal Government of the political entity known as the 'United States of America', and that all political connection between them is and ought to be totally dissolved;** *and that as free and independent states, they have the full power to levy war, conclude peace, contract alliances, establish commerce, and to do all other acts and things which independent States may of right do.*

And for the support of this Declaration, with a firm reliance on the protection of divine Providence, we mutually pledge to each other our lives, our fortunes and our sacred honor.

How the remaining story ends is up to us.

The words of our founding document are as relevant today as they were 240 years ago. They are the embodiment of the one political philosophy in human history that allows for the existence of individual freedom and real, God-given human rights – not the so-called 'privileges' granted, and just as easily curtailed or revoked, by the statists.

If we wish to restore to our nation the blessings of life, liberty, and happiness that such freedom provides, we must re-embrace the principles that allowed them to flourish in the first place.

As we celebrate this 240th July Fourth weekend, we should all reflect on what the words and ideas articulated in the Declaration of Independence mean to us.

Our future literally depends on it.

May God bless you all and may you have a safe and joyous holiday.

24 – A Week from Hell – The Tipping Point Reached

First published on July 14, 2016

This essay was written in the aftermath of two very ominous events for the future of the United States of America.

The first was the announcement, on July 5, 2016, by then-FBI Director James Comey (and later confirmed by former Attorney General Loretta Lynch) that Hillary Clinton would not face prosecution for her myriad crimes regarding her use of an illegal private e-mail server while serving as Secretary of State during Obama's first term.

This announcement made the following facts crystal-clear: The Rule of Law was dead in America; there was now one set of (mostly ignored and lightly enforced) rules for the globalist elites and another set of (very strictly enforced) laws we unwashed masses are expected to follow to the letter; and that the United States was officially on its way to becoming just another Marxist banana republic like Cuba or Venezuela.

Once a government declares that the Rule of Law no longer equally applies to all in a society, it ceases to be the guardian of the People's rights and becomes a government ruled by men, not laws. Once systemic corruption becomes embedded in the corridors of power that government loses its moral authority and legitimacy to govern. Once it has lost its moral authority, the only thing it can resort to in order to maintain its power is force, and that only works until the People muster enough force of their own to depose the usurpers.

Fortunately, Traditional America was able to muster enough political force this time around to remove the lawless, Marxist usurpers peacefully through the ballot box – but it was a very near thing. We may not be as fortunate next time.

The second event was even more threatening to America's future. On July 7, 2016, a Black Nationalist who was a former member of the US Army National Guard ambushed and killed five Dallas Police officers while they were protecting an anti-police 'Black Lives Matter' protest march. The irony couldn't have been more stark.

The massacre was the culmination of a nationwide wave of racially-motivated terroristic assassinations of police officers that exploded in 2016 and continues to this day as of mid-2017.

It turned out that the gunman in Dallas, like the vast majority of those who perpetrated the murders of other police officers during this time, were motivated by anti-White and anti-police hatred peddled by leftist politicians such as Obama, the mainstream media, and racist terror organizations such as 'Black Lives Matter'.

In this essay, I speak directly to the Blacks who have bought into this narrative of racial hate and warn them what consequences they will face if they continue down the dangerous path they are on.

In my estimation, these attacks are a precursor of an imminent race war that will be a major component of the next civil war in America. Civil war is the only result that can follow decades of ceaseless efforts by Cultural Marxists to divide this nation along racial, ethnic, religious, and class lines and to fan the flames of animosity between those groups.

The events that have transpired since July 2016 (the complete breakdown of civil discourse in this country between Left and Right; widespread leftist riots and attacks on conservatives; public calls for the assassination of President Trump and other Republican politicians, followed by an actual assassination attempt on a group of Republican congressmen) have only confirmed that America is on the road to conflict. The Cultural Marxists and their useful idiot minions on the Left will not rest until a civil war erupts in this country.

Prepare yourself accordingly.

***

Exactly one week ago as I'm writing this, the United States celebrated its 240th birthday. The horrible week that followed has made me seriously doubt it will reach its 245th – or even its 241st.

The very next day after our most important civic holiday, FBI Director Comey – looking more like a deer in headlights than the nation's top federal law enforcement officer – spent the first 13 minutes of a 15 minute statement spelling out, in detail, how Hillary Rodham Clinton lied in every public utterance to the American people and Congress regarding her illegal private e-mail server.

Then Comey pulled a complete 180 and stated he would not recommend she be indicted. Though he admitted she clearly broke the law, he characterized her actions as 'careless' rather than criminally negligent, and asserted that a 'reasonable prosecutor' would not press charges because there was no 'criminal intent' on Clinton's part.

That was enough for those on the Left, who immediately hit the airwaves and social media with the latest reality-defying Clintonian talking point – 'there's nothing to see here, America, it's time to celebrate and move on to Queen Hillary's coronation'.

The most surprising part of Comey's performance is that he delivered it with a straight face. The very fact that Hillary Clinton felt the need to create a secret, private e-mail server, outside the scrutiny of legally-required oversight, is prima facie evidence of criminal intent. Of course, being absolutely terrified will help a person keep a straight face. I can only imagine what horrifying fate the Clinton crime syndicate threatened the man's family with.

Not long after Comey's announcement, Attorney General Loretta Lynch formally announced Hillary Clinton would not face charges. What a shock. After all, Bill and Loretta only talked about grandchildren and golf on that plane on the tarmac in Arizona. Honest. It must be true because they said so. If you doubt their word in the slightest consider yourself a nutty conspiracy theorist who is dangerous to polite society.

In the days since, it's been revealed that Hillary was not even under oath when 'interviewed' by the FBI. Ain't that special. Nothing to see here either, people – move along.

On July 5, 2016, the Rule of Law officially died in the United States of America. Now, it can be convincingly argued that the Rule of Law has been dead for quite some time now, but that date will go down in history as the moment the-powers-that-be stopped pretending that we all are governed by the same law and formally announced there are no rules that apply to our elite masters.

The United States is now just another banana republic.

To anyone who isn't a Kool-Aid chugging, brainwashed Clintonista, that's a pretty big story. It would take quite a spectacular shock to kick it off the headlines and get Americans talking about something else.

Just such a shocking spectacle is exactly what America got on the evening of July 7th.

We all know what happened to those five Dallas cops, who died while protecting a mostly black crowd protesting against them.

We all know about the angry Black Nationalist who shot them.

We all know about the pathetic Community-Organizer-in-Chief, who inherited the dying embers of vestigial racial animosity in this country, and has since done everything in his power during the past seven-and-a-half years to race-bait, sow division, and generally piss gasoline all over that little fire until it's now erupted into a billowing conflagration of race hate.

I will not write about this tragedy. There is plenty of commentary out there already, and I'm not in a frame of mind to add anything insightful. Though I fully expected events like this to occur, for the trajectory our country is now on can lead to no other outcome, it has profoundly saddened and disgusted me nonetheless. The fact that it occurred in Dallas, a good city I once called home and is still near and dear to my heart, only makes it worse.

Instead, I will take this opportunity to speak to those who identify as supporters of the so-called 'Black Lives Matter' movement. Not those people in the black community who are good, traditional, red-blooded Americans who just happen to have more melanin in their skin than the rest of us – but to those who have bought into the siren song of grievance, entitlement, and angry victimhood peddled by race-baiting pimps like Obama, Sharpton, Jackson, and MSNBC.

You're being lied to, and you're being used.

You're being lied to when you're told that America is an inherently racist nation that has it out for you. A truly racist nation wouldn't have catered to your every whim for so long and would have put an end to your uncivilized behavior long ago.

You're being lied to when you're told that cops are the enemy and they just can't wait to kill you. Most cops would like nothing more than to have peaceful interactions with all they meet. Your dumb-ass, violent behavior is what makes your encounters with police dangerous for you.

You're being lied to when you're told you are 'entitled' to something, whether it's preferential treatment on a job exam or college application, or 'reparations' for slavery that was abolished in your great-great-great-great grandparents' time. Getting free shit, taken from someone else, solely because of your skin color, is what *real* racism looks like.

You're being lied to when you're told that acting the fool is the way to get your demands met. Violating other people's rights isn't going to win sympathy for your cause. Harassing and shouting at people who are trying to enjoy dinner in a restaurant or shop in a mall, or blocking traffic on a freeway, is only going to piss people off. Marching in the streets while calling for violence against 'whitey' or the cops, and then acting violent, is only going to make decent Americans realize that their country would be a much better place without you in it.

You're being used as a tool by those who would destroy our nation.

You're being used as a tool to keep us fighting each other so we don't pay attention to what our real, common enemy is doing to us.

You're being used as a tool to start a civil war that will destroy what's left of the United States of America – the last real obstacle in the elite's path to global domination.

Don't be a tool.

You need to pull your heads out of your collective asses, **now**, before it's too late. If you think that a revolution against 'The Man' is somehow 'cool' or 'trendy', you'd better think again.

Revolution isn't a game. Civil war isn't a sport. You want to see what the United States will look like after a civil war, take a look at Syria today. All the comforts of modern life you spoiled little asses take for granted now – running water; stores with shelves well-stocked with food; EBT cards to 'buy' that food; electricity to run your cell phones, TVs, and air conditioning – all will be seriously curtailed or completely lacking during a civil war.

You also might want to consider who your enemy will be in such a war. It won't be the neutered, roll-on-their-backs-and-piss-on-themselves white liberals you're used to intimidating – it will be Traditional Americans, an enemy you haven't faced yet.

If the United States does break up and descend into ethnic civil war, Traditional Americans will be, by far, the best-armed and disciplined faction. Even if dedicated traditionalists only make up 25% of the current United States population, they will still outnumber you 2 to 1. You don't want to pick a fight with them. If you do, they will kick your asses in short order – and all of your shit-talking and bluster won't save you.

You don't want to go there – but I know you will. Just don't say afterwards you weren't warned.

After the Dallas Massacre, the Affirmative-Action-Baby-in-Chief, the one man most responsible for fomenting the hate that killed those officers, had the gall to say that 'things aren't really so bad, America's not *really* that divided', and implied that those who say so are the real cause of the hate and division – a talking point quickly picked up and repeated by liberals across the nation.

Anyone with eyes to see and ears to hear knows that is bullshit. The half-century of relentless effort of Cultural Marxists like Obama and

226

his communist mentors to split the country into mutually-loathing hyphenated identity groups has finally borne bitter fruit. Kumbaya, group-hug, multicultural pablum parroted by well-meaning but naïve progressives won't stop what's coming.

They are right about one thing, however – the vast majority of the human race *are* decent people who, left alone, get along pretty well. They are usually not haters. The problem is, history shows that, when a society is pushed by agitators towards civil war, average people, who just want to be nice and 'go along to get along', don't set the agenda and drive events – the small percentage of ideologues do.

Eventually, a tipping point is reached, centrifugal forces start to rip the body politic apart, and society starts to slide towards chaos and dissolution. The moderates are then forced to pick a side or become 'collateral damage'.

At the beginning of this year, I predicted the tipping point for the world would come sometime during 2016. For those who care to look, here is a link to that essay:

http://www.counterrevolutionarycorner.com/2016/01/2016-tipping-point.html

For America, the tipping point was last week, with the final death of the Rule of Law in America, the Dallas Massacre, and the subsequent on-going attacks against police nationwide. All-out war hasn't arrived yet, but these events are this historical cycle's versions of the Boston Massacre, the Dred Scott decision, and Bleeding Kansas – harbingers of much worse to come.

If there is a silver-lining to this otherwise dark reality it is this – the Crisis that is coming to a head will finally settle, once and for all, what kind of nation America will be – communist or free; amoral or Godly; licentious or decent.

As Abraham Lincoln famously said three years before the last civil war began:

> *"In my opinion, (the agitation) will not cease, until a crisis shall have been reached, and passed. A house divided against itself cannot stand."*

Our divided house will not stand – one of the sides will either completely purge the other or the country will break up and each will dominate in their own areas. The two ideologies are mutually incompatible and cannot co-exist.

Once that occurs, we will finally be able to reclaim the free, Godly, and decent society that is our birthright.

25 – Unholy War

First published on August 6, 2016

The last two weeks of July 2016 saw the Islamic problem take center stage again in Europe and in the US Presidential Election.

The heinous mass murders in Nice and Munich were punctuated by a particularly grisly, symbolic act of religious terror – jihadists burst into a Catholic Mass in France, slit the presiding priest's throat at the altar, beheaded him, then proceeded to issue an ISIS-style Islamist 'sermon'/rant from the pulpit to the horrified parishioners in attendance.

Predictably, instead of identifying the Islamic problem for what it is, leftist apologists in Europe and America bent over backwards to try and claim the violent jihadists were not representative of Islam and repeated the stale old lie that 'Islam is a religion of peace'. Even the one person who should have been most outraged by the murder of the French priest, Pope Frances, toed the leftist party line and claimed that the people of the West were guilty of bringing the terror attacks upon themselves because young jihadis are motivated to commit murder by "a lack of economic opportunity" and because Europeans have left those poor youngsters "devoid of ideals".

American leftists displayed the same criminal-level dissociation with reality during the national conventions of the two major parties. During the Republican National Convention, Hillary Clinton and the Democrats shamefully called the Gold-Star mother of one of the four Americans killed in Benghazi in 2012 a liar when she reported that then-Secretary of State Clinton had blatantly lied to her about the real, jihadist motive for the attack.

*In reply, a week later at the Democratic National Convention, the Left trotted out a Moslem Gold Star father (who turned out to be a Pakistani legal activist who advocates for the integration of Sharia Law into our judicial system) to stand at the podium and cynically wave a pocket copy of **our** Constitution while lecturing Trump and Traditional Americans that trying to curb or control* *immigration from Moslem countries, in any way, makes them racist and is a fundamental violation of American constitutional principles.*

In this essay I explain why the Left is wrong about this, just as they are about nearly everything else. The United States, like any other nation in the world, has the fundamental right to protect itself from clear and present dangers such as that posed by the ideology of Islam. The Constitution is not a suicide pact.

A 2013 Pew Research poll of Moslems throughout the world found that nearly one-third agreed with the statement, "Violence, such as suicide bombings, is sometimes justified against civilians to defend Islam." That same poll found that 19% of Moslems in America felt the same way and that one-percent of them said that such violence is "often" justified.

*As I write this in late July 2017, Pew Research just released an updated poll that asked American Moslems the same questions as the earlier study. The number of them who stated violence against civilians is "sometimes justified to defend Islam" remained steady at 20%, **however the number who said it was "often" justified expanded five-fold to five-percent.***

That means, right now in mid-2017, one out of every twenty Moslems you meet in America believes (whether they say so outwardly or not) that it is "often" justified to kill you "to defend Islam".

Let that sink in for a moment.

Would we get in a car if we knew one in twenty of that particular model had a potentially fatal defect?

Would we board an airplane if we knew one in twenty of that type were manufactured in such a way that they had propensity to crash?

Would we allow our children to take an aspirin from a bottle if history showed one out of every twenty of those pills were likely to cause fatal side effects?

I should hope not.

Then why do we allow a group of people to freely associate with us when we know one out of every twenty are inclined to murder us and our loved ones because we don't share a belief in their death cult?

Up until now we've allowed this because we've been afraid of being called 'racist' or 'islamophobic' by our 'progressive' family members, friends, co-workers, and employers. That fear of being politically incorrect directly led to the deaths in Fort Hood and San Bernardino when people who'd witnessed strange behavior with the eventual Moslem terrorists failed to report their observations to authorities lest they be branded as racist.

No longer.

We the Deplorables, the proud members of Traditional America, have declared an end to this lethal stupidity. No longer will we listen to those who defend our enemies and blame us for being the cause of their attacks against us. No longer will we allow ourselves to be passive victims.

Just as the Democratic Party's endorsement of the racist ideology of hate spewed by minority groups like 'Black Lives Matter' directly led to the Dallas Massacre of five police officers and hundreds more across the United States, so has the Left's defense and enabling of the poisonous ideology of Islam led to the slaughter of innocent Americans at Fort Hood, Boston, Chattanooga, San Bernardino, and Orlando.

In my opinion, this unabashed, blatant support for America's enemies is one of the main reasons why Trump won the Presidency and why Democratic politicians have continued to lose in election after election. As of this writing, both Houses of Congress are in Republican hands (although far too many RINOs still remain), as are 34 of the 50 governorships and the vast majority of state legislatures.

No matter what may ultimately happen with the Trump Presidency, whether it succeeds or fails, whether Trump is able to serve out his term or is removed in a coup (pseudo-legally or the old-fashioned kinetic way a la Dealey Plaza), Traditional America has made its demands quite clear to the Democratic Party *and establishment members of the GOP – stop colluding with our **real** enemies. (As opposed to mythic collusion between Trump and the Kremlin.) Stop enabling foreign and domestic terrorists and the globalists who created them to destroy us.*

In other words – you Democrats, establishment Republicans and other denizens of 'The Swamp' need to stop committing treason against America.

Traditional America sent Donald Trump to Washington to make you do just that. But the clock is ticking – and the career members of the government that have become colloquially known as "The Deep State" have a limited window of opportunity to step up and support President Trump in his efforts to carry out our will and perform his constitutional duty to protect We the People "from all enemies, foreign and domestic".

If they fail to support him in that duty, or worse yet, demonstrate once and for all they approve of the treason by preventing our President from doing so, I have no doubt Traditional America will remove those traitorous elements of the government from power and deal with the threats themselves, one way or another, ***with Trump or without him.***

Traditional America has rediscovered its power and will not be denied.

One thing is certain – the Left, neo-conservatives, and their globalist patrons will come to rue the day that finally happens.

It won't be pretty.

***

Another line has been crossed in Islam's unholy war against the West.

On the morning of July 26, 2016, two knife-wielding Moslems burst into a Catholic Church in Saint-Etienne-du-Rouvray, in Normandy, France during daily mass and took Father Jacques Hamel, a couple of nuns, and several parishioners hostage.

While forcing one of the hostages to videotape the ensuing barbarity, the jihadists gave what was described by witnesses as 'an Arabic sermon' from the altar, then forced Pere Hamel to his knees. As he resisted they slit his throat and let him bleed out and, in a final indignity, beheaded him.

One other hostage was seriously wounded before the jihadis left the church shouting 'Allahu Akbar'. They were gunned down in the street outside by French police, who had been alerted by one of the sisters who'd slipped away when the jihadis began their attack on Father Hamel.

In a month filled with Islamic atrocities across Western Europe – a jihadist in a truck ran down hundreds of men, women and children during a Bastille Day fireworks display in Nice, killing 84; a mass shooting in Munich left 9 dead; a mass axe attack on a German train wounded 21; Germany's first suicide bombing wounded 12; and a pregnant Polish woman was hacked to death by a machete-wielding 'Syrian refugee' near Stuttgart – the murder and beheading of Father Hamel was, in many ways, the worst.

Not because Father Hamel's life was more important than any of the other victims (A statement he no doubt would have agreed with – by all accounts he was the kind of man who would have gladly given up his life to save others.), but because of the symbolism of the target.

By murdering a priest, in a church, *during mass*, and giving an Islamist 'sermon' from the altar, the jihadists have sent the clear and unmistakable message, to their followers and the world, that Islam is the soon-to-be dominant religion in Europe and that their enemies are too weak to stop them.

They're probably right. This is no longer 732, when a greatly-outnumbered Charles Martel heroically drove back the Moslem horde near Tours in France and saved Western Europe from being overrun; or 1492, when the Moslem Moors were finally driven out of Spain; or 1683, when the Ottoman Turkish siege of Vienna, Austria was finally broken and the Moslem army defeated; or even 1918, when the Ottoman Empire was defeated in World War I and the old Caliphate collapsed. Europe, the former center of Christendom, no longer seems to have the will to resist this latest, resurgent phase of Islam's 1,400 year assault on the West.

Europe's current leadership certainly doesn't. Following the attacks, French President François Hollande uttered his usual recitation of stale clichés in the wake of the now-routine atrocities – that the attack was a 'desecration of French democracy' (even though it was an attack on a church, not a government target), that the French government would do everything it could to 'confront' the jihadist threat (even though one of the murderers was a convicted wanna-be ISIS terrorist who was allowed, by that government, to take off his ankle monitor and run around free for four hours every morning), and that the French people would 'stand united' against terror.

If trite platitudes were weapons of war, the Islamic threat would have been obliterated long ago.

More tellingly, Hollande warned against the dangers of restricting constitutional liberties, saying that would only weaken the 'unity of the nation'. It appears he's only concerned about restricting the 'constitutional liberties' of Moslems, however, since his government has had no problem arresting non-Moslems in the past for the 'crime' of speaking out against the Islamic threat.

Marine Le Pen, the leader of the National Front party (the leading opposition party to Hollande's Socialists), was arrested late last year for making the accurate observation, during a speech, that Moslems packing French streets during 'prayer time' is de facto occupation of French territory akin to the German occupation during World War II.

For this innocuous and factual comment, Ms. Le Pen was prosecuted for 'hate speech' – yet Hollande has the audacity to warn that nothing proactive should be done to prevent Islamic attacks. Wouldn't want to offend the Moslems or make them feel unwelcome, after all.

Now, that kind of tepid, flaccid response from a French socialist to a sacrilegious Moslem atrocity in a Catholic Church should be expected – France is officially a secular state and Christianity is a mere shadow of itself there, with church attendance at miniscule levels. But we should expect some outrage from the Vatican, shouldn't we? After all, it was their priest that was killed, in their church. And if anyone should have some understanding of what such an attack signifies in the context of the millennia-long struggle of the Church to hold off Islamic invasion it should be them, right?

No. Not this pope.

Immediately after the attack the Vatican released a statement saying Pope Francis was 'shocked' because the attack 'happened in a place of worship' and that the Pope was 'praying for the victims of the attack.' OK – so far, so good. Not particularly forceful, perhaps, but a good start.

But then Pope Francis gave an interview on Sunday, July 31, and made his *real* position on Islamic terror quite clear. As reported in the Express newspaper in the UK:

> *Speaking aboard the plane taking him back to Rome after a five-day trip to Poland, he said: "I think it is not right to identify Islam with terrorism.*
>
> *"It is not right and it is not true."*
>
> *Francis was responding to a question about the killing on July 26 of an 85-year-old Roman Catholic priest by knife-wielding attackers who burst into a church service in western France, forced the priest to his knees and slit his throat.*
>
> *The attack was claimed by ISIS.*
>
> *He said: "I think that in nearly all religions there is always a small fundamentalist group."*
>
> *He then added: "We have them," referring to Catholicism.*
>
> *The Pope continued: "I don't like to talk about Islamic violence because every day when I look at the papers I see violence here in Italy - someone killing his girlfriend, someone killing his mother-in-law. These are baptised Catholics.*

"If I speak of Islamic violence, I have to speak of Catholic violence. Not all Muslims are violent."

He said there were various causes of terrorism.

The Pope said: "I know it's dangerous to say this but terrorism grows when there is no other option and when money is made and it, instead of the person, is put at the centre of the world economy.

"That is the first form of terrorism. That is a basic terrorism against all humanity. Let's talk about that."

When he started the trip last week, Francis said the killing of the priest and a string of other attacks were proof the "world is at war" but that it was not caused by religion.

He told reporters on the plane that lack of economic opportunities for young people in Europe was also to blame for terrorism.

He said: "I ask myself how many young people that we Europeans have left devoid of ideals, who do not have work. Then they turn to drugs and alcohol or enlist in ISIS."

Here is the link to the full article:

http://www.express.co.uk/news/world/695276/Pope-Francis-defends-Muslims-blasts-Islam-not-terrorism

Pope Francis made so many absurd statements in such a short interview I don't know where to begin to refute them. But I'll give it a shot.

First, Your Holiness, nearly all modern terrorists claim they've carried out their attacks in the name of Islam – and the Koran, Sida (the biography of Mohammed), and Hadith (traditional sayings attributed to Mohammed) are replete with calls to murder the Kafirs (infidels) and the 'People of the Book' (Jews and Christians). Spreading Islam into the non-Moslem world through jihad is an integral part of their belief system.

The beheading of your priest, in his church, *during mass*, while his murderers gave a sermon in Arabic from the altar and shouted 'Allahu Akbar', *is an Islamic terror attack!* If you are so deliberately obtuse as to not acknowledge something so blatantly obvious there is no hope for you, sir.

Then you say that all religions have a small fundamentalist group. You are correct – most do. But polls around the world consistently show that at least one-third of Moslems support violence against civilians (such as suicide bombings) to 'defend Islam'. One third is a lot more than a 'small fundamentalist group'.

You go on to claim that Catholics have them too. Perhaps – if you consider groups like Opus Dei fundamentalist. Of course, the only time I've ever read about Opus Dei committing violence against anyone was in a Dan Brown novel.

Then you prattle on about how if you 'talk about Islamic violence, you have to talk about Catholic violence', then bring up a bogus point about how there are Catholics, baptized in the Church, who commit violent crimes too. Of course there are – sin entered into human affairs as soon as Adam and Eve partook of the forbidden fruit, and there are violent people to be found in every race and creed. But the point you're missing is – in Islam the call for violence against non-Moslems is codified in their most holy texts, by Mohammed himself.

Unending war against the kafirs/infidels through jihad is a requirement of the devout Moslem. In their cosmology, there is no room on Earth for any other faith. In addition, Islam is the only 'religion' I'm aware of that insists that their 'religious' code (Sharia Law) is binding on those outside their faith.

There are Christians who believe the only way to heaven is through Jesus Christ, but they are content to leave ultimate judgement to God. There are Buddhists who believe the path they espouse is *the* way to escape the pain that results from what they see as an 'illusory world' – but if you choose not to follow them, they might feel sad for you, but won't hold it against you.

Not so with devout Moslems – Mohammed says we kafirs are

doomed by Allah to Hell, and tells his followers the quickest way for them to enter Paradise is to dispatch us to that Hell as quickly as possible.

Then, Your Holiness, you finally get around to talking about 'terrorism', but claim that "money, and not the individual, being the center of the world economy is the first form of terrorism...a basic form of terrorism against all humanity, and we should talk about that."

I'm not even sure what the hell you're talking about here – are you saying that capitalism is the first form of terrorism? In any event, Marxist sloganeering has nothing whatsoever to do with your priest having his head cut off by Moslem jihadis.

Finally, you say that, in essence, it's Europeans' fault that young Moslems are murdering them because those Europeans have left those poor youngsters 'devoid of ideals' and without jobs to keep them busy.

Just what 'ideals' should Europeans try to inculcate into the minds of those young Moslems that would displace the fiery allure of jihad? Patriotism is passé throughout the EU, now considered the province of the 'far-right', and does anyone really believe young Moslems are eager to become proud Frenchmen and Germans anyway? Judging from the unassimilated, no-go Islamic neighborhoods that plague most European cities, this is a pipe dream.

Encouraging them to adopt a more peaceful religion like Christianity is a non-starter as well – it would surely be 'offensive' to other Moslems if you did so and would no doubt be considered an assault on their cultural heritage. Besides, why should young Moslems convert to Christianity when the vast majority of native-born people across secular Europe no longer believe in it themselves?

As for your comment that a lack of jobs leads Moslems to turn to terrorism like other unemployed people turn to drugs, this also doesn't stand up to scrutiny. Many of most deadly jihadis had jobs prior to attacking – the Nice murderer had a delivery job, and used the very type of truck he was familiar with at work to crush those hundreds of victims; the Orlando killer worked for a security company with DHS contracts; the male San Bernardino gunman shot up a group of his co-workers at a department holiday party; and Major Nidal Hasan had a well-paying job with the U.S. Army prior to killing his fellow soldiers at Fort Hood.

No, Your Holiness, your comments make it unmistakably clear that you cannot be counted on to defend Western Civilization against the on-going demographic, and increasingly military, Islamic invasion that threatens its very existence. At a time when Europe desperately needs a new Pope Urban II to call for a 21st Century crusade to repel this Moslem takeover they have you – the Obama of Christendom.

Unfortunately, this type of leftist idiocy regarding the Islamic threat is not limited to the other side of the Atlantic. During Obama's entire presidency he has been little more than the Islamist-Enabler-in-Chief. Now Clinton and the rest of the Democratic Party have picked up the torch of Moslem disinformation and are running with it.

During the week of the Republican National Convention, the mother of one of the four Americans killed in Benghazi gave a testimonial about how then-Secretary of State Hillary Clinton lied to her face about the reason her son died (Clinton infamously claimed it was because of an internet video that was insulting to Moslems.) and rightly blamed Clinton's neglect and indifference for getting her son killed.

In response, Hillary Clinton called that Gold-Star mother a liar.

A week later, at the Democratic National Convention, the Clinton political machine paraded the parents of a Moslem Army officer, Captain Humayun Khan, onto the stage. Captain Khan was killed in action in Iraq in 2004. By all accounts he was a brave officer who stopped a VBIED before it could detonate near his men, giving his life to save theirs. All true Americans honor and are grateful for his service and sacrifice, and no words said by anyone can diminish that.

Not even the words his father spoke from that podium in Philadelphia.

In a disgusting display of rank partisanship, Khizr Khan invoked his son's memory as an excuse to unfairly mischaracterize Donald

Trump's positions on immigration enforcement and the need to restrict immigration from Moslem countries until those immigrants can be properly vetted. Mr. Khan then falsely called into question Trump's patriotism and called on America to vote for what he called the 'healing' candidate in the race – Hillary Clinton.

When Trump defended himself and criticized Khan's comments he was accused of being, you guessed it, disrespectful of 'a Gold-Star family'. Yet Hillary's the one who called a Gold-Star mother a liar. The double-standard couldn't be more blatant.

It didn't take long for information about Khizr Khan's background to come out – he is a lawyer from Pakistan who co-founded a law journal dedicated to integrating Sharia Law into Western legal systems and has ties to the Moslem Brotherhood.

Ain't that special. I'm surprised Obama didn't make him a cabinet secretary.

Since the Democratic talking point this week is the contribution of Moslems to our military, it would have been nice for the DNC to invite to their stage some of the parents of the 13 soldiers murdered by Major Nidal Hasan at Fort Hood. But that wouldn't have fit into their PC kumbaya multicultural bullshit.

With the election three months away, we can expect more red-herrings from the Democrats regarding Islam – and many progressive, low-information voters who get their information on the subject from Obama and the Council on American-Islamic Relations will no doubt be fooled.

But Obama and the other Cultural Marxists calling the shots in Washington and in the capitols of Europe know exactly what the real score is – for they're the ones who are deliberately making the problem worse.

The international socialists have entered into an unholy alliance with Islam against their common enemy, *us* – the remnants of traditional Judeo-Christian Western Civilization. They have deliberately expedited the Moslem invasion of first Europe, and now America by throwing open our borders to our enemies. They are actively aiding and abetting Islam's unholy war against us.

The violent jihadi terrorists who directly attack us, as evil as they are, are just the tip of the spear. Even more destructive to us long-term is the demographic and cultural jihad being waged against us. This type of jihad has manifested itself in Europe in the form of rampant criminality and intimidation by Moslems against native non-Moslems – whether the mass rapes of European women on New Year's Eve; 'Sharia Patrols' harassing 'infidels' in the UK for drinking alcohol or women who they say dress 'immodestly'; and aggressively threatening or killing any who dare to criticize Islam.

Now cultural jihad has come to America.

On June 28 of this year, in an upscale suburb of Minneapolis, a group of about 20 to 30 Moslem Somali men terrorized the neighborhood – speeding down streets, driving across lawns, firing bottle rockets and shouting jihadist slogans at residents and, even worse, threatening to kidnap and rape women because "Sharia Law allows (them) to do so". Here is an excerpt from an article on the incident:

> *It happened in an upscale Minneapolis neighborhood near Lake Calhoun last week. A mob of about 20 to 30 young Somalian refugee men came parading through the neighborhood about 9:30 Monday morning, making terroristic threats.*
>
> *The men stopped in front of one woman's house, and the ugly comments turned to threats. "They were screaming at the house that they were going to kidnap you and they were going to rape you," one Minneapolis resident told <u>ABC5 EYEWITNESS NEWS</u>. "It was a very traumatizing experience."*
>
> *The neighbors told the news media on Thursday that the Somali men have been harassing them throughout the week, but Monday was the most violent and scary.*
>
> *They reported the men were driving onto the sidewalk and lawns, shooting off bottle rockets and screaming. One resident said, "The entire neighborhood is up in arms."*

Another neighbor said, "We couldn't get them out. We didn't know what to do."

The woman whose home they stopped in front of and yelled the threats to on Monday had just recently moved to the neighborhood, and said she never expected this kind of problem."

One neighbor said, "It needs to get nipped in the bud before it gets any worse because the escalation that occurs over a matter of hours could potentially kill or harm someone."

In their online report of the incident at ABC5 Eyewitness News, they are only described as "multiple young men", but the news broadcast version admits the men were Somalis.

The U.S. State Department, in cooperation with the United Nations, has reportedly resettled at least 132,000 Somali refugees into America since 1983, but others have reported that the numbers are much, much higher.

Here is a link to the article: http://dennismichaellynch.com/mob-of-somalian-refugee-men-terrorize-minnesota-neighborhood/

This intimidation is pure cultural jihad. The resident who said this needs to be nipped in the bud before someone gets killed is absolutely correct. However, nothing meaningful has been done – police came and talked to the 'young men', took statements from the terrified residents, and promised to increase the number of patrols in the area.

Perhaps the Minneapolis Police Department is afraid to get tough with these jihadist thugs because of their boss, Mayor Betsy Hodges, who is quite the 'multicultural progressive'. When she's met with leaders of the Somali community in her city in the past she's made sure to wear a hijab so she would not 'offend' them.

I wonder if she knows or cares that her wearing a hijab is a sign of submission to those Moslem men. If leftists like her have their way, America will soon be in full-surrender mode like Europe.

Except for a few stories on local media, the mainstream did not cover this terroristic incident in Minneapolis. It doesn't fit the Cultural Marxists' agenda to keep us in the dark about the Islamic threat until it's too late for us to do anything about it.

I cannot help but wonder how many other stories like this aren't getting reported, just how many Moslem 'refugees' the Obama Administration is *really* importing into our country, (it's many, many more than 10,000) and how large the threat has already grown.

Update – It turned out the situation regarding Minneapolis Mayor Betsy Hodges is far worse than I realized when I originally wrote this essay.

Not content with merely having the city's police look the other way when residents complain about Somali terroristic threats, Hodges has actually put Somali immigrants on the Minneapolis Police Department.

One of those new Somali 'policemen', a 32 year-old named Mohamed Noor who had only been on the force for 21 months, responded on July 15, 2017 to a 911 caller who'd reported a possible rape in progress.

He was patrolling in a vehicle driven by his partner, a 25 year-old rookie who'd only been on the force one year. When the complainant, an Australian yoga instructor named Justine Damon, approached the police vehicle, Noor fired past his partner (through the driver's-side window) and killed her.

As of this writing in early August 2017 'Officer' Noor and the City of Minneapolis have not been forthcoming with any meaningful information about the suspicious killing.

The Minneapolis Star Tribune reported that Noor was placed on the force after completing an accelerated 7 month cadet program that provides a way to "attract more diverse people with broader life experiences" to the Minneapolis Police Department. Well, it's certainly done that.

Noor had three formal complaints against him in his 21 months on the force, one for allegedly assaulting a woman, prior to the shooting.

Mayor Hodges, meanwhile, no doubt drunk on the wonderful optics of 'diversity', had lauded Noor upon his joining the Minneapolis Police Department in 2015.

Multiculturalism works great until the Moslems you've invited in start gunning down innocent citizens.

The Cultural Marxists will keep doing anything and everything they can to keep the American people confused and impotent in the face of this enemy. They will keep using political correctness to try and intimidate us into silence. They will keep calling any who challenge their 'Islam is a religion of peace' narrative 'racists', 'bigots', and 'islamophobic'.

They will continue to have Gold-Star Sharia Law advocates deceptively lecture *us* on what they claim *our* Constitution means.

We Traditional Americans need to continue to ignore the blatant lies of the Left about Islam. That is the first step to defeating jihad in America.

Second, we must stop thinking about Islam as a religion – it is not. It is a political ideology, geared towards global conquest, which is thinly-disguised as a religion. That is what confuses many Americans as to what counter-measures to this threat are constitutional or unconstitutional. By thinking of it as a religion, they believe any action taken to counter Islam's aggressions is a violation of Moslems' religious liberties.

They could not be more wrong – a person's religious rights end when the religion in question advocates, in its most sacred texts, the murder of those who don't believe in that religion.

But what about all those Moslems that we've met who are nice and decent people? There are many people who were raised in Moslem countries who are good people. I lived in a Moslem country and knew many of them personally. *The problem is, if they are genuinely good people, and treat all people, including non-Moslems, with dignity and respect, they cannot be good Moslems.* The vast majority of the passages in the Koran, Sida, and Hadith forbid it.

The sad fact is that the ISIS jihadis are 'better' Moslems than the so-called 'moderates', for they have the bulk of Islamic scripture on their side. That's why there will be no 'reform' of Islam – the 'moderates', even if they truly want to change their belief system into something 'kinder and gentler', have nothing in their holy texts to point to that will outweigh the more militant, evil portions of Mohammed's teachings and life example.

Which brings us to the third thing we must do – we must stop referring to our enemy as 'radical' Islam or 'extremist' Islam or 'fundamentalist' Islam. *Our enemy is the ideology of Islam itself.*

Many don't want to accept this idea because they think it means that we will be potentially at war with 1.5 billion Moslems. In practice, that is not going to be the case. But we must have the courage of our convictions to unequivocally declare our undying enmity to the dehumanizing ideology that is political Islam. (i.e. How Moslems treat those who don't share their beliefs.) We must be unyielding and merciless against those who would force this evil ideology upon others – just as our fathers were with the evil ideologies of Nazism, Fascism, and Bushido during our nation's last great crisis in World War II.

Which brings us to the last thing we must do. We must acknowledge the 800-pound gorilla in the room and address the one topic that even many on the Right are still too timid to openly speak of – that *if we are ever to live safely and at peace again in the West, we must purge our societies of political Islam.*

If a person wants to believe in Allah and Mohammed, and feel that belief is the best way for their soul to avoid hellfire and reach paradise, that is between them and their god and is none of our business. That is religious Islam, and is protected by the freedom of religion clause of the First Amendment.

If however, their 'religious' beliefs extend into dictating how non-Moslems are going to live their lives, or worse yet, whether they are allowed to live at all, then that *most certainly is our business.*

Moslems' rights end when they begin to infringe on other peoples' rights.

Since Mr. Khan waved around his pocket Constitution at that podium on that stage in Philadelphia, let's revisit the preamble of that document:

> *We the People of the United States, in Order to form a more perfect Union, establish Justice, insure domestic Tranquility, provide for the common defence, promote the general Welfare, and secure the Blessings of Liberty to ourselves and our Posterity, do ordain and establish this Constitution for the United States of America.*

Mr. Khan implied that Donald Trump's proposal that all Moslem immigration be temporarily halted from hotbeds of jihadism such as Syria and Libya, until those immigrants can be properly vetted, is unconstitutional. *He could not be more wrong.*

Looking at the intent of the Constitution, as summarized in the preamble above, Khan is claiming that any reduction or pause in Moslem immigration would be a failure of America to 'establish Justice' and 'secure the Blessings of Liberty' for Moslems. (He also implied that it would violate the 14th Amendment's 'equal protection clause', but he is wrong about that too – there is no constitutional right for foreigners to enter the United States.)

Khan conveniently ignores the rest of the preamble – especially the parts about 'insuring domestic tranquility', 'providing for the common defence', and 'promoting the general welfare'. The first two of these things are the most basic function of any government.

If a government fails in its duty to protect its citizens from hostile, foreign threats, that government has no further reason to exist. At that point, the People should abolish it and institute a new government that will defend them – just as the Declaration of Independence says.

The Constitution is not a suicide pact. The Founding Fathers never would have agreed that the interests of a hostile foreign ideology takes precedence over 'the common defence', 'domestic tranquility', and 'general welfare' of the American people. They also became very familiar with Islam during their confrontation with the Barbary pirates and, after studying the sacred texts of Islam, had an exceedingly dim view of the 'faith of the Mohammadans'. They would be appalled at what the Cultural Marxists are now inflicting on their posterity.

A significant percentage of Moslems world-wide, approximately one-third, when polled by Pew Research in 2013, said that violence against civilians (such as suicide bombings) is justified in order to 'defend Islam'. That is not some idle threat from a fringe minority. This cannot be characterized as 'extremist' or 'radical' Islam – this is damn close to being mainstream.

The numerous Islamic massacres of non-Moslems that have since littered the headlines shows this to be true – and clearly demonstrates that those who espouse political Islam are a clear and present danger to the safety and security of the American people.

Therefore, here is the necessary final step to reestablishing peace and security in our nation – all Moslems *must* be required to publicly renounce Sharia Law and any part of Islam that advocates violence against or violating the rights of others. In addition, they must also be required to take a public loyalty oath to 'preserve, protect, and defend the Constitution of the United States against all enemies, foreign and domestic'.

Those who refuse to publicly renounce Sharia Law and swear allegiance to our Constitution and acknowledge it as the highest law of the land, whether they are citizens or not, must be given one-way plane tickets out of the country. (Preferably to Saudi Arabia – the country most responsible for encouraging violent jihad across the globe.)

Finally, it should be made clear to them prior to taking the oath that taqiyya (deception that Moslems are scripturally allowed to engage in with non-Moslems to further the cause of Islam) will *not* be tolerated – once they have sworn allegiance to the United States, any act which gives aid and comfort to our enemies will be considered treason, and those who do so will be subject to the traditional and constitutional penalty for that crime – death.

We must be resolute and steadfast in the implementation of these measures. They will not be pleasurable, nor desirable – but they are necessary. The unending and continuously escalating evil acts of our enemies have made them so.

Very many in the West will find these measures unacceptable. 'These fly in the face of our most cherished values', they will declare. 'If we violate Moslems' civil liberties, the terrorists will have won', they will claim.

Once again, they will be wrong, for they will have failed to make the critical distinction between Islam as a religion and Islam as a political ideology.

How many more innocent people have to be slaughtered because of sloppy thinking by those on the Left? How many more priests have to have their throats cut, like some pagan sacrifice, because of the squeamishness and moral cowardice of progressives? How many children have to be crushed under truck tires because Western citizens are too apathetic to care, and would rather pay attention to the latest celebrity gossip than take the effort to understand the Evil that is thriving in the world?

Perhaps they will begin to care when the jihadists start kidnapping movie stars and post videos of them being beheaded on the internet – but probably not before then.

One thing is certain – those traditionalists who still believe in the values of Western Civilization do not have infinite patience for tolerating this type of naked Evil. There is a limited window for the current governments in the West to take meaningful action, or the People will remove them and do it themselves.

At some point, perhaps in a year or two, after we've suffered through another 50 to 100 Nices and Orlandos, (perhaps sooner if jihadists deploy weapons of mass destruction against us) the proposals I've made in this essay will seem tame and inadequate.

At that point, the people of the West will feel like their backs are against the wall and will demand truly draconian measures, by today's standards.

If current trends continue, I have no doubt that the Islamic threat will eventually be neutralized, one way or another, and that those Moslems who end up rounded up and thrown into camps will be considered the lucky ones.

If the Left truly cares about Moslems, they will do everything in their power to nip this problem in the bud before that happens. That would be *real* compassion.

I'm not holding my breath.

Hang on folks – the next few years are going to be a **very** bumpy ride.

26 – Time to Boldly Speak Hard Truth

First published on October 15, 2016

This essay was written in the weeks leading up to the Great Presidential Election of 2016. In it I delineated the profound differences in world-views of the two competing sides, then argued that, at that late hour, it was pointless to try and persuade those on the Left to change their minds and vote for sanity – by that time the chasm between them and Traditional Americans had grown unbridgeable.

At that point I believed all that was possible was to remind that group of disgruntled Traditional Americans, who were displeased with the thought of voting for Donald Trump and considering a protest vote for the Libertarian or some other small party's candidate, of the very real danger a President Hillary Rodham Clinton would pose to the safety and well-being of us all and to please reconsider. I pointed out that a Trump Presidency, although it was not likely to be peaceful, would be infinitely better and far less likely to result in another American Civil War. (At least not as quickly.)

I, along with many other Traditional Americans, spent many sleepless nights in the days and weeks leading up to the election praying to God and begging for our People's deliverance from Evil.

America was teetering on the edge of a precipice, and everything had to break our way to prevent us from plunging into the Marxist hell that awaited us if we failed.

This essay was my last humble attempt to prevent such a calamity – a 'final argument' to my fellow Traditional Americans to do what had to be done. I like to believe it may have played a small part, like so many tens of millions of others, to help in our group efforts to save our country.

It turned out that every vote was necessary after all.

***

The 2016 election campaign, arguably the most contentious since 1860, is now in its final month. For some time, since Clinton and Trump secured their nominations, I have tried to write something meaningful about the general election.

In a draft essay, I wrote many thousands of words rehashing, in excruciating detail, Hillary Clinton's nearly 50-year, well-documented public record of lies and deceit, brazen graft and corruption, criminality, and outright treason. I called on my fellow Americans to come to their senses and articulated that, although Trump is a flawed person, handing the keys to the highest office of the land to Hillary Clinton would be an immediate and unmitigated disaster that would ultimately result in the final demise of the United States.

Then, after many weeks of monitoring the mood of the American people, of all political persuasions, in personal conversations, television, and especially on social media, the weight of truth finally struck me – the essay I was working on was a complete waste of time.

It was a waste of time because Democrats and their supporters *are absolutely indifferent* to the evil, corrupt things that Hillary Clinton has done, and no amount of conversation or presentation of evidence will change their minds. They are either willfully blind, phenomenally gullible, completely amoral – or all of the above.

Even more important, writing that essay was a waste of time because, in spite of knowing better, I was still operating on long-held, unconscious assumptions that I, as an American, have had instilled into me since I was a child – that the United States is 'one nation, under God, indivisible' and that this election is a venerable civic duty to determine who will be charged with the responsibility to ensure that 'liberty and justice for all' is fact and not mere words.

I was still operating on the false assumption that 'my fellow Americans' on the Left care about what's true, or right, or about the well-being of this country.

Nothing could be further from the truth.

There is no 'United States' anymore. It is dead. To be sure, there are political entities and states that still invoke that name to claim the legitimacy to govern – but they are not united. There is no 'one nation' anymore. There are no united American people either – hell, we can't even agree on the most basic questions such as: what the definition of an 'American' is; whether America is a good place that is worth defending or not; or what it should stand for.

Even worse, since a large plurality of the American people have chosen to become God-less, we can't even agree on what is right or wrong.

What Traditional Americans loathe as perversion, deviancy, and an assault on ethical norms in the realm of sexual behavior and the family – 'progressives' celebrate as 'free-expression of diversity'.

What Traditional Americans distain as laziness, sloth, and unearned hand-outs – 'progressives' champion as 'economic justice'.

What Traditional Americans consider to be racist, undeserved redistribution of wealth and jobs – 'progressives' label as 'affirmative action' and 'checking white privilege'.

What Traditional Americans condemn as infanticide – 'progressives' **demand** as a constitutional 'right to choose'.

What Traditional Americans view as the coddling of an increasingly violent and aggressive racist, minority subculture – 'progressives' encourage as 'social justice'.

What Traditional Americans identify as prudent measures to defend our borders and secure our nation's people against foreign criminals and terrorists – 'progressives' deride as 'racist', 'islamophobic' and 'jingoistic'.

What Traditional Americans cherish as an inalienable, God-given right to effective self-defense against those foreign and domestic enemies – 'progressives' haughtily dismiss as a dangerous 'gun-fetish'.

What Traditional Americans hold most dear, their Faith and reliance upon God's grace – 'progressives' mock as outdated superstition and consider Christians fools who 'cling to their guns and bibles'.

Traditional Americans see America as a force for good in the world – while 'progressives' declare America evil and actively work to undermine her strength at home and abroad.

Not since before America's first Civil War have its people been this divided on core philosophical values. And just like then, the Election of 2016 has become a no-holds-barred, winner-take-all political war to determine which side gains control of the levers of power of the Federal Government – for Traditional Americans, to use that power to attempt to preserve their liberty and way of life against further attacks by the Cultural Marxists on the Left; for 'progressives', to aggressively wield that power to dominate and impose their world-view upon all others. (They are 'tolerant' of everything except diversity of ideas.)

This ever-widening chasm between the two sides will not be bridged by this election – if anything, the divisions have been made far worse by it. No matter which side wins, the other will feel disenfranchised by the result. One month from now, the election will finally be over – but the people of the United States will wake up on November 9th to find the feuds between them escalating and the nation still on the path towards civil war. The only question that will remain is – how fast will we get there?

If Trump wins, it buys us some time, even though he is not really a philosophical conservative. As a result, he will most likely be lured by the temptation to 'do some good' with the power of government rather than just aggressively cutting back its scope as a more strictly constitutionalist president would. Still, if he also wields that power to shore up American strength against our foreign enemies, and to protect our national economic interests against globalist schemes to defraud us and destroy our sovereignty, that will be a huge improvement over the globalist minions, *of both parties*, who have occupied the White House during the past 25 years – especially the blatantly anti-American, pro-Islamist quisling that has pretended to be president the past eight.

More important, Trump is unlikely to continue to use the power of the Federal Government to attack Traditional Americans and their culture as the current president has. That will give those Traditionalists breathing room and time to try and roll back the decades-long Cultural Marxist assault on them through peaceful, political means. Getting two or three Scalia-like justices on the Supreme Court would go a long way towards accomplishing that.

Should Trump win, we can expect much wailing and gnashing of teeth on the Left, but little direct action – at least not initially. What we *will* see, however, is the same unholy coalition of powers who so vehemently opposed his election – the leadership of the Democratic and Republican Parties, the media, Hollywood, socialists and communists at home and abroad, globalists like George Soros and their cronies – do everything in their power to sabotage and undermine a Trump presidency. In addition, this coalition will accelerate their efforts to fund and foment violent revolution through groups such as 'Black Lives Matter' and 'La Raza', with the intent of forcing crackdowns by the government that will lead to further Marxist uprisings. Unfortunately, a Trump presidency will likely not be a peaceful one.

If, however, Clinton wins, much more severe, nation-threatening conflict could develop quickly. With her arrogant, pathological personality, it won't be long before she decides to use the power of the Presidency to attack her enemies, real and perceived. She will use the power of 'the pen and the phone' (as Obama infamously put it) to impose her will through executive fiat, escalating the abuses of presidential powers already exponentially expanded by her predecessors Obama and Bush, and will have a stacked, hard-left Supreme Court in her corner to rubber stamp her actions. And, if she is indeed in as poor health as has been reported, she will no doubt feel great urgency to implement her agenda while she is able.

She will expedite and expand the importation of aliens into the United States and will grant them the vote as soon as possible. Very quickly it will become impossible for Traditional Americans to win a national election or meaningfully affect policy at the national level. That avenue of peaceful change will be closed to them forever. Then the Marxists will have free reign to do whatever they wish.

Of all the characters in United States political history, Hillary Rodham Clinton has the most potential to morph into an American Hitler. Never before has there been the union of Hillary's level of megalomania merged with the power of the modern Orwellian super-state.

(Obama is the current worst example but, even though he is an ideologue, and a clear enemy of Traditional America, at his core he has proven himself to be more interested in the trappings of power rather than the wielding of it – i.e. he'd rather be golfing. Hillary appears not to share this 'moderate' tendency.)

In addition to expanding on Obama's habit of using the power of Law to persecute Christians and other Traditional Americans through the courts, Clinton is likely to move as quickly as possible to disarm them as well so they cannot effectively resist further encroachments on their rights. This may take some time, perhaps a couple of years, but once again, the Supreme Court will be instrumental in any such effort.

Like Marxists everywhere, Clinton will no doubt keenly remember Mao's dictum that 'all power comes from the barrel of a gun'. But *freedom* also comes from the barrel of a gun, when those guns are in the hands of liberty-loving people, so she will make every attempt to remove the 'ultimate veto' on her policies that privately-owned firearms represent.

This is how serious conflict, if it comes, will start. Traditional Americans know the importance of firearms in citizens' hands as much as Clinton does and will not surrender them willingly. Firearms ownership and possession will be increasingly criminalized, as has already occurred in Europe, Australia, and Canada, but Traditional Americans will not comply with what they will rightly consider illegitimate decrees.

Eventually, Clinton and her Marxist cohorts will be unable to resist the urge to enforce their decrees by force of arms and there will be a 21st Century version of 'the shot heard 'round the world' – some new Lexington and Concord that will trigger an all-out civil war and eventual Traditionalist counterrevolution against the Cultural Marxist regime. (Remember, the first American Revolution was also triggered by a government gun-control raid that was resisted – and then went *very* badly for those trying to do the confiscating.)

Those are the stakes in this election – one fork in the road gives us time to, hopefully, peacefully roll back the Cultural Marxist revolution that has nearly destroyed our nation, while the other leads to a significant risk of armed conflict on American soil within the next few years.

I, like most people, have no desire for war, and recognize what an utter disaster such a conflict would be to our homeland. I am morally bound to do everything in my power to prevent such a calamity from occurring. Therefore, I **must** cast my vote for the only remaining candidate who can stop Hillary Rodham Clinton from becoming President of the United States – Donald Trump.

I will do so with a clear conscience and with the full knowledge that he is a far-from-perfect man and a far-from-perfect candidate – but he is profoundly better than the alternative. If there ever was an election where the 'lesser of two evils' argument is valid, this is the one.

Finally, there is one more aspect of this election that needs to be discussed – what is the proper attitude that should be taken towards those Americans who support the other side?

This is a tough one. On the one hand, there is a sentiment expressed in numerous memes floating around social media that say something to the effect, "I will still respect you and not 'unfriend' you just because you hold a different political view than mine. That is the essence of democracy."

That is a noble-sounding sentiment, and one that would have been eminently sensible in elections 40 or 50 years ago. Until the late 1980s/early 1990s or so, though the Republican and Democratic Parties may have differed over specific policies, they never disagreed on the ultimate goal – to keep the United States prosperous, strong, and the champion of freedom around the world.

Even the most liberal Democrat in 1960 had no doubt that America was a force for good in the world, and no American then had reason to doubt the heroism, loyalty or patriotism of Democratic politicians. John Kennedy was a decorated war hero who'd fought the Imperial Japanese in the Pacific in World War Two and personally saved several of his crew when his patrol boat was sliced in half by an enemy destroyer. Likewise with 1972 Democratic presidential nominee George McGovern, who'd volunteered to serve in the Army Air Corps following Pearl Harbor and piloted a B-24 on 35 bombing missions over Nazi-occupied Europe. Jimmy Carter entered the US Naval Academy in 1943, and participated in the early development of nuclear powered ships. In 1952, he heroically led a team in the Chernobyl-style cleanup of a partially melted-down experimental reactor at a research facility in Canada.

But today's elections are not our fathers' elections. The heroes of the old Democratic Party have long-since retired or passed away, and the modern Democratic Party has been taken over by leftists who came of age in the 1960s – Saul Alinsky-worshiping hippies who bought into Marxism in all of its forms, particularly Cultural Marxism. Many, if not most, of the Boomer Generation matured and out-grew their infatuation with the Left, but a hard-core cadre remained and became the instrument by which older Marxists injected their poison into America's culture and body politic. That hard-core group, of all Americans alive today, is the one most personally responsible for the nearly-complete destruction of Traditional American culture. Those evil Cultural Marxists are now the leaders of the modern Democratic Party.

Therefore, the noble-sounding sentiment I mentioned earlier, that says we should respect someone who holds a different political view than us, is no longer necessarily valid – it depends on the political view in question.

Just as it would have been considered ridiculous and un-American during World War Two to have said that Nazi-sympathizers in this country should have been 'respected' because they 'merely' held a different political view than the rest of us, so should it be with those who support Globalism, Cultural Marxism, and Orthodox Islam today.

The ideologies of Globalism, Cultural Marxism and Orthodox Islam are just as much existential threats to America today as Nazism was in the 1930s or overt, Soviet-style Communism was during the Cold War. Globalism works tirelessly to destroy America's economic lifeblood and our sovereignty, Cultural Marxism attacks us at the core of our national soul while their unholy allies, the jihadi armies of Orthodox Islam, seek to ultimately conquer us after our will to fight has been sufficiently sapped.

Just as Americans who chose to actively sympathize with and support the Nazis and Communists were rightly considered traitors to their nation and people back in the last century, those who now knowingly support groups who actively try to subvert and destroy Traditional America, especially its core ethos of individual liberty and constitutional freedom, are equally treasonous. That would include most of the leaders and operatives of the Democratic Party, especially Obama and the Clintons; a significant number of the Republican Party's leadership; those in academia who developed political correctness as the enforcement tool of Cultural Marxism; those who incite racial violence and hatred such as the organizers of the so-called 'Black Lives Matter' movement; and those who support and act as apologists for jihadist organizations such as the Council on American-Islamic Relations (CAIR).

To 'respect' any of those enemies of our people is absurd – to ask us to even 'tolerate' them is too much.

But what about the vast majority of those who have been duped into supporting the enemies of America? Are they evil because they unwittingly enable and strengthen evil ideologies through their political support, or are they merely the 'useful idiots' Lenin identified as essential to every socialist revolution? How should we feel about them?

That's another difficult question, especially since most of us likely have at least some friends, family, or co-workers who fit that description – earnest 'liberals' and 'progressives' who truly believe that the Left is a force for positive change and ignore the darker consequences of who and what they support. (Such as dismembered baby parts peddled for cash by Planned Parenthood.)

I don't believe most 'liberals' and 'progressives' *intend* to be evil – but they are clearly gullible at the very least. Most I've interacted with are deliberately obtuse and ***absolutely refuse*** to examine any evidence that calls into question their leftist world-view.

These are not respectable character traits. But it's worse than that. Foolish, willfully ignorant people may be annoying in everyday life, but are usually harmless otherwise. Unfortunately, they become dangerous when they vote.

Just as history has not been kind to the German people who voted Hitler to power in 1933, and has assigned them the collective guilt of inflicting Nazism on the world, so it will be with today's 'liberal' and 'progressive' voters. By continually electing Cultural Marxist politicians into positions of power over the past half-century, they are directly responsible for the cultural and spiritual rot we and our nation have suffered.

At the risk of appearing 'insensitive' or 'closed-minded', we cannot be 'reasonable', or 'tolerant', or 'willing to compromise' with them.

Not this time. There can be no compromise with evil – or those who enable evil. The stakes are too high.

If feelings are hurt, so be it.

Ecclesiastes says there is a time for everything – a time to be born and a time to die; a time to reap and a time to sow; a time to embrace and a time to refrain from embracing; a time to love and a time to hate; a time to keep silent and a time to speak.

Now is the time we must show resolve, harden our hearts, and speak the truth – regardless of who may take offense.

If we do, then perhaps, God-willing, there will be no need for a time of war or a time to kill.

Our futures and those of our children literally depend on it.

Go out and boldly spread the word – vote for Trump and keep the Clintons out of the White House.

Go and save our country.

27 – The Day After

First published on November 10, 2016

Most key turning points in history come as surprises like the proverbial 'thief in the night' – the Boston Massacre and the Battles of Lexington and Concord; John Brown's Raid and the first shots fired at Fort Sumter; the Stock Market Crash of 1929 and the attack on Pearl Harbor; the assassination of President John F. Kennedy; the terror attacks on 9/11. Very few are recognized and anticipated in advance.

Election Day, November 8th, 2016 was one of those rare exceptions. Months in advance it became clear that something momentous and pivotal awaited all of us on that night. As it turned out, reality exceeded expectations in epic fashion.

My wife Jill and I spent the long election night with my oldest friend and Brother-in-Arms Al and his dear wife Sue, to provide moral support to each other come what may. We were on the edges of our seats the entire time as results trickled in and sent us all on an unforgettable emotional roller-coaster ride.

Although my reading of the political tea-leaves and the sentiment of people in the month or so leading up to the election left me intellectually open to the possibility that mainstream media polls were significantly underestimating Trump's support and that he actually had a chance to win, my guts were twisted in knots of anxiety anyway. No one knew what to expect.

My heart began to sink as the earliest results showed Clinton ahead with an approximately 5% lead in state after state in the critical southeastern United States. Even media outlets sympathetic to Trump began to talk about the ever-shrinking path he would have to navigate to get to 270 Electoral votes, and the hubristic, imperious confidence of those networks hostile to him (which were nearly all of them) made me concerned that the fix might be in. What better way to steal votes than during absentee and early voting, when oversight would be minimal compared to that on Election Day?

Then Trump started closing the gap, until he got within striking distance of Clinton in his first must-win state – Florida. Clinton held onto a thin lead as the nation had to wait another excruciating hour as the votes in the Panhandle (located in the Central Time Zone) were counted. Miraculously, the voters in a handful of counties in the far west of the state gave Trump the come-from-behind win with a slim margin of 1.2%.

Most other states, with a few exceptions here and there, went as expected to either Clinton or Trump. Trump still faced an uphill battle and the daunting task of breaching the so-called 'Blue Wall' states of the Upper Midwest – Wisconsin, Michigan, Ohio, and Pennsylvania.

Those largely rust-belt states, home of numerous under-employed, white, culturally-conservative, blue-collar, historically pro-union working class folks had not been convincingly carried by a Republican presidential candidate since Ronald Reagan in the 1980s. Now Trump would have to carry three-out-of-four to beat Clinton.

The first to go to Trump was Ohio by a resounding, and unexpectedly amazing 8% margin. Suddenly the liberal talking heads on CNN, MSNBC, ABC and CBS weren't looking as cocky as they were earlier. Then, the shock of the night came when Wisconsin, long-considered to be such a lock for Clinton that she hadn't even bothered to campaign there for months, went for Trump by a margin of 22,748 votes (0.77%). In a historically-progressive state like Wisconsin, that was a veritable landslide for Trump.

I have never been more proud of the people of my adopted state than on that night. They stepped-up and did their part to save our nation.

Nearly as surprising was the fact that Trump nearly put Clinton away early by narrowly missing carrying the neighboring, and even more historically left-wing, state of Minnesota by a mere 44,765 votes (1.52%) – a state that wasn't even supposed to be in play at all. Things were really starting to look bad for Hillary.

Improbably, Trump was now just one state away from winning the whole damn thing – either Pennsylvania or Michigan would be enough. He was one state away from becoming the 45ᵗʰ President of the United States. (The expressions of total astonishment and dawning despair on the liberal talking heads' faces at this point of the night were priceless – if you ever want a good belly laugh check out 'MSNBC and CNN 2016 election night coverage' on YouTube. Yes, I'm all about wallowing in sweet schadenfreude when it comes to the Left wailing and gnashing their collective teeth over a well-deserved defeat.)

Trump was still 13 electoral votes away from the 270 needed to win. Pennsylvania's 20 electoral votes could put him over the top. So could Michigan's 16. He could also win with Arizona's 11 plus New Hampshire's 4 or Alaska's 3.

Then, even though poll results had been steadily coming in all evening, everything inexplicably and suddenly stopped. Dead silence. For approximately two agonizingly-long hours everything seemed to be in a holding pattern.

It was understandable that Alaska, being so far west, or even Arizona, might take some time to finalize their results, but the sound of crickets coming from Pennsylvania and Michigan seemed mighty suspicious at the time.

It turned out that Trump won Pennsylvania and Michigan by razor-thin margins – Pennsylvania by 44,294 votes (0.72%) and Michigan by 10,704 (a miniscule 0.23%). If one is inclined to give election officials in those states the benefit of the doubt, it can be argued they were likely recounting the votes to be extra certain they got it right in such a close race.

However, the more cynical side of me cannot help but entertain another possibility – that the globalist powers-that-be spent those two hours calculating if it would be worth it to try and steal the Pennsylvania and Michigan votes since they were so close. For that to work however, Arizona's had to be close enough to steal as well. (Alaska and its 3 electoral votes were already projected to be solidly in the Trump column.)

I suspect what they were really waiting for from approximately 1 a.m. Eastern Time on November 9th to 3 a.m. was to see which way the wind was blowing in Arizona. Trump eventually carried the state by 91,234 votes (3.54%) – far more than could be stolen by any but the most blatantly obvious methods.

So, the globalists decided to throw in the towel (at least on that glorious day).

The most amazing upset in a Presidential race in American history was complete. Donald Trump was the new president-elect.

Hillary Clinton would go on to win the official nationwide popular vote by 2,828,691 votes, giving disgruntled leftists an excuse to declare that Trump was an 'illegitimate' president and generating the inevitable calls for the abolishment of the 'antiquated' Electoral College system.

However, when one considers that California alone, where Clinton netted 4,269,978 more votes than Trump, accounted for more than Clinton's entire margin of victory in the nationwide popular vote; and that the three states of California, New York, and Illinois netted her 6,951,282 more combined votes than Trump; and that all three of those heavily blue states have very powerful Democratic Party machines, extremely high populations of illegal aliens, and no voter-ID laws – then suddenly Clinton's alleged 'victory' doesn't pass the smell test at all.

Even using the official numbers, Trump won the popular vote in the other 47 states by a margin of 4,122,591 votes.

In essence, had Hillary Clinton won she would have become President thanks to the legal and illegal occupants of New York City, Los Angeles, and Chicago. Not exactly a recipe for long-term stability in a country, especially with Hillary's 'let them eat cake' mentality towards us unwashed masses in 'flyover country'. Thank God for the Founding Fathers and their wisdom in creating an Electoral College system (instead of a straight-up one-man, one-vote democracy) that was designed to prevent that very thing – otherwise a presidential candidate could campaign in a handful of the largest metropolitan areas and carry an election, thus running roughshod over the interests of the rest of the country.

By 3 a.m. on November 9th, 2016, when Clinton finally conceded and Trump gave his acceptance speech, all of us at our election-watching party/support group felt like wrung-out dish rags. I will admit that I may have drunk a little more Jack Daniels that night than I should have. But I was sober enough to give thanks to God for His mercy and deliverance. After more than 50 years of decline and defeat, He had granted Traditional America a blessed victory against the globalist Cultural Marxists and a reprieve from their seemingly unstoppable agenda to destroy us.

What we do with that reprieve is up to us – but we'd better not waste it. The electoral victory we won was a very near run thing, and our enemies aren't going away. We will not win the next election unless we put in at least as much work, if not more, than we did for this one.

And if we don't win again in 2020, we might as well go back to oiling-up our ARs and buying more ammo – because any future president spawned from the anti-American, communist-dominated modern Democratic Party will surely make us need them.

*** Note – all voting statistics cited are taken from the Federal Election Commission's Official 2016 General Election Results. *Here is a link to a PDF version of the official document:*

https://transition.fec.gov/pubrec/fe2016/2016presgeresults.pdf

***

The Election of 2016 is now in the history books and Donald J. Trump is the 45th President-Elect of the United States. Thanks be to God.

I will examine where we go from here in another post in the near future – after I've first had a chance to soak in the tremendous relief Trump's victory has brought.

It's only been a couple of days since our nation was delivered from the clutches of Hillary Clinton, but I sense some people are already choosing to forget (or perhaps never quite realized) the extent of the mortal danger we were all in – and that, for many of us, the result of this election was potentially a matter of life and death.

On Tuesday, the United States came within a frog-hair's breadth of handing over the most powerful office in the world to arguably the vilest, most corrupt, pathologically-dishonest, and power-lusting character in American history.

I have no doubt that Hillary Rodham Clinton would have quickly used that power to persecute Traditional Americans at the very least and, at worst, to attack them directly with force of arms. As I said in my last essay, such an attack would have been vigorously resisted by Traditional America, and a Second Civil War likely would have quickly followed.

The dissolution of the United States vs. hope for a renaissance of American pride, prosperity, and might; war vs. peace; the specter of Syrian-style destruction from sea to shining sea vs. continued life in a modern, functioning society – those were the stakes of last Tuesday's election.

During the excruciatingly long hours of Tuesday evening into the wee hours of Wednesday morning, America, and the indeed the entire world, hung in the balance like Schrodinger's Cat – uncertain as to which diametrically-opposed fork in the road their future would lay.

The margin of Trump's victory was as narrow as it was miraculous. The result reaffirmed my assertions in earlier essays that, in light of the demographic changes engineered by Cultural Marxists over the past half-century (changes designed to increase the voting base of the Left through mass importation of immigrants from nations and cultures with little to no tradition of limited government) it has become increasingly difficult for Traditional American candidates to win national races. Add to that the extensive voting and election fraud the Left engaged in as revealed by the heroes at WikiLeaks and Project Veritas – legions of dead, illegal alien, and felonious votes for Hillary and countless reports of computer voting machines switching Trump votes to Clinton – and it became nearly impossible.

In state after state, early results showed Clinton significantly ahead right out of the gate – even in states where Trump eventually caught up and won. This pattern became so obvious and noteworthy that Lou Dobbs commented on it during Fox Business News' election coverage.

I believe this phenomenon was likely the result of the built-in lead Hillary was spotted over Trump by the aforementioned voter and election fraud. It is much easier to steal absentee and early votes because there are fewer observers keeping the process honest than there are on Election Day.

Trump must have benefitted from an overwhelming turnout indeed to overcome Hillary's 'margin of fraud'. (Thanks to my brother Wayne for that catchy phrase.) Just how large that margin was we may never know – but it wouldn't surprise me if it was as high as 5-7%.

In the end, even though Trump won enough votes to carry the Electoral College, initial counts have Clinton supposedly 'winning' the national popular vote by approximately 200,000. The Left will use this 'fact' to attack the Electoral College system and undermine the legitimacy of Trump's Presidency before he even takes the Oath of Office.

Which brings me to one final observation. There has been an impulse among many well-meaning (and not-so-well meaning) Americans to push for 'unity', 'healing', and the traditional 'peaceful transition of power' in the immediate aftermath of the election. Hillary Clinton's belated concession speech and Obama's comments were in this vein, while Trump's effusive praise of his recent enemies (Clinton, Obama, Ryan, McConnell, et al.) extended beyond mere courtesy and creeped dangerously close to absurd hypocrisy.

Don't believe these newfound professions of good will – they are dangerous chimeras. Our Cultural Marxist enemies on the Left will not give up their war against us just because of one setback, however severe it may have been to them, and will not rest until they destroy us and our way of life. While Obama plays nice with Trump in the White House, Democratic operatives continue to organize anti-American riots, marches, and protests across the country.

Likewise on social media. There have been numerous comments and memes expressing the idea that, now that the election is over, we can all reunite, let bygones be bygones, and put 'mere politics' behind us.

I cannot accept this. In an election this close, with stakes so high, every vote potentially carried the fate of our country with it. Those who made the decision to vote for Hillary Rodham Clinton, or those 'Republicans' who deliberately attempted to sabotage Trump's campaign, were willing to risk a Supreme Court dominated by socialists for 40 years – with all the irreparable damage to our nation and culture that would entail. They were also willing to overlook

Hillary's vast, well-documented history of criminality, treason, and evil.

Their poor choice put the lives of me, my family, and my friends at grave risk. That I cannot forget, and will not forgive – certainly not mere hours after they attempted to destroy all I hold dear.

We must not let our euphoria over our miraculous deliverance blind us to that fact that they, our supposed 'fellow Americans', supported those who have provided aid and comfort to our enemies.

We must never compromise with evil or those who seek to destroy us.

That's how we got into this mess in the first place.

28 – The Counterrevolution Begins

First published on January 16, 2017

This essay, written the week prior to Trump being sworn in as President, explores why Traditional Americans can be considered 'counterrevolutionaries' against the decades-long Cultural Marxist revolution that has nearly destroyed our nation and culture.

It explains how, in country after country over the past century, communists have always hid their real identity behind masks of 'compassionate progressivism', 'liberalism', or 'socialism' – at least until they gain power, at which point the masks come off and they reveal their true, totalitarian nature. Then the gulags open for business.

Nothing in the Left's incessant unhinged, blatantly anti-American and seditious speech and behavior (such as repeatedly and publicly calling for the President's assassination) during the first half-year of the Trump Presidency has given me any reason to reconsider my assertion that 'progressives' and the modern Democratic Party in America are, in fact, blatantly communist – if anything it's only confirmed that.

To reiterate the obvious – communism is not compatible with a free society.

Neither is the modern Democratic Party.

Traditional Americans now have awakened to the fact that those on the Left who seek to impose the hostile foreign ideology of Cultural Marxism on them are their enemies. Unfortunately, those who, wittingly or unwittingly, provide political support to those enemies have set themselves up as de facto enablers of them. It is my sincere hope that those misguided people see the error of their ways before it is too late and they become seen as enemies too.

We have reached the point in this country where the Left have openly declared political war against us and vowed unending 'resistance' to our lawfully-elected President in an effort to render the United States ungovernable. What they fail to realize is, now that they've killed the time-honored American tradition that the out-of-power party should act as the 'loyal opposition', it works both ways.

Once the Left divorced the spirit of civility and fair play from politics, the only remaining way to settle differences is violence and force. Thus far, the only ones on the receiving end of that political violence have been Traditional Americans who have been attacked while trying to play by the old rules and peacefully exercise their rights to free speech and assembly. But that won't continue indefinitely.

The Left are in for a very rude surprise when Traditional America finally decides it is no longer willing to play by the old rules either, to continue to allow themselves to be victimized by leftist thuggery, and to remain at a perpetual disadvantage with their morally-challenged, self-declared enemy. Then there will be hell to pay.

The Left have thrown out the old rules of the game. Traditional Americans have taken notice. The Left, for many decades, have taken for granted Traditional America's historic tendency of exhibiting good will and following the old rules. But they have confused our civility for weakness, and have finally used up that good will.

Should the Left and their globalist masters ever succeed in removing Trump and replace him with someone more amenable to their agenda, or should the time come when the Democrats win a future presidential election, Traditional Americans will remember how leftists behaved when Trump was elected.

If the Left thinks they are good at being ungovernable, they haven't seen anything yet.

Traditional America will never allow themselves to be ruled by an anti-American communist like Obama again, no matter how he or she comes to power.

We will never surrender to this enemy.

***

When I first began writing this blog in May 2015 I decided to call it 'Counterrevolutionary Corner', but never defined what I meant by the word 'counterrevolutionary'. I've intended to do so for some time, as some have erroneously confused the term with radicalism or the desire to overthrow the existing government. This is not the case.

Webster defines 'counterrevolution' as:

1. A revolution directed toward overthrowing a government or social system established by a previous revolution and

2. A movement to counteract revolutionary trends.

In America today, and indeed the entire West, the 'revolutionary trend' that needs to be resisted is a Marxist one that has been underway for nearly a century. This would-be revolution seeks to impose a collectivist, utopian, and ultimately totalitarian philosophy upon formerly individualistic, reality-based, free nations and peoples.

Its conceptual roots trace back to the mid-19th century with the writings of Karl Marx; its economic expression was first fully enacted in the early 20th century with the Bolshevik takeover of Russia and the creation of the Soviet Union; and its all-out assault on the Traditionalist cultural foundation of the West began in the 1960s with the rise of the 'counterculture' movement.

When this Marxist revolution first infiltrates a society it cloaks itself with benign terms to disguise its true intent – 'liberal', 'progressive', 'socialist', 'democratic'. It claims to be the 'voice of the people' against evil 'capitalists' and the 'bourgeois' (i.e. individuals who have worked their way to some modicum of success).

Only later, after they've fully seized the levers of power in a country, do they pull off their masks and reveal what their true character was all along – blatantly communistic and totalitarian.

In the United States, the Marxist revolution has made great inroads into our economic system and largely succeeded in corrupting the culture, but it hasn't completely won yet. So, the current intended meaning for the term 'counterrevolutionary' in my blog's title contains aspects of both the first and second Webster definitions cited above – to seek the overthrow of those portions of the government and social system which are either creations of or completely overrun by Marxists (such as the IRS, the 'public' education system, most of academia, the 'mainstream' media, etc.) while advocating resolute resistance and counterattack against Marxist revolutionary trends in all other areas of our lives.

To a Marxist, on the other hand, 'counterrevolutionary' is one of the worst pejoratives that can be directed at a person. In their world-view, a counterrevolutionary is one who stands in the way of progress towards their promised utopia on earth and is an 'enemy of the people'. If one views Marxism as the secular religion it is, the term 'counterrevolutionary' carries the same semantic meaning as 'infidel' or 'kafir' does to a Moslem jihadist – and those who have that label slapped on them and have the misfortune to be caught in territory controlled by Marxists usually suffer the same fate.

A staunch counterrevolutionary can't be 'reeducated' in gulags to renounce their faith in God or human freedom, so they must ultimately be 'liquidated'. Hundreds of millions of individuals around the world were accused of the 'crime' of 'counterrevolutionary activities' prior to being murdered by communist regimes over the last 100 years. So, to honor and remember all those martyrs of freedom who came before us, I wear the title 'counterrevolutionary' with pride.

When I took the oath of enlistment to serve in my nation's military I swore to 'preserve, protect and defend the Constitution of the United States against all enemies, foreign and domestic' and to 'bear true faith and allegiance to the same'. That wasn't just an oath to some antiquated piece of parchment with fading ink locked away in the National Archives. It was an oath to defend the principles that document was based on – that societies are composed of free individuals with inalienable rights derived from God, not men, and whose governments are subject to and limited by His Natural Law. Therefore, all forms of totalitarianism, by definition, are enemies of the Constitution and the United States.

Although I didn't realize it at the time, when I took my oath of enlistment I also took an oath to be a counterrevolutionary against the on-going, totalitarian, Marxist revolution targeting my country. That oath does not expire. I will continue to fight that hostile, alien ideology for as long as I live – I will wage philosophical battle against it in the war of ideas, will call out its supporters and adherents in the political sphere and, should those battles ever go against us to the point our Marxist enemies seize the levers of power and move to extinguish freedom, by force of arms.

I will **never** surrender to them. I will **never** be 'reeducated'. I will always be a 'deplorable, bitter clinger'. And I swear I will do my best to ensure that any who attempt to 'liquidate' *this* counterrevolutionary, his family, friends, or countrymen will pay a high price for the opportunity.

That being said, I will admit that when I first began writing my blog I was near despair for the future of my country. For nearly my entire adult life, I had watched my nation's economy be eroded by thinly-disguised communists and her soul rotted by Cultural Marxists – all coordinated by the evil globalist cabal that is the ultimate manifestation of the totalitarian impulse. I watched them erase my country's borders and open her up to invasion by countless millions from lands that don't share our traditions of individual freedom or limited government. I watched them infiltrate their Islamofascist, jihadi allies into our midst under the guise of 'welcoming refugees'.

I watched any patriots who dared to speak up against this assault have their livelihoods destroyed by political correctness until most of the rest were demoralized into sullen silence. I watched our enemies grow increasingly bold and brazen, and began to wonder if the battle was already lost – if there were too few of us left to effectively resist and whether such resistance could be organized in time. I sensed our last chance was approaching, and feared that our ultimate fate would be to fight a desperate, never-ending, rear-guard action, without any hope of victory, merely to preserve some remnants of decency from the wreckage of our once-great civilization.

What a difference a year-and-a-half makes. It turned out there were far more Traditional Americans remaining than I'd dared hope. Far more who share the same disgust at the cultural sewer our society has become. Far more who have had enough of being blamed by our

272

enemies for all the evil in the world while being forced to pay for our own destruction. Far more who are tired of letting real Evil go unopposed. Far more who are ready to take their country back.

John Adams, long after the successful end of the American Revolution, wrote, "The Revolution was effected before the War commenced. The Revolution was in the hearts and minds of the people; a change in their religious sentiments of their duties and obligations. This radical change in the principles, opinions, sentiments, and affections of the people, was the real American Revolution."

Likewise with the current counterrevolution against Globalism, Marxism, and their Islamofascist allies. I believe the arrogance and overconfidence of the Marxists during the Obama Presidency was the final trigger that launched the counterrevolution that is only now starting to outwardly manifest.

Long before Donald Trump came onto the political scene, every Leftist abuse of power; every time government agencies were used to persecute political enemies of the regime; every time they destroyed the Rule of Law to protect leftist criminals and traitors such as the Clintons; every time they used the power of government to give aid and comfort to America's enemies; every blatant lie their allies in the 'mainstream' media peddled to cover up the truth; every time they tried to turn the United States into just another Third World banana republic – ever-increasing numbers of Traditional Americans awoke to the horrific truth that the band of merry Marxists occupying the corridors of power were not just some opposing political party who could be civilly-disagreed with, they were potentially an existential threat to their very lives.

By the middle of Obama's second term, many Traditional Americans had come to the conclusion that the Marxists in power, led by the so-called 'President' himself, were anti-American traitors, even if few dared to say so publicly. Just like the American colonists before 1775, in their 'hearts and minds' Traditional Americans knew they were being governed by agents of foreign ideologies and powers hostile to their essential interests.

To paraphrase President Adams, *that* is when the *real*

counterrevolution occurred. The only question that remained was what form that counterrevolution would take. Would a shooting war be sparked, or could that righteously-angry, counterrevolutionary energy be somehow channeled into the political process to effect peaceful, yet meaningful, change back towards sanity and Traditional American values?

Enter Donald Trump. He was the wildcard no one anticipated, and is the one person in America who was best positioned to defy political correctness and speak the truth at the very time Traditional America was desperate for both. He is independently wealthy, placing him beyond the need for political donations, and appears beholden to no one, despite leftist fairy tales of Russian blackmail to the contrary.

Even more important, Trump is brash and confident, and he vigorously took the rhetorical fight to the politically correct elites in a way that had never been seen before. His unapologetic, in-your-face attitude towards them instantly won over Traditional America. He became our champion, and we propelled him to the most unlikely presidential election victory in American history.

In this final week before his scheduled inauguration it remains to be seen exactly what a Trump Presidency will bring. With his executive leadership experience, Republican majorities in both houses of Congress, and seemingly limitless energy, he has the potential to be the most transformative president in his first 100 days since Franklin Roosevelt.

However, regardless of what Trump eventually does or does not accomplish as president, he's already done his country a tremendous service and we owe him a great debt of gratitude. He has destroyed political correctness and exposed it for the paper tiger it is. He has emboldened millions of Traditional Americans, who are now freely speaking out against the Left like never before. Greater still, he's shown Traditional America just how many of us remain and helped us realize how powerful we are. We triumphed in spite of rabid opposition from nearly all of the major media, academic, and governmental elites from around the world.

Even if the worst-case scenario should now befall us, and the globalists engineer a way to take Trump out of the equation, either by assassination, prosecution over false charges, or some other unforeseen treachery, it won't matter. Thanks to him, the Traditionalist, populist genie is out of the bottle for good, and is now spreading like wildfire throughout America and Europe.

Traditionalists across the West have scored crucial first victories in the Brexit vote of last summer and in Trump's election, but the great struggle of our time has just begun. The globalists' century-long campaign for world domination may have suffered a setback, but they will regroup and renew their attack in unexpected ways. They have worked too hard against us, and for too long, to just give up now after a couple of defeats. They are capable of nearly any evil imaginable, including 9/11-style false flag operations employing weapons of mass destruction, provoking a race war at home or World War Three among the great powers abroad, or perhaps even worse. We must remain ever vigilant and prepared for any contingency.

That said, the easy victory the globalists had hoped for, against demoralized, dispirited, Traditionalist populations, is no longer in the cards. The American Spirit of our Forefathers has risen like a phoenix from the ashes.

We are awake, and we're not going anywhere.

29 – Leviathan Unbowed

First published on March 24, 2017

This essay discusses the ongoing efforts the globalists and their minions (both on the Left and within the Republican Party) have undertaken to undermine Trump's Presidency – efforts that began long before he even took office.

Seven months in, those globalist forces continue their obstruction and sabotage. They've successfully promoted the false narrative of Russian 'collusion' with the Trump campaign during the 2016 election, which led to Trump unwisely allowing the appointment of a Democratic special prosecutor to 'investigate' the matter and go on endless fishing expeditions that have mired his Administration in scandal. Deep state operatives resist every directive and initiative from the President, while the media distorts his every statement and lies about his intentions.

This has had the effect of dissipating the President's populist political momentum and derailed efforts to repeal Obamacare. It has also delayed the implementation of Trump's campaign promises to cut taxes, build a wall on the southern border, rebuild the country's infrastructure, 'drain the swamp', and to 'lock her up'.

Traditional America elected Trump president to enact these necessary, long-overdue, and non-negotiable reforms of the hopelessly corrupt, globalist-dominated power structure in Washington. As I write this in August 2017, it remains to be seen how much of that reformist agenda will be blocked by our enemies. But one thing is certain – we will not be denied.

If our enemies successfully prevent meaningful reforms during Trump's Presidency, or even worse, nullify the election by removing him prematurely through impeachment or assassination, I have no doubt Traditional America will do whatever is necessary to take their country back. The election of Trump was just the beginning of our counterrevolution against the globalists and their Cultural Marxist agents embedded in our society.

We Traditional Americans created the Trump phenomenon, not the other way around. Even if the 'Powers-That-Be' take him out, this fight will have only just begun. We're not going anywhere, and we will settle for nothing less than real reform.

President Kennedy once said, "Those who make peaceful revolution impossible will make violent revolution inevitable."

Real reform or violent revolution – that is the only remaining choice available to the so-called 'elites' who think they run this country.

So far they are foolishly choosing the path to violent revolution.

***

It's been two months since President Trump was sworn into office and he's done some great things – such as signing an executive order on Day One pulling the United States out of the globalist wet-dream known as the Trans-Pacific Partnership; launching aggressive, real attacks against ISIS as opposed to the kabuki theater fake air campaigns Obama forced our military to play-act in; standing up to the rogue regimes in Iran and North Korea; signing executive orders to initiate extreme vetting of individuals from Moslem failed states throughout the Middle East; making good on his promise to deport criminal illegal aliens; and nominating Judge Gorsuch to the Supreme Court.

Those accomplishments alone are more than enough to justify our votes for President Trump, and our nation is infinitely better-off today with him in the White House than it would have been with Marxist Hillary Clinton as President. However, as expected, the vast array of forces that conspired to deny Trump the Presidency – the hordes of Democratic, socialist, politically correct, pussy-hat/hijab-wearing, social justice warrior, wanna-be-anarchist, snowflake-enabling members of the Left; the Cultural Marxists that dominate the media and Hollywood; the careerist globalist minions who inhabit every dark nook and cranny of the 'deep-state' and permanent government bureaucracy in Mordor-on-the-Potomac; foreign globalist governments and institutions across the world; and many, many others – have pulled out all the stops to do everything in their power to make America ungovernable and sabotage the Trump Presidency.

Relatively insignificant leftist federal district court and appellate judges (at least compared to the Office of the Presidency) have blocked President Trump's clear constitutional and legal authority to order extreme vetting of aliens, thus establishing a de facto 'right' to every foreign national in the world to enter the United States. Leftist politicians have blatantly and seditiously declared their cities and states to be 'sanctuaries' for illegal aliens in open violation of longstanding federal immigration law. Globalists within the intelligence agencies and federal bureaucracies have tirelessly worked to subvert and sabotage every Trump initiative with unprecedented leaks and obstruction. Senate Democrats have threatened to do something not seen in the history of the Republic – filibuster a nominee to the Supreme Court. All while the so-called 'mainstream media' continues with an unparalleled torrent of lies, distortions, double-standards, misrepresentations, and character assassinations of everyone, from Trump on down, who is not a Democrat, socialist/communist, Cultural Marxist, member of one of the enshrined 'victim classes', or politically correct globalist.

I fear those efforts to block the political counterrevolution we initiated last November have started to have an effect. The ongoing debate on what should be done about Obamacare is a case in point.

If there's one thing that modern American history shows us it is that government programs and agencies, no matter how unnecessary, unconstitutional, or idiotic they may be, *NEVER* get repealed once they are enacted. Think of the useless, expensive, and counterproductive Education and Energy Departments or the Environmental Protection Agency as examples – all of which Republicans promised, then failed, to repeal. That's because new government programs and agencies quickly gain constituencies with a vested interest in perpetuating them and make spineless politicians too afraid to touch them, lest those constituencies turn against those politicians in the next election cycle and label them as 'heartless', 'cruel', and 'uncaring'.

Obamacare is no different. In spite of its many flaws, it has succeeded in one thing – planting in the minds of many Americans that they have a 'right' to universal, taxpayer-funded health care. Republicans have promised for the past seven years to repeal Obamacare – the best, least-expensive option that would allow insurance to be bought in the open market (just like any other service or commodity) where innovation and competition can keep costs down. But now, with more and more Americans believing they have the 'right' to a health care 'entitlement', it won't happen – the establishment Republicans have chickened-out and pivoted to 'repeal and replace' instead.

Then the GOP leadership tried to 'tweak' that steaming pile of freedom-killing crap the Democrats shoved down the American peoples' throats back in 2010, slapped an establishment Republican label on it (the 'American Health Care Act'), and hoped to declare the problem "fixed". But it would still have just been Obamaclusterfuck-Light. Fortunately, enough Tea Party Representatives and members of the House Freedom Caucus said 'no' today to 'Ryancare' and forced the GOP leadership to pull the faulty legislation because they didn't have the votes to push it through.

This is the fatal flaw in our current political system, the one that has allowed government to metastasize into nearly all areas of our economy and personal lives – areas government *never* had the moral or constitutional right to insert itself into in the first place. The current health care debate is just another sad example of how our country has moved inexorably towards ruin – Democrats aggressively push us two steps towards more socialism/communism, then Republicans timidly half-undo one of those steps. Then the process repeats the next time Democrats get into power.

America began dying as soon as Americans started viewing Government as Santa Claus and the Solution to All Problems. It began dying as soon as we tried to outsource our responsibility for our own well-being to others. It began dying when Americans started voting to use the power of the state to steal 'free' shit from other people and have them pay for it.

Traditional America, fed up with this freedom-crushing growth of the government leviathan, voted in Trump as a political attempt to fight back against it. However, although he's made some very good moves in his first two months, it's starting to look like Trump will not be able to fundamentally change this dynamic. The imperial (as opposed to small-'r' 'republican') 'deep-state'/perpetual government bureaucratic system appears to be too entrenched.

Unfortunately, I'm beginning to believe his Presidency will become more of a holding action against the march towards socialism rather than a transformative break away from it. In my opinion, Trump has made some critical unforced errors that have helped the globalist/leftist opposition sabotage his agenda, the largest being trying too hard to reach out to the very establishment he railed against during the presidential campaign. Bringing establishment Republicans like Reince Priebus into his administration as White House Chief of Staff wasn't a good start. Even more problematic was keeping Obama holdovers in key positions like FBI Director Comey.

That's already started to bite him in the ass. Worse yet was Trump aligning himself with Paul Ryan and establishment Republicans on the Obamacare 'repeal and replace' bill, then trying to throw the conservative Republican members of the House Freedom Caucus under the bus to get it passed. The President's tweet last night that the members of the Freedom Caucus, by opposing the fatally-flawed 'Ryancare' bill, were violating their pro-life beliefs because there was one part of the bill that de-funded Planned Parenthood, was clumsy at best and disingenuous at worst. Either way, it was an overly-simplistic thing to say and poorly thought-out politically. The Representatives in the Freedom Caucus are Traditional America's voice in the House and it's not a good idea to alienate them, and by extension, *us*. If Trump *really* wants to make fundamental change and 'drain the swamp' in Washington he needs to learn pretty damn quick that we Traditional Americans are the *only* ones who've got his back. The more he doesn't do that the more he risks looking like one of the 'swamp-things' himself.

In any event, it's become increasingly clear that it's probably going to take something even *more* counterrevolutionary from We the People than just the election of Trump to restore prosperity, sanity, and decency to our nation and culture.

Just what form that next phase of the counterrevolution takes remains to be seen – but Republicans continuing to behave like the

'Democratic-Light' Party isn't going to get it done. Perhaps this over-bloated government leviathan will collapse under the unsustainable weight of debt and unfunded liabilities it has accumulated over the past century and we'll be forced to rebuild a (hopefully) better system from the rubble. Or perhaps we're going to have to take more direct action before then to save our nation and our culture. Either way, we 'Deplorables' need to fight complacency and continue to consider ways to work to Take Our Country Back and Make America Great Again. That includes holding President Trump's feet to the fire if need be.

We won a great battle last November – it bought us invaluable time to regroup, threw a giant monkey wrench into the globalist, Cultural Marxist agenda our enemies were steamrolling over us, and forced them to play defense for the first time – but this war has only just begun.

It's going to be a long, difficult one. We need to keep our powder dry.

30 – The Cauldron Bubbles Over

First published on June 16, 2017

This essay was written in the aftermath of the attempted mass murder of a group of Republican congressmen at a public park in Alexandria, Virginia as they practiced for a charity baseball game. The would-be assassin was a socialist supporter of Bernie Sanders who repeatedly and publicly expressed the extreme hate towards President Trump, Republicans, and conservatives that is typical of the modern Left in America.

In the aftermath of that shooting, the leftist establishment tried to spin the event to advance the meme that both sides of the current political divide in America are equally culpable in creating the climate of hostility that led to the attack on the Republican congressmen.

This, of course, is demonstrably false – nearly all of the political violence that has plagued this country during the 2016 presidential campaign and subsequent Trump Presidency has been fomented and initiated by the Left, as the extensive list of unprovoked leftist attacks included in the following essay exhaustively demonstrates.

The attack on the Republican congressmen in Alexandria was the direct result of the unprecedented level of hate and vitriol the Left has directed towards Traditionalists – hate that now saturates the popular culture in the West.

I warned in this essay that poisonous atmosphere would inevitably lead to a backlash from the Left's Traditionalist victims. Hate will breed counter-hate. Even decent people can turn the other cheek only so long before their patience and good-will are exhausted.

In the two months since I wrote this essay these trends have only accelerated. 'Antifa' and 'Black Lives Matter' violence has escalated so much in places like Berkeley and Charlottesville that even some staunchly-leftist media outlets and politicians have felt compelled to condemn them.

Likewise, in Charlottesville, a group of alleged 'white supremacists' and 'neo-Nazis' arrived at a 'Unite the Right' rally, to protest the Cultural Marxist demand to remove a statue of Robert E. Lee at a public park, well-armed and ready to battle Antifa and BLM. This led to violent clashes which culminated in the death of a leftist protester and the wounding of scores more when a young alleged white supremacist drove his car, ISIS-style, into a pack of Antifa and BLM marchers. Republicans reflexively felt the need to condemn the violence from the so-called 'Alt-Right'.

Unfortunately, regardless of who condemns the ever-increasing wave of political violence sweeping the country, it is far too late to close the Pandora's Box of mutual loathing and hatred the Cultural Marxists have tirelessly worked for decades to pry open. Tepid and tardy 'condemnation' from Nancy Pelosi and MSNBC commentator Joe Scarborough won't deter the woefully-ignorant wanna-be communists in Antifa or BLM (who believe anyone who doesn't agree with them is an evil 'fascist' or 'racist') from violently striking out at those who they see as their enemies. Rebukes from country-club Republicans like Mitch McConnell and Paul Ryan won't stop neo-Nazis from taking to the streets to give Antifa and BLM the fight they claim to be looking for.

So far the pervasive hatred and violence of the Left towards Traditional Americans have only been opposed by the least-reputable, tiniest minority of extremists on the 'Alt-Right'. But that doesn't mean the vast majority of Traditional Americans (We the Deplorables who demonstrated our power by electing President Trump) haven't been taking note of the vile, intolerable conduct of the Cultural Marxists and their minions. We have, and have become quietly enraged by that behavior and the failure of government authorities to put a stop to the anarchy and lawlessness.

Traditional America has, reluctantly, finally realized that there can no longer be peaceful co-existence with the Cultural Marxists on the Left. The only remaining question is what to do about that new reality.

The violence seen to date is but a harbinger of far worse to come. There will come a time, in the not-too-distant future, when Traditional America decides our nation would be far better off without the leftist enemies in our midst. That will be the true game-changer. Then the Second American Civil War will begin.

The Left, emboldened by their earlier 'victories' over unarmed Trump supporters and a handful of neo-Nazis with shields and clubs, will then face tens of millions of righteously angry, extremely well-armed and trained veterans, hunters, and sportsmen.

They won't know what hit them.

***

Two days have passed since a socialist gunman opened fire on a group of Republican congressmen at a park in Alexandria, Virginia, wounding five, including Representative Steve Scalise of Louisiana. Representative Scalise was struck in the pelvis by a rifle round, and the resulting bone and bullet fragments damaged numerous internal organs. He remains in critical condition at this time, has endured multiple operations, and faces many more to come.

Ironically, in one way the fact that Representative Scalise was present during the attempted mass assassination may have been a blessing-in-disguise – as the Majority Whip and third-highest ranking member of the House of Representatives he was one of the few assigned a two-officer security detail from the Capitol Police. They immediately engaged the gunman, whose level of hate was clearly more developed than his martial capabilities, and swiftly dispatched him. But for the grace of God, and had that security detail not been present, I would now be writing about the mass murder of a large number of United States Congressmen.

Law enforcement quickly identified the shooter (no doubt because he was a white male whose name isn't 'Mohammed') as 66-year-old James T. Hodgkinson of Belleville, Illinois.

It also came to light that he was sympathetic to left-wing causes, including having supported Bernie Sander's presidential campaign and being vehemently opposed to President Trump and the Republican Party.

This excerpt from an article about Hodgkinson from the BBC summarizes his political views:

> *"A Facebook account that appeared to belong to Hodgkinson was filled with anti-Republican and anti-Trump posts, as well as expressions of support for former Democratic presidential candidate Bernie Sanders (the page has since been removed).*

On social media, Hodgkinson railed against Donald Trump, writing on Facebook, "you are Truly the Biggest A** Hole We Have Ever Had in the Oval Office" and calling Trump a "traitor".

He also belonged to many Facebook groups with names like "Terminate the Republican Party" and "Donald Trump is not my President".

Local media unearthed a 2012 photo of Hodgkinson protesting outside a downtown Belleville post office holding a sign that read, "Tax the Rich".

The Belleville-News Democrat also compiled his letters to the editor in 2012, when he railed against conservative tax policies and praised President Barack Obama."

The full article can be found here: _http://www.bbc.com/news/world-us-canada-40280034_

In the immediate aftermath of the shooting the mainstream media tried to portray Hodgkinson's comments as an 'extreme' example of leftist thought, but that is simply untrue. His comments are actually quite mainstream among what passes for leftist commentary nowadays – whether placed on social media by hordes of run-of-the-mill liberal/socialist/communist 'useful idiots' spouting the kind of banal shit Hodgkinson did; high-profile celebrities such as Madonna (who proudly and publicly rhapsodized about thinking 'a lot about blowing up the White House') and Robert De Niro ('I want to punch Donald Trump in the face'); or mainstream media idiots such as MSNBC 'counterterrorism expert' Malcolm Nance tweeting that he nominates Trump Towers in Istanbul 'for the first ISIS bombing of a Trump property'.

And it's not just commentary anymore – the Left have escalated their hate-spewage to include 'performance art', with Kathy Griffin's photo of her holding, ISIS-style, the realistic-looking decapitated head of President Trump and the liberal 'reinterpretation' of the Shakespeare play *Julius Caesar* to have the murdered tyrant dressed obviously like Trump being only the latest examples of this kind of criminal incitement. They join numerous rap videos that called for and showed the mock-shooting of President Trump. (The rappers get a free pass on their criminal incitement because they're black and no one in the media has the stones to call them out for fear of being labeled a 'racist'.)

Their armies of low-information, high-rage, 21st century Brownshirts have repeatedly acted on this incitement in a campaign of political violence (i.e. 'terrorism') against Traditional Americans and Trump supporters – a campaign that has lasted over a full year now (the wave of violence started months before the Republican convention) and has been largely buried on the back pages by the mainstream media. The Daily Caller put out an amazing list of the numerous attacks, with links to the original articles, on their website today:

This List Of Attacks Against Conservatives Is Mind Blowing

Posted By Dave Brooks and Benjamin Decatur On 12:54 AM 06/16/2017

A wave of liberal rage has marked the last 11 months since the rise and subsequent election of President Donald Trump.

Antifa protestors clad in black masks shut down college campuses, destroy property and indiscriminately attack those they disagree with, whether women or the elderly. Meanwhile, CNN fires Kathy Griffin for taking photos with a bloody replica of the president's decapitated head.

Amid this backdrop, The Huffington Post publishes an article calling for the execution of Trump and "everyone assisting his agenda."

Then, shots ring out as a man gorged on media hysteria attempts to slaughter Republican congressmen while they practice for a charity baseball game.

The aggression since Trump's nomination is difficult to enumerate, but nevertheless, The Daily Caller News Foundation pored over media reports to compile a close but non-exhaustive list of violent acts against conservatives in months following the Republican National Convention.

In creating the list, The DCNF reviewed numerous articles detailing attacks and violent threats against conservatives and Trump supporters. While there are examples of anonymous threats, The DCNF chose to include only those that resulted in the cancelling of events and two to members of Congress deemed credible. Some instances of violence between rival protestors were not included as it was difficult to ascertain who initiated the event.

Events Over Time:

July 2016:

-A Hillary Clinton supporter lights a flag on fire and attacks a Trump supporter in Pittsburgh.

-Protesters jumped on cars, stole hats, fought with and threw eggs at Trump supporters outside a Trump rally in downtown San Jose. Trump supporters sued San Jose over the violence.

August 2016:

-Anti-Trump protesters attacked, pushed, spit on and verbally harassed attendees forced to walk a "gauntlet" as they left a Trump fundraiser in Minneapolis, Minn., and beat an elderly man. Protesters also attacked Trump's motorcade.

-A Tennessee man was assaulted at a garage sale for being a Trump supporter.

-A Trump supporter in New Jersey was attacked with a crowbar on the street.

September 2016:

-*Protesters in El Cajon, Calif., chased and beat up a Trump supporter.*

October 2016:

-*A GOP office in North Carolina was firebombed and spray painted with "Nazi Republicans get out of town or else."*

November 2016:

-*A high school student was attacked after she wrote that she supported Trump on social media. The perpetrator ripped her glasses off and punched her in the face.*

-*The president of Cornell University's College Republicans was assaulted the night after Trump won the election.*

-*Students protesting Trump punched and kicked a Maryland high school student wearing a Make America Great Again hat.*

-*A high school student was arrested in Florida after he punched a classmate for carrying a Trump sign at school.*

-*A group of black men in Chicago attacked a white man while raging against Trump.*

-*Maryland high school students punched a student who was demonstrating in support of Trump, and then kicked him repeatedly while he was on the ground.*

-*"You support Trump. You hate Mexicans," a California high school student yelled at a Trump supporter, before viciously beating the girl.*

-An anti-bullying ambassador was arrested for shoving a 74-year-old man to the ground in a fight outside Trump tower where people upset over his win had gathered. The woman tied to Black Lives Matter caused the man to hit his head on the sidewalk.

-A Texas elementary school student was beaten by his classmates for voting for Trump in a mock election.

-Two men punched and kicked a Connecticut man who was standing with an American flag and a Trump sign.

December 2016:

-A Trump supporter was beaten and dragged by a car.

January 2017:

-A Trump supporter was knocked unconscious after airport protesters repeatedly beat him on the head.

-A Trump supporter was attacked after putting out a fire started by anti-Trump protesters.

-When Trump protesters encountered a driver with a pro-Trump flag on his car, they surrounded the vehicle, ripped off and began burning the flag, and pounded the car. They also punctured the tires.

February 2017:

-California GOP Rep. Tom McClintock had to be escorted to his car after a town hall because of angry protesters. The tires of at least four vehicles were slashed.

-Protestors knocked a 71-year-old female staffer for California GOP Rep. Dana Rohrabacher unconscious during a protest outside the representative's office.

-Milo Yiannopoulos' speech at the University of California-Berkeley was cancelled after rioters set the campus on fire and threw rocks through windows. Milo tweeted that one of his supporters wearing a Trump hat was thrown to the ground and kicked.

March 2017:

-Masked protesters at Middlebury College rushed AEI scholar and political scientist Charles Murray and professor Allison Stranger, pushing and shoving Murray and grabbing Stranger by her hair and twisting her neck as they were leaving a campus building. Stranger suffered a concussion. Protesters then surrounded the car they got into, rocking it back and forth and jumping on the hood.

April 2017:

-A parade in Portland, Oregon was canceled after threats of violence were made against a Republican organization.

-Fears of violent protests shut down Ann Coulter's UC Berkeley speech. Campus police had gathered intel on protesters who were planning to commit violence.

May 2017:

-Republican Rep. Tom Garrett, his family and his dog were targeted by a series of repeated death threats deemed credible by authorities.

-FBI agents arrested a person for threatening to shoot Republican Rep. Martha McSally over her support for Trump.

-Police in Tennessee charged a woman for allegedly trying to run Republican Rep. David Kustoff off the road.

-Police in North Dakota ejected a man after he became physical with Republican Rep. Kevin Cramer at a town hall.

-A former professor was arrested after police said they identified him on video beating Trump supporters with a U-shaped bike lock, leaving three people with "significant injuries."

June 2017:

-James Hodgkinson opened fire on a congressional GOP baseball practice, injuring five, including House Majority Whip Steve Scalise.

-Republican Rep. Claudia Tenney received an email threat that read, "One down, 216 to go," shortly after the shooting at the Republican congressional baseball practice.

-A man driving a white Malibu reportedly fired several shots at a man driving a truck displaying a "Make America Great Again" flag in Indiana.

The entire Daily Caller article can be found here:

http://dailycaller.com/2017/06/16/this-list-of-attacks-against-conservatives-is-mind-blowing/

In all fairness, by comparison, when I searched for 'conservatives attack liberals' I was able to find *two*. (If any leftists are accidentally reading this essay and can find other examples I've missed, please do share. I guarantee you won't find anywhere near as many as the list above.)

On April 28th of this year in Lexington, Kentucky a 19-year-old man named Mitchell Adkins walked into a coffee shop on the campus of

Transylvania College with a machete and a knife and started attacking those who identified themselves as Democrats. Two women were injured, but fortunately not severely.

An article in a local newspaper had this to say about Adkins' motives for the attack:

In November 2015, the Transy campus newspaper, The Rambler, published a letter from a student named Mitchell Adkins who complained that he was harassed on campus because he was a Republican.

"Being a Republican in this school makes me such a minority that I've had to face discrimination on a daily basis," Adkins wrote in that letter. "Transylvania is a predominantly Democratic school. I'm always happy to listen to other people's opinions, but as soon as I give my own, I'm called a 'bigot,' an 'a----le,' some even go as far as 'fascist Nazi.'"

"With the election of (Republican) Matt Bevin as governor, I've become even more of a target for people claiming that I'm 'responsible for ruining this country' and that, somehow, I'm an evil person for what would make this state great," he wrote.

That letter was signed "Mitchell Adkins," along with a university email address that began "madkins19."

Separately, in a November 2015 community blog post on the website Buzzfeed, a user with the name MAdkins19 identified himself as a Republican at Transylvania University who suffered political discrimination at the hands of "hardcore liberals."

The writer referenced the election of Bevin as Kentucky's governor that month, which he said "resulted in ugliness for all of his supporters."

"I was at lunch when someone told me Bevin was elected, and my cheer of pride was met with looks of disgust and hatred," he wrote. "People left the table, saying things along the lines of I was responsible for ruining this state and country, that my political opinion was wrong just because it was different. I have never been afraid to share my opinion, but being in

this college has made me reluctant due to the backlash which I know is inevitable."

In an update to the post, MAdkins19 said he had dropped out of Transy.

"The constant bullying and lack of friends drove me to an overdose, a trip to the hospital and two trips to a mental hospital," he wrote.

The complete article can be found here:

http://www.kentucky.com/news/politics-government/article147447274.html

Obviously, Adkins was ultimately responsible for his decision to physically attack those he identified as liberals and should be criminally prosecuted for his violent acts. However, there can be no denying that the climate of politically correct, liberal bullying of conservatives in America that Adkins cited is a very real phenomenon and is prevalent on college campuses across the nation. That hostile climate was obviously enough to set off this 19-year-old. Unfortunately, I would expect more of this kind of thing in the future. Hate always eventually breeds more hate in return.

The other 'assault' I found was the now-infamous punching of a Black Lives Matter protester by a 78-year-old man at a Trump campaign rally in North Carolina in March, 2016. The BLM punk was shouting profanities and flipping off the crowd at the family-friendly event when the Trump supporter punched him. In my opinion, this was not an unprovoked assault – the uncivilized thug had it coming and the elderly patriot is worthy of our praise for standing up against it. Engage in that kind of provocative, unmannered behavior and you deserve what you get.

Another incident liberals like to blame on conservatives is the recent attack on a train in Portland, Oregon by a man named Jeremy Joseph Christian, who the mainstream media identified as a 'white supremacist' and who had reportedly 'shouted anti-Islamic slurs' towards two women who were wearing hijabs. Christian then stabbed to death two men who came to the women's aid. Upon deeper investigation, however, the situation wasn't so cut-and-dried. It turned out that Christian was in fact a fervent supporter of Socialist Bernie Sanders and Green Party candidate Jill Stein. (Not surprisingly, that part didn't make the mainstream news.) Looking at screenshots of some of his Facebook rants, it is clear to me this guy was a total whack-job and not a real conservative at all. Here is a link to an article about him and his mindset:

http://dailycaller.com/2017/05/28/portland-killer-is-an-anti-circumcision-bernie-sanders-supporter/

In a similar vein, in the wake of Wednesday's attempted mass assassination in Arlington the mainstream media unsuccessfully tried to draw parallels with the 2011 shooting of Representative Gabrielle Giffords in Tucson, Arizona by 22-year-old Jared Lee Loughner. Although the Left tried to paint Loughner as a right-wing extremist, his expressed political views were all over the map. His trial was repeatedly postponed by the federal judge who presided over the proceedings because he was diagnosed as a paranoid schizophrenic and it wasn't resumed until Loughner was forcibly given antipsychotic drugs to make him 'competent' enough to understand the charges against him.

Not so with Hodgkinson, the would-be assassin in Arlington. Although he certainly appears to have harbored extreme anger towards his targets, there is no indication that he did not know what he was doing. In fact, his extensive planning and preparation for the attack, as well as his long productive work history, indicates a high-functioning mind. (At least compared to a schizophrenic.) His comments clearly indicate he was immersed in the extreme ideology that has now become mainstream among the Left in America.

The hypocritical spin by the Left to try and equate Hodgkinson's evil crime with alleged, nearly non-existent violence committed by Traditionalists would be laughable if it wasn't so nauseating. The immediate 'kumbaya' calls in the mainstream media and among establishment politicians from both parties for 'all sides to unite and ratchet down the incendiary rhetoric' is disingenuous and implies a moral equivalency between the modern Left and Traditionalists in this country that simply doesn't exist. The Left have been overwhelmingly guilty of openly inciting political intimidation and violence against their opponents for at least the past half-century. The shooting in Alexandria was only the next logical consequence of their long campaign of incitement that will no doubt lead to far worse atrocities in the future.

No, liberals, no matter how much you spin it, this guy is yours. You own him. Although he holds the ultimate responsibility for pulling the trigger on those men, your incessant hate towards those who don't agree with your extreme political agenda was most certainly a major motivation for Hodgkinson to commit his heinous crime.

Contrast the Left's current efforts to distance themselves from James Hodgkinson with their reaction following the equally-heinous mass murder of nine black Christians in a church in South Carolina in June, 2015 by 21-year-old Dylan Roof. When Roof's Facebook profile showed that he'd latched onto far-Right extremist and racist rhetoric, the Left didn't extend the same courtesy to Traditionalists (to not unfairly paint them with a broad brush) that they now demand for themselves. On the contrary, they used the Charleston shooting as an opportunity to smear, in essence, all white people in America as being guilty by association. Uniter-in-Chief Obama blatantly said so when he provocatively lectured White America for having "racist DNA". When photos of Roof were discovered with him posing with a Confederate battle flag, the Left initiated a purge of all things Confederate that continues to this day – there isn't a statue of Robert E. Lee anywhere in the nation that is safe against this politically correct, Taliban-like campaign of cultural cleansing.

There can be no meaningful or productive dialog with those who habitually and blatantly lie about you and distort the truth. There is no point in even trying. Traditional America finally awoke to that fact about two years ago, tuned-out the leftist bullshit, and decided to take matters into their own hands. Fortunately, they had one, long-shot, peaceful political option remaining to them to express their righteous anger and, being for the most part decent people, they took it – and thus propelled Donald Trump to the White House as the only public figure that was even remotely expressing their frustration and Traditional worldview.

But that was more an act of desperation, a last-gasp reaction of political counterrevolution against the incessant Cultural Marxist assault on them and their Traditional culture they had silently suffered under for decades, rather than a sign of a healthy, fully-functioning republic. If the Left succeeds in paralyzing Trump's mandate to 'drain the swamp' and enact meaningful reforms of the corrupt globalist, leftist, welfare-warfare state-supporting, mainstream media/academia complex, thus closing off the only viable peaceful option available, the tsunami of righteous disgust and anger will no doubt manifest in other, more unpleasant ways. The days of Traditional America allowing themselves to be the quiescent piñatas of the Left are over.

When the gulf between the worldviews of opposing sides becomes so vast that meaningful dialog becomes impossible, the only remaining way to resolve differences between them is violence. That is the sorry state of affairs in America in mid-2017.

Just as the incessant, racist, inflammatory rhetoric of the 'Black Lives Matter' movement, publicly endorsed by President Obama and the rest of the left-wing politically correct machine, led to a wave of slaughter of police officers across the country and culminated in the murder of five officers in Dallas and three in Baton Rouge this time last year – so has the incessant, hateful, inflammatory rhetoric against Trump, his supporters, and the Republican Party in general led to last Wednesday's attempted assassination of those GOP congressmen gathered at that ballfield in Arlington.

For the past half-century, the Left have worked tirelessly to create a toxic witches' brew of hate-filled, group-identity/tribal politics and division in America, accentuating the historical differences between people rather than the common Traditional American heritage we share. Then they have turned up the heat for years until the contents of the cauldron (which used to be America's great 'melting pot') have finally started to boil.

Last Wednesday morning one of the bursting bubbles splashed over the side, giving us a painful taste of what's to come if the Left doesn't turn down the heat soon. I'm not getting my hopes up – in fact I'll go out on a limb and predict that, notwithstanding their current calls for 'unity', the Left's campaign of hate and incitement will fully resume within one to two weeks at the most.

Unless this prediction is somehow miraculously wrong, it is only a matter of time before the cauldron boils over completely. Then those who lovingly cooked up the toxic cocktail will be the primary ones to be scalded – and they will fully deserve it. Unfortunately, if history is any guide, a lot of innocent people will end up burned in the process too.

I sincerely hope I am wrong on this, but fear I'm not.

This week's attempted mass assassination of Republican congressmen, along with the massacre of the policemen in Dallas and Baton Rouge last year, is akin to the types of events that became commonplace in the 1850s – such as 'Bleeding Kansas', the vicious caning of Senator Charles Sumner on the Senate floor, or John Brown's raid on Harper's Ferry. We should all reflect on how that turned out.

America is once again on the brink of civil war.

God help us all.

Afterword – The Coming Crisis

When I started writing political commentary during the dark days of early 2015, little did I realize that the frustration, disgust, and anguish I felt at the near-ruin of my country resulting from the evil schemes of the Cultural Marxists was shared by tens of millions of Traditional Americans. It was beyond my wildest hopes that my humble collection of essays would inadvertently encapsulate the spirit of the uprising of an 'Army of Deplorables' that would successfully challenge the entrenched, and up until then seemingly-invincible, globalist power structure.

But where do we go from here? What does the future hold for our country, ourselves, and our posterity?

Trying to predict the future is an endeavor akin to peering through the proverbial dark looking-glass at best, but current trends and the echoing themes of history provide clues that allow us to make an educated guess. All those historical themes and trends point to an imminent period of crisis, tumult, and conflict both here in the United States and abroad.

The Cycle Theory of History so well described in *The Fourth Turning – An American Prophesy* by William Strauss and Neil Howe indicates America is due for a crisis climax to rival the severity of the most traumatic and nation-threatening events of the Great Depression and World War Two, The Civil War, and the American Revolution. This crisis climax will consist of a myriad collection of seemingly-intractable issues and problems that were exacerbated or neglected for the past sixty years.

Foreign enemies such as China, Iran and North Korea have been allowed to grow into existential threats to our nation, while armies of people hostile to our Traditional American culture have been allowed to immigrate but not required to assimilate with us.

Our economic power and sovereignty, along with our once-thriving middle class has been destroyed by the evils of globalism.

Meanwhile, a decadent culture of entitlement has been fostered to go along with an endless series of unnecessary globalist-initiated interventions and wars against nations and peoples who posed no meaningful threat to America's security, thus creating a cancerous, perpetual welfare-warfare state that has mortgaged our children's future and financially and morally bankrupted our nation.

Decades of eroding social, cultural, and moral standards have rendered America a cesspit of glorified irresponsibility, vice, and criminality.

Our once-united Traditional American culture has been ripped asunder by racial, ethnic, and tribal divisions.

This varied collection of seemingly-intractable issues and problems share one common trait – they were all the result of failed Leftist philosophies and dogma.

I use the term 'seemingly-intractable' because all those issues will become simplified and quite solvable once we eliminate the power of the globalist Left to rule over our lives and destroy our traditional, once great culture.

That is the choice we face – surrender to them and watch once prosperous and free America transformed into the starvation of Venezuela, the cannibalism of North Korea, or even the killing fields of Cambodia – or fight back now, *hard*, before it's too late. If that sounds extreme, just ask yourself what the people who brought us Antifa, Black Lives Matter, La Raza, and the Nation of Islam will do when they gain total power and give the fanatical 'social justice warriors' of today badges, guns, and the authority to use them tomorrow.

Surrender is not an option. Therefore, we will have to do whatever we must to root out, discredit, and destroy every bastion of totalitarian globalist and leftist power and influence in our society, wherever it lurks.

The news media, entertainment industry, government, and especially academia must be purged of all socialists and communists in a sweeping program of demarxification patterned after the denazification of Germany following its defeat in World War Two. Communism must be declared the enemy ideology it is and its adherents dealt with accordingly.

All globalist 'think-tanks' and foundations must be disbanded and every globalist embedded within the dark and secret recesses of the so-called 'deep state' must be exposed and removed from their positions of power.

Our enemies on the Left will claim these objectives are extremist, nationalistic, and fascist. Nothing could be further from the truth – *they are the real fascists, as the only difference between the Godless totalitarian creeds of Marxism and Nazism are superficial and semantic only. Both claim the total primacy of the State – one to allegedly benefit a mythical, utopian collective representing the 'New International Man'; the other an equally-mythical, racially-based collective called the 'Volk'.*

We, on the other hand, are fighting to preserve and restore the principals of the Declaration of Independence – that all power is granted to sovereign individuals by the Creator, and those free individuals delegate that power and sovereignty to governments for the express purpose of preserving their God-given liberties.

That is a profoundly radical and unique political philosophy not seen before or since America's founding. Being in tune with both the reality of the Universe as designed by the Creator and with human nature, it is a philosophy that has allowed America to thrive and blossom into the wealthiest, most powerful nation in recorded history. It has also benefitted those nations wise enough to emulate America's example with freedom and prosperity as well. To all freedom-loving individuals, it is a philosophy well worth fighting for.

We should not hesitate to proudly and unabashedly proclaim American Exceptionalism to one and all, for it is the Truth. When our enemies then label us as 'extremists' we should remember that, to paraphrase the great patriot and defender of freedom Senator Barry Goldwater, *Extremism in defense of liberty is no vice. Tolerance in the face of tyranny is no virtue.*

Senator Goldwater said something very like this in 1964 during his acceptance speech for the Republican nomination for President. During that speech he eerily and presciently predicted the rise of the politically correct, totalitarian Cultural Marxist mortal enemy we face today when he stated:

"Those who seek absolute power, even though they seek it to do what they regard as good, are simply demanding the right to enforce their own version of heaven on earth. And let me remind you, they are the very ones who always create the most hellish tyrannies. Absolute power does corrupt, and those who seek it must be suspect and must be opposed. Their mistaken course stems from false notions of equality, ladies and gentlemen. Equality, rightly understood, as our Founding Fathers understood it, leads to liberty and to the emancipation of creative differences. Wrongly understood, as it has been so tragically in our time, it leads first to conformity and then to despotism."

There is no better description of the current tyranny of 'tolerance' and the deliberate confusion of equality of opportunity vs. equality of results (The so-called 'rights' to receive money taken from others through income-redistribution, 'free' healthcare, food, education, housing, phones, etc., ad nauseum.) championed by would-be totalitarians Barack Hussein Obama, Hillary Rodham Clinton, and their fellow leftist ilk. That road leads to destitution, starvation, and an American version of the *Gulag Archipelago*.

That is unacceptable. We have no choice but to defeat the enemy philosophy of collectivism by any means necessary. The future of our culture, our nation, and our people are at stake. Our very lives and those of our children depend on it.

Hopefully, we will be able to accomplish this non-negotiable objective politically through peaceful means. Unfortunately, in light of the globalist Left's exponentially-escalating hostile and bellicose conduct during the 2016 presidential campaign and subsequent Trump Presidency, that appears to be increasingly unlikely. After the Left's defeat, they ripped away, once and for all, the false mask of 'love', 'peace', 'coexistence', and 'tolerance' to reveal their true evil visage hidden underneath.

The past two-and-a-half years have been among the most tumultuous in over 150 years. The next five to ten will 'try men's souls' as much as our ancestors were tested by World War Two, The Civil War, and the American Revolution. We must trust to our faith in God, the strength He gives us to hold fast and defend what is right, and the goodness of our fellow Traditional Americans. With His help, we will prevail.

To my fellow Traditional Americans, thank you for taking the time to read this book. Hopefully, my humble efforts will provide some benefit to you during this troubled time. Thank you for being there, and for mustering the courage to speak out and begin the long struggle to retake our country and to Make America Great Again.

God bless We the Deplorables!

Shawn L. Belisle – September 3, 2017

ABOUT THE AUTHOR

Shawn L. Belisle is a lifelong student of history, sociology, and politics. He served over 25 years in the military, security, and law enforcement fields, first as an Air Force Security Policeman; corporate security at a Fortune 100 corporation; a civilian Security Policeman at an Air National Guard base; and at a correctional facility. He considers his oath of enlistment to "support and defend the Constitution of the United States against all enemies, foreign and domestic" to be a sacred one that doesn't expire. Neither does his training.

He lives happily with his wife Jill, a pride of obnoxious but lovable rescued cats and a dog in the quiet woods of rural Wisconsin.

He prays every day for peace, and for the necessary strength and courage should that prove to be impossible. His working philosophy of life is to 'Hope for the best, but prepare for the worst.' So far, it has served him well.

His writings and commentary can be found at counterrevolutionarycorner.com and the Counterrevolutionary Corner Facebook page.

www.ingramcontent.com/pod-product-compliance
Lightning Source LLC
Chambersburg PA
CBHW061957280526
45787CB00005B/1901